D1101741

FROM WARD TO WHITEHALL:

THE DISASTER AT MID STAFFS HOSPITAL

By Julie Bailey

12462281

Published in the United Kingdom by:
Cure the NHS
5b Lichfield Road
Stafford
ST17 4JX

Contents and Illustrations
Copyright Julie Bailey & Cure the NHS 2012

No portion of this book may be reproduced, stored in a
retrieval system or transmitted at any time or by any means
mechanical, electronic, recording or otherwise without the
prior written consent of the publisher.

First Printed August 2012 by
4 Sheets Design & Print Ltd

Available on Amazon Electronic Books

ebook pdf ISBN 978-0-9573826-1-9
ebook e-reader ISBN 978-0-9573826-2-6

ISBN 978-0-9573826-0-2

Contents

Acknowledgements

I would first like to thank the group, the members of Cure the NHS who I am so proud of. Without them, without their courage and determination to put their own grieving aside and try to help others no one would have listened. Also, I must thank them for the support and encouragement that they have given me during the writing of this book.

Special thanks must go to James Duff, now my dearest friend and Castell Davis for giving me the time and space to complete it and to Ken Lownds for helping me to produce it.

And last but not least my children who have helped to support me through the painful journey I have had to venture, during the writing of this book.

Foreword

Patients trying to make complaints about the quality of care in the NHS, especially the hospital services, can have considerable difficulties. In general, they are not experts on medical matters and they don't usually have access to information about other complaints so they may be told that theirs is a unique complaint and others have not found any problems. If they do find others who have complained about the care at a particular hospital, or they find other evidence of such problems, then they may have the strength to persist with their complaints.

Julie Bailey's book tells the story of how difficult making a complaint can be but how, when she persisted, she was able to find others who were having the similar difficulties and how this led to a group of patients forming CureTheNHS, a campaigning group attempting to improve the National Health service, and, in particular, the care at the Mid Staffs NHS Foundation Trust in Stafford, England. Eventually this group pressed for a public inquiry into the problems at that hospital after these had been revealed by the year-long investigation carried out by the regulator, the Healthcare Commission, and published in March 2009.

In May 2008, shortly after the Healthcare Commission announced their investigation, when the group were having great difficulties getting anyone to listen to them, having tried several of the organisations that were meant to be doing just that, the Chief Executive of the Regulator, the Healthcare Commission, accompanied by the Chairman, met the Chief Executive of the NHS and told him of the overwhelming response that they had received from local people regarding questions of quality of care at Mid Staffs. The Chief Executive of the NHS cautioned them about listening to 'a local campaign group' that might be 'simply lobbying' rather than expressing widespread concern.

A report from the Institute of Healthcare Improvement, commissioned by Lord Darzi, Parliamentary Under-Secretary of State at the Department of Health, submitted to him in 2008 but released, as a result of a Freedom of Information request, in 2010 stated: "The NHS has developed a widespread culture more of fear and compliance, than of learning, innovation and enthusiastic participation in improvement."

There have been many concerns about poor care received by the vulnerable and elderly in the NHS. A report from the Care Quality Commission, successor to the Healthcare Commission, in June 2012 warned that 131 hospitals (22 per cent) were failing to meet the standards required by law to ensure the safety and basic care of patients.

The 'second level' complaints (those not resolved in the local hospital) were given to the Healthcare Commission for analysis but they were unable to cope with the work and the job was passed to the Parliamentary Health Service Ombudsman. In 2008/09 she only 'accepted' 401 of the 16,317 enquiries she received from the public and only 32% were for hospital services. In that year there were 89,319 written complaints about hospital and community health services in England.

What chance do patients have in this climate of fear if, when the regulator receives an overwhelming number of complaints from the general public about a hospital, it is considered 'simply lobbying?' Complaints are like gold dust — they should be used for improving the service. I hope that Julie Bailey's book will help to make this happen in the NHS.

Brian Jarman
9 September 2012.

Prologue

It's not every day that you decide to write a book but today isn't any other day. It's not that I haven't thought of it before but today it continues to gnaw away at me. It won't go away I try and push it out of my mind as I have so many other things to do. I've put it off so many times because I know how painful it will be. I will have to reflect on one of the most traumatic periods of my life, revisiting scenes that I never wanted to return to. But I can avoid it no longer.

What happened five years ago changed my life and set me on a course of action that I never ever expected. I lost my dear Mother through what I believe was cold neglect, at the same time I was forced to witness many others being cruelly neglected within what should have been a place of safety and care.

At the time I thought I was alone but I soon realised that I wasn't, Mid Staffs Foundation Trust hospital (MSFT) had been harming and abusing patients for years. And it wasn't until they harmed my Mum and I launched the campaign Cure the NHS (CTNHS), that others including myself realised that we were not alone. We would no longer suffer in silence.

It's ironic that the Staffordshire Newsletter, the newspaper that initially helped me at the beginning of the campaign is now criticising all that I have worked for and that is now the impetus for me to start my story. Inside today's edition are letters that criticise me and the campaign for exposing the failures at MSFT hospital. It's not the first time and I'm sure it won't be the last but it really niggles at me today, for some reason.

I've put up with enough and it is now my turn to have a voice and tell the reader how hundreds of people are needlessly dying throughout the NHS. I want to tell the reader about the fatal flaws within the NHS and the harm that is caused on a daily basis by an unrestrained culture of apathy and ignorance. Five years ago I believed that the NHS was something to be proud of. I never thought for one minute I would be sitting here writing a book criticising it. But that is what I am about to do.

I've sat all day at the Mid Staffs Public Inquiry (MSPI), as I have done every day since it started, listening to the Chief Nursing Officer (CNO) of the NHS telling us that there had been a problem with nursing. That it had lost its way. But now things have improved and are back on track. Problem solved. Move on. Forget about it.

Dame Christine Beasley claims she has no real concerns about the standard of nursing in the NHS, acting as if she is oblivious to the fact that she is sitting opposite twelve people who have had their lives destroyed by the grave lack of care at MSFT hospital. On a daily basis we continue to hear of appalling practice from all over the country often because of poor nursing and I sense absolutely no urgency from her that something radical needs to happen, within the nursing profession. What hope have we got when she is leading the profession? I despair.

With her evidence still ringing in my ears and the criticisms from the editor of the *Staffordshire Newsletter* questioning the need for the MSPI and the cost to the public, I put my boots on and take the dog for a walk. It's the part of the day I normally most enjoy but all I want to do is get home, despite a late sun to warm me. I'm not sure if I need to eat something but my stomach aches, it feels tight, knotted and I just need to go home. I park the car without thinking and lift Jess, out of the back, without saying a word to her. I throw the ball a few times for her but my heart's not in it and my mind's elsewhere. Jess knows this. She sits down with the ball and refuses to bring it back, like a moody teenager.

I get home and start cleaning, I need the distraction, it's what I always do. I start to mop the kitchen floor. I want to cry but I won't, it takes energy I haven't got and I try not to. I bite my lip. The floor has been mopped, what now? I climb the stairs, Jess sits at the top watching my every move. She knows something is wrong I can tell by the way she watches me, as I pass I stop to quickly smooth her but only briefly to reassure her. She hates it when I cry, I know it. I bite my lip and begin to clean the bathroom. The distraction is working.

I try to empty the bin and as I do, a bleach bottle drops out on to the floor. I grab it with such force and begin to bash it against the bath in temper, over and over. My strength and the

Erratum: the date at the bottom of this page should read 18th March 2009

anger surprises me and the tears come and just flow as I continue, crash, crash. I sob, crumpled on my knees. I'm broken. The ache in my stomach feels tighter and the anguish in my voice alarms me. It all comes back to me now. The negative comments, the dirty looks in the street, the horrible feeling of hopelessness. "No! No!" I hear myself saying as I continue to bang the bottle down. The time I have given. The life I have sacrificed. What for? Over the last four years I have given my life, my heart, my soul, my everything to campaign for a safer NHS. Every waking moment is spent fighting. And for what? What has it all been for? I feel so helpless. So alone.

Jess is at my side, she cries too and I can see her distress. She jumps and barks with real concern. What's happening? I wipe my eyes with my hand but the tears continue, I moan aloud. Her bark jolts me. What the hell am I doing? Get up, get up woman! I can control this, what has happened to me? I feel the strength rise inside me and I'm back on my feet. It's over. OK, I'm hurt but why? The Newsletter has printed countless articles I'm not happy with, some weeks there are even letters that name and criticise me. What's so different about today's article?

That I don't know. Maybe I've just cracked under all the bitterness and resentment I've felt over the last few weeks as many in the community have questioned why we need this inquiry. So many just want to forget about it, an inconvenient uncomfortable, truth. "It was horrible, yes, but why can't you forget about it?" I'm that mad woman who just won't let it go, just seeking publicity, my fifteen minutes of fame. Believe me, if I had a choice I'd rather have my Mum. Perhaps it's the editor's comments when she says the least we can expect from the MSPI, is that it stops others being harmed. If that isn't enough, then what is?

It quickly dawns on me that covering the last five years in one book will not do our struggle justice. I have chosen to separate the periods and events as this will allow me to tell you about our difficult journey properly. In this first book I will cover from the day my Mum went into the hospital which was 25th September 2007 until the 18th March 2008 when the first investigation into the hospital was concluded. It is my intention to tell you about the further investigations into the hospital in another book at a later date.

Part One

A New Beginning

The day my life changed forever didn't quite begin like any other. I was up early to take my only daughter to Swansea University, a new stage of her life was about to begin. My Mum was 86 and wasn't in the best of health. She'd been a smoker in the past diagnosed with chronic obstructive airways disease and now susceptible to chest infections. Over the last year she had been diagnosed with a hiatus hernia, which had restricted her diet, to soft foods. It had been diagnosed in the summer and it had been a pain in the behind as she really loved her food, except anything that had come within twelve feet of garlic.

I hardly had time to speak to my Mum as all my energy was put into getting Laura finally packed and into the car. There was an air of anxiety in the room, but no one wanted to talk about it. I was losing my daughter, Mum was losing her granddaughter but at the same time we knew we had to be strong and support her. Mum helped as best she could, reminding us of things that we needed to take. She was like that, the matriarch, the organiser within our little family.

She'd had a rough night and hadn't slept much and would get dressed later. She'd be alright. That was Mum, it was the sort of woman she was, never one to make a fuss if there was someone else who needed the attention. And today it was Laura's turn for a fuss, it was her day.

It was an emotional hour or so getting Laura ready, a big day for her leaving home for the first time and of course I was losing my daughter. I knew life would never be the same again but I didn't quite expect it to change in the way it did. I'd tried to equip the kids with the confidence to challenge their comfort zone and it was always expected that Laura would go to

University. My son, Martin, had gone to Bristol a few years earlier and was now a graduate, teaching and living in Southampton. I knew he was ready for that adventure but I wasn't so sure about Laura. Or was it me that wasn't ready for her to start that adventure?

The car was packed and we were waving Mum off at the door, she didn't look well but then she hadn't slept. I tried to do the goodbyes quickly, I knew Laura would be upset leaving her Nan, they were very close. But this is her new beginning, the first day of the rest of her life. As I drive I wrack my brain trying to remember everything we needed to bring, praying there's nothing we've forgotten! It's like a full house move in a Volvo v40, if that's possible. Laura had brought along her boyfriend, Dan. They'd been together about 2 years, I was sure he was upset but he didn't show it. It was a miserable day but the drive is straightforward and passes quickly. Laura's tears at leaving her Nan have quickly passed with so much more to think about.

Three hours later we arrived and the shock at what we find is something I have to try to hide. The student accommodation she was allocated was like a large broom cupboard. There were kids everywhere, all different nationalities and types. All busy making their little nests, some confident, some shy, all thrown together for a new stage in their lives. We quickly empty the car and try to help her to make this dark, dingy, room her home. We knew it wouldn't be easy, especially as the view was of a solid brick wall. 'Anyway this is the student village and she will soon make friends and her new adventure will begin', I tell myself.

The drive home is painful. I wanted to cry but how could I, I try to avoid talking to Dan it's not that I don't want to. I pass the time by flicking through the radio channels looking for something to distract me, I find nothing. Before we hit Ross on Wye Laura has phoned, she's unhappy but she is bound to be. Dan holds the phone out so she can hear me and I tell her she will quickly make friends. I was dreading that call and was hoping I would at least have made it home before she rang.

Stafford is the same. It's still raining, but it's now dark and the lights are on, it's early evening, when we arrive home. Mum's room was at the back of the house. She had moved in with me about 2 years before. It wasn't that she really needed to. She was mostly self caring but found it hard to cook for herself and she needed the company. Old age can be a lonely time and with me working full time running my own business, it made life easier all round. The house was big enough, she had her own unit looking out onto the garden and we shared the kitchen and living room.

As I walked through the living room door I see my Mum sitting on her recliner and I collapse into her, throwing my arms around her. She's taken aback but she comforts me all the same, holding me to her, half on the chair. "We will all miss her Jude but we must let her do as she wants". I dry my eyes and tell her that she has already rung, she wants to come home. Mum holds me closer and I don't know it but this is the last time that she will hold me in this way, to comfort me as a Mother does, and has, all these years.

She'd been poorly all day and hadn't managed to eat or drink anything but an early night will do it, she tells me. It doesn't. She's up all night and she finally sleeps around 4am, with me curled up on the bottom of her bed. The following morning she's still poorly and I mention calling the doctor. She's reluctant but she knows that she has no alternative and the disappointment is evident in her face. Her hope was that she would wake this morning and be fine, but she isn't and she knows it. Mum's glass was always half full, she always saw things in a positive light, perhaps it had been her hard life that gave her a strong sense of optimism. 'Things can only get better' had more than not been the case.

Isabella Emily Ivy Bailey (Nee Rayment) was born on the 16/2/1921 in Edmonton, North London and until her late teens she lived a relatively comfortable life, totally adored by her Father. Her Mother had always suffered with ill health which sadly meant they never had a particularly close or warm relationship. It was left to her Father to do what he could to fill that role. As a young woman she saw the early war years as an opportunity to party with friends and family. The stories she told us about the air raid shelters brought them alive many years later. Mum had that ability, she was able to reminisce and you felt part of that experience. You would hang on her every word, just waiting for what happened next. They danced they sang and they made many friends, the camaraderie was infectious between them. She believed that life was for living and that's what she did and so did all of her family. She had several brothers who she was very close to and a younger sister. By 19, she was engaged, very much in love and waiting for her fiancé to return from France. He never came home. She heard from her Mother in Law to be one day that he had lost his life, serving his country.

Mum tried to mourn but with each day that passed more and more people around her had lost loved ones too. It was very much expected that the war would take lives, it was something they had to get used to. Despite her reluctance she ended up serving in the Women's Royal Air Force but hating the discipline only lasted a few days. She absconded and tried to return home but instead was sent to a munitions factory in Staffordshire, her life was then changed forever.

One fateful evening following a dance she met my Father and her family in London were none too happy with her choice of husband. Despite Mum's appeals to them they never really took to him and their first assessment of him turned out to be correct. She went on to lead a miserable married life, providing him with six children. Her first child, Stan, died a few months old and she often spoke about him even seventy years later, his death lived with her always.

My Father left her when I was young, they divorced and Mum struggled to keep her family together. It is to his shame that in his absence he failed to provide any means of support for us and Mum struggled to put food on the table. At one point she had four jobs, leaving one to start another just to keep a roof over our heads. In those days there were no free meal tickets, you went out and worked to survive. Sometimes we were closer to the edge than I dare to remember.

I try the doctor's number again but it's engaged, there must be an awful lot of sick people in Stafford. I put the kettle on, anxiously keeping my hands busy, and return to the phone. Finally I get through to the surgery, they tell me the doctor will be with us as soon as he can. This reassures us a little bit. I finish making my tea and take it into Mum's room, she looks exhausted. If she could just stop being sick she would be alright, I'm convinced.

I heard the car pull up before I heard him knock the door. Mum was familiar with this doctor, Dr Wilson, because he only lived a few doors away and he would call in on his way home if we had rung for a house call. She loved his jovial manner and I often teased her that she was attracted to him. He was a tall handsome man with a slightly greying beard and he was always casually but smartly dressed. I wasn't attracted to him like Mum, it was his car I fancied. He drove an old red sports car and I looked with envy at his parked next to my newish Volvo. "The doctor's here Mum" I shout from the living room.

This doctor had been involved with Mum's care for a while now ever since she had developed the hiatus hernia. Over the last year he had chopped and changed her medication hoping it would do the trick. It had and after each visit she had benefited from either a change in her medication or an increase in her current medication. A "slight tweak," the doctor had called it but this time it wasn't working.

"Has this old classic had it" Mum asks lifting her head off the pillow hoping that he will tell her what she wants to hear. Mum tries to sit up but she hasn't the energy and he tells her not to get up just for him.

"For today you have," he tells her. "I need to send you to the hospital because we can't stop you being sick". He sits down at Mum's dressing table stool and begins to write a letter. His long legs look daft sitting on the tiny seat and I stand there hoping it won't give way on him. He sits writing for several minutes and fills a page before he stands and hands me an envelope to give to the hospital.

He apologised to Mum "Adjusting your tablets won't do the trick today but I'll make sure you get the best bed on the wards."

Mum liked him, he didn't speak to her like a decrepit old woman and he was usually full of chat. Mum's face said it all, she was relieved that she would soon be in more capable hands. Or that is what we thought. Both Mum and I were proud of the NHS, she had only had good experiences. We both respected doctors and nurses and had always felt that they gave their lives to help others.

The ambulance was outside the house for ages. Or did it just seem like ages? The house suddenly became silent and I could even hear the clock ticking, it felt very strange. Being in the house alone was odd as Mum was normally always here she loved the TV and it was strange not hearing it on this morning. They didn't have room for me so I had to follow in the car. I quickly found a few bits from her room not really knowing what she would need. I made sure I took all of her current tablets thinking she would definitely need those. I found her a night-dress, the best one I could find in a hurry, and her favourite slippers, I knew they were old but she loved them. I quickly grabbed my phone, handbag and was turning the key in the door when the ambulance pulled off. I drove to the hospital full of hope that she would soon feel better and be home with us. She'd been admitted with the same thing last year and had only been in overnight.

Stafford Hospital (or Mid Staffs Hospital before it was rebranded) is a mile or so outside of the town, a short drive through leafy suburbs and some open countryside before it rises out of the green earth like a concrete fortress. It seemed like ages until I managed to park the car, several times I waited thinking people were pulling out. Eventually I found a space and pulling my coat around me made my way into A & E, passing under the ubiquitous ambulance canopy like you find in a petrol station. As I pass through the automatic doors it looks like I've come to a shopping centre, all I can see are shops and cafes, I thought this was a hospital? In the middle of the entrance people sit along a seating area with both sides filled with people eating their lunches. People are bursting out the door of the cake shop I found the ambulance staff still with Mum, she looked so small on a hospital trolley. I followed them up to the emergency assessment unit (EAU), which I later learned the staff called *Beirut*. Mum was wheeled into a single room and I thought, 'This does look like the best bed in the house.' She even had an ensuite!

Nurse after nurse arrived, all very busy, doing different tasks and asking different questions, all of them very pleasant. Mum was hard of hearing but had never taken to wearing an aid so I ended up answering most of the questions for her. I could tell by her face that she had had enough and as the ques-tions continued she carried on retching into a cardboard bowl that one of the nurses had given her. She was exhausted but as each nurse arrived she rallied round to be pleasant to them.

It was now around 7pm and a doctor was on their way a kind nurse told us. She had been in a few times to see us and ask how Mum was. She had a lovely smile and bright blue eyes. She had a Swedish look about her with long blonde hair tied tightly behind her head and not a split end in sight. As soon as she spoke you could tell she wasn't Swedish, her Cannock accent was evidence of that. But her voice was calm and quiet and I had to repeat everything she said because of Mum's hearing. Apart from Mum constantly being sick she had pain in her back and chest, just to add to her misery. A nurse had already tested the heart monitor on her but we hadn't heard the results yet. I didn't think for one minute it was her heart, she had always been proud of her strong ticker.

Mum tried to doze off, she was exhausted but the constant retching stopped her, as soon as she closed her eyes, again the retching would start. I sat in the chair next to her and could have easily nodded off if I had been alone but for poor Mum. I really felt for her and if I could I would have gladly shared her discomfort. It had now been over 24 hours since she had had anything past her lips and yet she continued to retch. I was starting to worry that something was seriously wrong. Why was she still retching?

Not one but three doctors appeared and one seemed to take charge over the other two. They all looked young but I could see that Mum was relieved. One would have been enough, but three! Mum tried to keep up with his questions but with her eyes she passed it over to me to answer for her. One of them sat Mum up and tapped at her back and put the stethoscope here, there and everywhere. Mum looked at him in hope, hope he would soon ease her discomfort. He was clearly the senior doctor, older but smaller than the others. The lead was doing all the talking and the other two mostly listened. What struck me about him was how scruffy he looked. His hair was everywhere, wavy black and thick, it looked as if he was long overdue a haircut. He wore a scruffy pair of baggy beige trousers and loose flip flop sandals. He looked as if he was going to the beach and not attending to sick people.

He reread the admission letter that her GP had written and asked again where the pain was coming from. He asked if Mum had pain down her arm and I sensed he thought it was her heart. I suddenly remembered the electrocardiogram (ECG) and wondered if the results had indicated a problem. I remind him of her hiatus hernia and if he thought the retching could be what was causing the pain. The three medics talked amongst themselves and it was hard to hear or understand what they were saying. They leave quite abruptly, stopping only to tell us

17

they would be back later after blood results had returned.

I sat there making eyes at Mum wondering if they realised we were even alive and in the room. I'm sure if they could have got away with it they would not have spoken to us at all. The lead doctor barely acknowledged us the other two did at least make eye contact as they left the room. The lead doctor was very abrupt and didn't respond to any answers we gave. I felt he wasn't listening to what either of us was trying to tell him.

We don't wait long before another nurse arrives to tend to us but I recognise this one. She is a customer of mine and immediately puts our minds at rest. I ran a dog grooming salon in the town and I had several nurses who were customers. I had retired from social work and returned to Stafford from South Wales, to care for Mum a few years ago. I had been grooming this nurse's spaniel for some time and she was a regular visitor to the salon. She assures us she will chase up Mum's results and get her some pain relief. Within fifteen minutes she was back. She told us that Mum's heart was fine and she had called the Dr to prescribe something for the pain. It was now 11ish and I was shattered but Mum is now eased and the nurse reassures me that she will keep a close eye on her. They are going to try another drug to try and stop her sickness and I'm confident she is in safe hands. It was such a relief to hear some positive news from all the tests she had had done. It was also a comfort to see someone that I knew and could talk to. This nurse would now be on duty until the morning, having been on nights all week. You couldn't tell though, her face was fresh and she looked full of energy. She wore her long hair tight in a bun and Mum commented that she had once worn her hair in the same way. This nurse also wore small round glasses that made her face look even sweeter.

I left the hospital tired and drawn, struggling to control the car on the windy country lanes. I was still worried but with the sense of relief that she was in the best place and now free from pain I managed to get a few hours sleep.

I return first thing the next morning, a hot flannel across my face and a scalding cup of tea before I'm out of the door. I've no idea of the visiting times but I'm unable to settle at home not knowing how she is. I tried ringing the ward a few times but there was no answer, it just rang and rang, so I decided to get there early. Perhaps, I thought, I would be in time to catch the doctor on the ward round. Luckily I was, but we just seem to go through the same questions as yesterday. It seems odd but every time they ask her why she is here and each time they ask she is being sick into a cardboard bowl. They also ask her if she is in pain and where the pain is coming from. Once again the heart monitor reappears but this time it's a different nurse doing it. By this point I'd sussed that the staff in the lilac over-alls are Health Care Assistants (HCA) not nurses and one was struggling to attach stickers onto the appropriate places on Mum's body. She's very friendly and chats while she struggles with the stickers but I sense she's wasting her time. Mum tries to smile at me and we make small talk but we both know an echocardiogram is not what is needed, or that's what we both hope.

Mum thinks she's got a chest infection, she's started to cough a lot and she continues to retch. There are developments though as a nurse is putting up a saline drip. Mum tells me several doctors had tried to get a cannula into her arm very early this morning, with the third doctor succeeding. They were all relieved. Her face is ashen but the fluids will help her. That's if she can stop being sick. The anti sickness tablets haven't helped but they are going to try another type. I wonder how many types there are because her GP had tried a couple before she had been admitted. I push these thoughts out of my mind and try reading the day's newspaper to Mum. It's a bit like trying to read the bible to an atheist. She's not interested and neither am I really. She's unable to settle but I chat about Laura and that distracts her. We decide between us that we won't tell Laura about Mum's admission to hospital. There's no point she will only worry, want to come home and anyway Mum will probably be home in a few days. We decide to stick to the story if she calls.

I daren't answer my phone when Laura rings, it's on silent but I feel it vibrating. After the third call, I pluck up the courage, I leave Mum and stand outside the ward and ring her. I'm dreading it, I talk to her but at the same time I'm not really listening, just going through the motions, I try and avoid the subject of her Nan and try and focus on what she has been doing. But she wants to talk about her Nan and I find that hard to deal with, has she guessed something is wrong?

"How's Nan?"

"Oh yeah, she's fine." I hear my voice quiver, I hope she can't.

"Can I have a word with her?" I freeze.

"Oh...She's having a nap at the mo."

All of a sudden the lift doors swoosh open and a bed begins to emerge as two porters manoeuvre it out onto the ward.

"Sorry, Lorz. A customer's just come in. I'll have to go."

"Ok. I love you, Mum."

"I love you too Lorz." My voice cracking as I pull the phone away. I feel so guilty. I can't imagine what she's going through and all I want to do is get her off the phone.

Mum continues to cough and her sputum is a horrible greeny colour, she must have a chest infection. She was right. She tries to hold her head back at the same time as she coughs to try to ease her pain. I struggle for the rest of the day to get a doctor to understand that it's likely that she has a chest infection, I'm unable to get them to understand what we are trying to tell them is the problem. It's a combination of a language barrier and the added complication that Mum also has the hiatus hernia, with its own symptoms. She spends the day retching and coughing, she's exhausted. As yesterday, every few hours a posse of doctors arrive, all very young and with no-one seeming to be in charge or to give us any idea of a plan of care, or even what they are thinking. Once again they ask the same questions as previous visits and I feel like telling them that everything has been asked before, but I don't.

That evening my brother visits and his presence has the potential to lighten the mood, all three of my brothers are born jokers and Pat's no different. We hope he'll cheer us up when he gets here. We have lots to talk about as we haven't seen him for a while, but she's just feeling too unwell to chat. She's so tired and tries to close her eyes but she's also too unwell to sleep, the retching startling her awake.

"Urgh. Get that one, Jude."

"What, Mum?"

"That spider." She's pointing at the wall next to her bed.

"Where?" I squint at the wall but can't see any spider.

"There!" She insists, annoyed I can't see it. There was not much that frightened her but she didn't like spiders and we had some laughs over the years with plastic, joke shop spiders but today isn't one of them. The nurse explains that Mum must have had a reaction to the anti-sickness drug she is taking, lots of people do. She says they should stop giving it to her. I worry we are running out of options with anti-sickness drugs. Despite the nurse putting it in her notes over the next few weeks she is continually given or they try to give her the drug.

Pat leaves around 8pm and I try to give Mum a rinse with a dried out flannel, it freshens her up a bit, but her pain is evident as I gently move her. I sit back down and try stroking her hand, hoping to soothe her off to sleep. It works and I hear her chest rattling as she breathes, it's horrid to listen to but her eyes are firmly shut.

As I begin to doze too, the night shift nurse arrives she's also a customer of mine. She brings me a small spaniel to bath and brush out. She suggests I go home as I look shattered. I am and Mum is sleeping although not peacefully, more of a forced sleep because she is too exhausted to stay awake any longer. The thought of going home and Mum being in pain worries me but the nurse assures me that she will keep an eye on her and give her painkillers as soon as she wakes. I know Mum won't ring the bell but I leave it next to her, more to reassure myself than Mum.

I check my watch, it's 11.15pm. The hospital is deserted, my shoes make the only noise on the long deserted corridor and I try to walk quietly, not to wake anyone. I take the stairs and out through the main entrance, as I approach the main doors a buzzer sounds and I notice a woman in a room opposite the entrance. The doors are now locked and she has released the doors to let me out. The cold hit's me as I take in a gulp of early September air, it's damp but welcome. I fumble first for the car park ticket that I took from the machine fifteen hours ago. I empty out my bag, where is it? I just want to get home. Once found I then fumble for change, or should I say notes. The price shocks me but I have to pay, I just consider myself lucky that I have that much in my purse. The car park is deserted unlike this morning as I once again searched for a space. Tonight there's just me and I hope I will get through the barrier without any fuss. I do and I drive home struggling to concentrate on the roads. I climb into bed but toss and turn all night, I sense Mum is doing the same. I'm tempted to ring the ward and ask if she is ok, but I don't. She's in safe hands, I tell myself.

The Awful Truth

The following morning I have the same trouble as yesterday parking the car, but today I remember to put my parking ticket somewhere safe to avoid spilling my bag out later. I call for the newspaper on my way up in the hope that Mum will be interested in the news today. She isn't, she looks worse than yesterday and she tells me that no one has entered her room all night, until the early hours of this morning. I doubt this and suspect perhaps Mum is mistaken. As the day goes on she convinces me that she is right and the nurse didn't, as she had promised, keep an eye on Mum.

You see Mum isn't a complainer, she will put up with most things and hates to make a fuss. Nurses and doctors are gods in Mum's eyes and I suppose mine too. It seems odd that a nurse would show concern over my wellbeing and then ignore my vulnerable Mother all night. I'm not convinced until later that day I find Mum's drug chart and like she has been saying all day she was given no medication all night. Mum was right and it's very unlike her but she continues to tell me throughout the day about her awful night. She tells me how she called out for the staff during the night and at one point she heard them outside the door and they had then shut the door, ignoring her calls. I try to change the subject as I find it hard to believe that the nurses would do this. I try to distract her and although I know it is unlikely because of her persistence, I try to push it out of my mind because I don't want to believe it.

The paper doesn't distract her and she tells me that she had to be sick on the bed sheet as she didn't have a bowl to be sick in. The nurses had ignored her calls and she continues to tell me about her night at every opportunity that she gets.

"It was horrible Jude" her face now in a grimace, "I tried to get out the bed, to get a cloth". But I could see it wasn't going to go away I tried to keep talking trying not to let her return to the subject but it isn't working.

'Get out of the bed? She wouldn't have got out of the bed?' I try to keep telling myself. It must be the medication that has confused her.

"I didn't want the nurses to see I had been sick in those clean sheets either," she reaches out for the newspaper stopping me from reading it.

She's determined that I listen to her, I can see the determination in her face now.

"The smell all night was terrible," she is almost pleading with me but still I resist believing her version. She begins to retch again and I can see that she had tears in her eyes and an anger I very rarely see. But even this I try to brush off and convince myself I just need to change the subject. I need to distract her from some sort of hallucination she must have had about her night on the ward.

The following morning I am there when the Consultant arrives, at least that's who I think he is. He has a posse of other doctors with him but he is the one in charge, the one that walks several paces in front of the others. You can tell by his whole persona that he is in charge as the others hang on his every word. He's quite odd looking as he is quite tall with a moustache that seems to fill his face. He's wearing an expensive suit and the others look as if they are trying to emulate him in their less expensive outfits.

He tells us it is likely that it is the hiatus hernia playing up and because Mum had an endoscopy in May it is unlikely there will be any changes, therefore there is no need to do the procedure again. The plan will be to observe her. I mention the chest infection but he doesn't seem to want to listen. I try again and mention that Mum is under a Consultant at the hospital as she is prone to chest infections. Before I know it the posse is out of the door and gone. He hasn't listened. They will try another sickness drug but nothing for the chest infection. I feel exhausted asking, it's my heart that's racing not Mum's. What can I say? What can I do? I know it's a chest infection but I just feel so small next to them with their knowledge and authority. I can see the disappointment on Mum's face, she knows she needs to get the antibiotics down her soon, I can see the worry on her face and I feel I've failed her.

Later that morning I try again with a young doctor that we met yesterday, like most of the doctors we met during her three days in the EAU, we are unable to communicate properly because of language problems. She looks South American, with light brown skin and dark attractive eyes, although they look heavy as if she has gone without sleep or had a heavy night. She looks too young to be a doctor, I would guess around twenty but her clothes make her look even younger. Around her waist she is wearing a thick jewelled belt that holds her waist in tightly. Over her shoulder is what I could only describe as a hippy bag that hangs at the side of her and flops around as she moves around the bed. I dread to think what germs she has collected on the bag and instead of watching her I'm more interested in watching if the bag touches Mum's skin.

I look up and she's once again holding on to Mum's notes as if she is trying to read them. I feel I must point out that both Mum and myself had believed passionately in a diverse society, reflecting Mum's Jewish roots, and our family has always been very left-leaning but it seems folly to employ doctors who lack the language ability to communicate with patients. How on earth can they diagnose if they don't understand a patient's description of their symptoms?

In desperation I show her the bowl of green sputum and grimace as I gently touch Mum's back, trying to indicate that the pain in her back is connected with the green sputum she is coughing up. I feel daft but I will try anything to help Mum. I can see the hope in Mum's eyes and her vulnerability hits me like a hammer at the back of my head.

It works and within fifteen minutes her first antibiotic is being administered intravenously, the relief on our faces would have made a good picture. I don't bother to mention the steroids that she usually takes along with the antibiotics, we're just relieved she has these. I'm so happy I decide it's a good time to call Laura.

I stand out in the hallway and hope no one passes as I don't want her to know where Mum is. When I return to the room and sit back down, Mum is sleeping. I pick up the paper but I can't read, my mind is in Swansea with Laura. My eyes wander and as they do I notice a plastic tube coming out the side of Mum's bed. Is it a catheter? What? Yes, it is! What's happened? Why have they done this? What's wrong? What's going on? I sit there in a blind panic for what seems like an age, until a nurse calls in and I find out it's the nurse who fitted the catheter. She tells me that Mum has a blockage and that was the reason it was fitted. I'm still pondering what she has said as it seems odd that they have found a blockage and I had only been gone for 10 minutes at the most. I want to ask lots of questions but her demeanour puts me off doing so.

She's a Staff Nurse I can tell by the colour of her uniform and I must say something but I can sense she isn't the explaining type. She's blonde with a short sharp bob and is already at the door before I even have chance to say anything.

"You will feel better soon." And she is gone out the door. Mum didn't hear a word she had said and I repeat it to her.

"She says you will feel better soon," I tell her as I reach for her hand.

"Why?" she asks full of inquisition.

I smile but shrug my shoulders at the same time as I have no answer for her as I'm as bemused as her.

"There was nothing wrong with my water works, Jude, never has been." She now sounds as confused as me.

Just as I'm thinking that's peculiar, a couple of HCA appear and break the silence. Mum's being moved and once the porter arrives she will be moved to Ward 10, we have a few minutes to gather her things before the porter arrives. I quickly pack her bits and at the last minute remember her slippers from under the bed, only because she has reminded me. They're her favourite slippers but she hasn't needed them for the last three days as she has hardly got out of bed. They probably smell and need replacing. It's a joke between us that they have done some miles but she loves them. We don't have to wait long before the porter arrives, stinking of hair gel and cheap aftershave, and we're off.

The two health carers come with us and chatter amongst themselves on the journey, seems they cover a few hospitals and they socialise together. Mum is irrelevant but I don't care I'm so happy that she has got her antibiotics. By tomorrow morning the drug will be in her system and by tomorrow night her pain should ease. But then she isn't going to have her steroids. I push that out of my mind quickly, I can only fight one battle at a time. They are going to try another drug to stop her sickness and she will probably be home tomorrow. Fingers crossed.

Mum is pushed into a room with four other beds, all empty and unmade. There's a little old lady sat in an armchair with a tray attached to the chair. She's doesn't look up as we come into the room, despite all the noise. She's just sat there in a pretty summer dress, looking down at her lap. It struck me as odd that she doesn't have a nighty on and was perhaps waiting to be admitted to the ward, like us.

The room is cold and I shiver myself at the chill as I wrap my cardigan around me tightly but the lady continues to stare at her lap, unaware of our presence. Mum and I say nothing, the uncomfortable silence stops us and when we do we whisper to each other. After packing her things into her cabinet I finally sit. The silence now is deafening. Mum looks at me and nods. That's all it takes, she doesn't have to say a word. A look and a nod from my Mum speaks a thousand words and I know exactly what she wants me to do. My Mum's sick, exhausted and in pain but can't rest at the thought that someone needs help. She was one in a million. There was the right thing to do and the wrong thing to do, it was as simple as that.

I turn and say hello asking how she is, she doesn't move, I suspect she is confused, some form of dementia perhaps. I can tell by Mum's face that she is relieved that I have tried to make conversation. I'd worked in social care from when I had left school and most of my career had been working with people with dementia type illnesses. Over the last few years I'd worked as a Senior Practitioner within a social work team in Carmarthenshire. I'd reached a point in my life where I thought I desperately needed a change and circumstances allowed me to try something new. I'd spent my life working for someone else and had always wanted to work for myself, but in what capacity that could be I did not know. Mum had instilled in me her work ethic, although from a working class background she taught me that if I worked hard I could achieve something. I loved dogs, always had, unlike my Mum who could take them or leave them and she would rather leave them. I can still see her wrinkling her nose up as Jess would come up to lick her. I decided to take a short course and qualify as a dog groomer. I'd put all my savings into renovating a shop in the town and had become a well-respected dog groomer with an expanding client list. I loved my job, what dog lover wouldn't? Very often Mum would come with me to avoid staying home alone. Luckily September was often a quiet month as owners often missed a visit and saved their dog for a Christmas bath instead. I wouldn't be missed so much in September but In October I would be busy as I groomed a lot of dogs for a big, local dog show.

We sit in silence but just as I'm wondering how much longer we will sit here waiting a HCA brings in a meal tray to the old lady next to us. Not a word is spoken until Mum knocks me to help her with the food. I try to make conversation again asking her if she needs any help with the plastic covering, but she seems oblivious to me. Shortly after the HCA returns picks up the untouched meal tray and goes to take it out the door, not saying a word to either of us. I'm too concerned myself to say nothing and I know full well that Mum is too. Every now and again Mum strained her head round to see if the lady had started to eat her dinner.

"She hasn't touched it?" I ask but really only wanting her to show some concern for the lady.

"She never does," and with that she is gone out the door and along the corridor. I can hear her heavy footsteps echoing along the corridor. She was really tall and a large woman but the sound of her feet along an empty corridor make her sound much larger than she really was.

Again there is a period of silence and then I hear footsteps along the deserted corridor. This time it's a Staff Nurse and as she passes the bay we are sitting in I run out and try and catch her attention. I ask her if Mum will shortly be seen as it must now be several hours that we have been here waiting.

"Who are you?" she asks.

I'm a bit taken aback with her response and her sharpness especially when she tells me to go and sit down and wait a bit longer.

After much deliberation and more waiting we find that we have been taken to the wrong ward and will now need to be moved to another ward. It was just lucky that I had been with Mum when she had been moved. I dread to think what would have happened had I not been there, although I was about to find out.

The same nurse seems to stomp back into the bay and break the silence "Who brought you here?"

Despite trying to tell her that we had been moved here by HCAs from the last ward I sensed she didn't believe what I was telling her. Her face looked at me with total mistrust and disbelief at what I was telling her.

Ward 11

The first thing that struck us as we arrived on Ward 11 was the noise. Compared to the silence of the last ward, the contrast was striking. Where you could have heard a pin drop this ward was buzzing. It seemed like there were people everywhere. As Mum was wheeled right to the bottom of a long corridor, people stood outside of the bay doors, waiting. For what, at this stage I didn't know. They looked old, confused. But within days I was fully aware of why. As we came along the corridor we heard a scream. It's a real, chilling sound, not like the fake screams you hear in the movies, this one is true. Someone is in pain, someone is suffering. Mum hasn't heard it but she notices the amount of people compared to the bareness of the last ward, her eyes scanning around. I don't sense fear at this stage, no it's concern she still has the strength to be concerned about others.

Mum is wheeled into a room with four beds and is pushed into the bed nearest to the window. Two of the beds were vacant and a young woman was in the other bed with what looked like her Mother sitting next to her. She is in pain, that's clear. She has her knees raised up towards her chest in a foetal position and she has been crying. Was it her who was screaming? I can see by her face it was.

Mum is quickly transferred to the bed by two pleasant looking nurses. I look at my watch. Oh my God! It's seven o'clock! She was due her medication at four o'clock!

"Erm, Is it possible for Mum to get her medication now?" I didn't tell them she was due at four or that it had taken me three days to get the antibiotics prescribed. "My Mum's in pain. She needs pain relief," I plead but it is done unconsciously, just falling out of my mouth.

Their faces change and instead of kind, caring nurses I see a completely different side to them.

The taller of the two speaks, "We were ready to give your Mum her drugs at teatime but you weren't here".

"Oh sorry, they took us to the wrong ward." I say, still taken aback by her response.

"Well, that's not our fault is it? She will have to wait for the night drug round now." She said sharply to me, before they both walked briskly out of the room leaving Mum in pain, the woman in the opposite bed without assistance and me open mouthed.

I'm so shocked at their response I'm shaking. I find it hard to even look at Mum, when I do, I touch her hand to try to reassure her. I want her to think I have things under control but I haven't and we both know it. I look over at the woman in the bed opposite. I'm embarrassed. I know my face is flushed, I can feel it. She has heard it all before and so has her Mother.

"We've been waiting for over an hour to see a doctor now." The girl's Mother says to me. She has a kind face, full of concern for her child. She's trying to ease my embarrassment, showing me she understands. She tuts and taps the buzzer again, knowing it won't help but it's all she can do.

I start to unpack Mum's things, trying to distract myself from the situation but it can't be ignored, what am I going to do? The bedside drawer is filthy and I take a wet wipe and clean it out. I need another and another, really I need bleach and a scouring pad but these luxuries I haven't got. Damn! It's the last wet wipe but that really is the least of our problems. I can easily just avoid the drawer but the staff I can't.

Just as I'm thinking this, I hear a woman's heels coming down the corridor, getting closer and closer. Louder and louder. She storms into the bay and starts to shout at the poor woman opposite, she has her arms folded and stands menacingly in front of her. She's not a nurse because she is wearing a suit, be it an ill fitted suit. The trousers are too long and they drag on the floor and the sleeves partly cover her hands. The suit makes her look daft but she must be some sort of manager, a wedge of anger wrapped in polyester. I wonder who she can be and what position she holds.

"You are used to being in charge and today you are not in charge and that is the problem. You have been seen by two doctors already and there is nothing wrong with you,"

She unleashes on the tormented woman in her thick Stoke accent. And with that she turns off the buzzer and walks out the door. There is a painful silence punctuated only by her sharp heels on the lino.

The woman curls herself into a ball on her bed and sobs and sobs. It's horrible, I sit there pinned to my chair, I want to cry too but how can I? Why would I cry? I hate to hear anyone crying. No, that's not true, I hate to hear people crying that I'm unable to comfort. But I will and it will happen regularly over the next 8 weeks. It was a sound I would hear almost every night. I can sit here now, nearly five years on, and describe time after time the suffering. Some days it feels like a paper cut in my stomach, I can recall with such detail those times, often like it was yesterday.

I later learnt that this was the Ward 11 manager and the following day she was proven wrong. The poor woman had been bitten by a spider and if she hadn't got the attention she did, she may have lost her life. She had resorted to phoning a doctor she knew and asked him to speak to the junior doctor on the ward. After the conversation the very junior doctor prescribed the correct medication, luckily.

I arrive the following day around 1pm Mum finally got her drugs last night at 11pm, to much relief. I had left here around 12am and didn't sleep a wink, worrying. I went home in shock I never thought nurses would behave in that way. Even when I had said Mum was in pain they did nothing. Why? Aren't nurses supposed to be caring and kind? Selfless people who give their lives to others? What is wrong here?

The day passes quickly, Mum continues to be sick and as yet she has been given no fluids on this ward. It's hard to find anyone to ask and when you do they are vague as to who Mum is never mind specific questions about her care. Her room is right at the end of a long corridor and you only see a member of staff if they come into the room which isn't very often. I go home and worry about her until the following morning.

Overnight Mum tells me that she met a lovely nurse who had attached a bag of fluids and another one had been attached this morning. But she tells me how sore her arm is and I take one look at it and know there is something wrong. Her hand and arm is swollen and in places her arm is blue. It looks so inflamed and I suspect infected. I ring the call bell immediately, something is wrong and Mum knows it. She then tells me that she had shown the nurse that morning.

For the rest of the afternoon no one answers the call bell. Not just mine but anybody's call bell along the corridor. This probably means twenty patients. There are four in Mum's bay, six next door and six opposite and two side rooms. I search the ward for staff and can find no one. Where are they? As I walk along the corridor the buzzers echo in my ear and also the shouting from some of the other patients. I return to Mum's bay and help the woman opposite onto her commode, there is no option. I had worked as a home care assistant when I was a student at Swansea University. I had been trained how to move someone safely onto a commode, but it had been several years ago. I didn't feel I had any choice, if I didn't help her, who would?

By teatime Mum's bed is soaking wet, her catheter is leaking for some reason. We have been told for the last three hours that someone will come and change her soon. We hear it over and over again but no one comes. I wander off to look for a nurse and on my travels I don't find a nurse but I do find a cupboard with dry linen in. I take a couple of sheets and I gently try to push Mum onto her side and push the dry linen next to her skin. I'm unable to change her bed myself because of a cannula she has in both arms and there's the catheter to contend with. The one arm is so swollen and sore I'm frightened of hurting her more. I feel out of my depth and unable to help. I have the clean bedding but I feel there's little more I can do, I feel powerless. Mum nods in and out of a restless sleep, she looks so uncomfortable. I want to scream out for help but whom to? There's nobody here.

We wait hours for a nurse to help her and all the time she is in pain. By the time a nurse arrives she is crying out. Her arm is now twice the size it should be and the alarm on her monitor has been going off for over two hours. Luckily the other patients seem understanding, although it must irritate them because it does me. To make matters worse the woman in the room opposite has a buzzer that seems to have been going off for hours too. I have to go home and leave Mum in their hands but I worry all night and sleep is impossible. There just doesn't seem as if there is anyone on the wards to care for the patients. Nobody seems to be in control or to be managing the ward, the place seems out of anyone's control. It's bedlam!

All I can think about is Mum but at the same time I can see and hear others suffering. The old woman in the next bed, Lillian, is immobile and Mum tells me that she just sits in her wheelchair all day from early morning until late evening. I smile as I arrive and she looks up and raises a hand to me. Dinner is given out and she struggles to open the plastic covering her plate until I offer her help. But even I struggle to open the plastic container. Turns out it's hardly worth opening, the food's so dried up I can't even tell what it is. I watch her as she struggles to eat it, it doesn't look appetising at all. Mum catches me watching her.

"Have you eaten, Jude?" Poor Mum. She hasn't eaten in days and yet she thinks of me. It doesn't surprise me a bit, that was the way she was made, to always think of others. One of my Aunties once told me that they had seen my Mum give her last penny to the woman next door for the electricity meter. Minnie had just lost her husband and Mum wouldn't see her go without heat and light even though it meant she had to go without. It's just the way she was.

It's like a military operation when the nurses do arrive, barking orders at the patients and expecting lively co-operation. There are two of them and they ask me to leave, not pleasantly either. No apology, nothing and hardly a word to Mum. I hardly get chance to grab my bag before the curtains are pulled and they attend to her. I stand outside the curtain not really wanting to leave, although I feel awkward standing around like this. The two nurses talk between themselves and I cannot hear Mum at all. It seems like barely a minute or two and the curtains are thrown back with such haste. They leave as quickly as they've arrived. One with a bowl of water in her hand the other carrying the dirty laundry under her arms, I'm not an expert in infection control but I suspect this isn't the most sensible thing to do.

Mum's now clean and dry but what about the patient opposite, she has been ringing for ages for assistance. On the way out one of the nurses walks over and turns off the buzzer, promising to be back in a minute. Now how many times have I heard that so far this week?

I got there late in the morning on the fourth day of Mum's admission and if I thought things had been bad so far, I had seen nothing yet! As I walk in the ward manager is standing to attention behind her desk. If there's one thing that has struck me about the staff it's the lack of eye contact. No one looks up from what they are doing and they're normally talking to each other behind their desk. Others stare at the computer but so far this week not one nurse has greeted me on entering the ward. The atmosphere is cold not only towards relatives but the patients too. There have been a couple of nurses who seemed interested in the patients but the others are just doing a job. So far Mum has said nothing but her eyes say it all as she looks from them and then over to me.

Mum tells me about her night and how Lillian was awake till the early hours but was still hauled out of her bed at 7am, where she will stay for the rest of the day until she is put back into bed by the night staff. Before she finishes telling me of the time since I left last night a porter and a HCA appear.

"Hello Isabella. We're here to take you for an endoscopy." The sweet HCA says. She's really young and I suspect new to the ward. Her face is round and she wears glasses that seem to perch casually on the end of her nose. Petite with short, dark, brown hair which is held back with pretty butterfly clips.

Mum and I look at each other, then at the HCA and repeat in unison, "What for?" "She had an endoscopy a couple of months ago and the Consultant said she wouldn't need another one as it was unlikely it would have changed," I continued. "Has something changed"? Has something happened overnight? "Did you see a doctor last night Mum?"

"No." She answers, wrinkling her forehead.

"I'm really sorry to ask but would you mind double checking?"

"Yep, no problem." I can tell she doesn't want to but she's got a genuine enough nature to not want to do the wrong thing. Mum and I just look at each other, knowing something's not right but wanting to believe it will be soon.

"Yeah, it's right. Isabella Bailey." She reads from the file. I'm still not sure it's right but I don't feel it's my place to question.

The next hurdle is oxygen. Mum has been using oxygen constantly since she has been admitted although she hasn't had her oxygen levels checked. The HCA searches around for a portable bottle to help Mum to breathe whilst she is taken to the endoscopy unit. She tries three different bottles but they're all empty.

"I've only got thirty minutes between patients and I'm already behind." The porter huffs. Mum, putting herself out, offers to go without oxygen as long as she is reconnected once she is on the unit. The porter is pleased with this and the HCA seems relieved too, she has already searched the ward for the last five minutes.

I can hardly keep up as the porter races along the corridor. As we go he knocks over a couple of empty large oxygen bottles that are situated outside the bay door. They go crashing but he doesn't stop to see what damage they have done. Everyone seems to be sleeping in their chairs and as we race by the HCA has a hell of a job keeping up too. She is running at the side of Mum's bed pushing her medication stand. The bumps mean nothing to this porter as he races over them Mum grimaces and occasionally calls out with the pain. The HCA can do nothing but run alongside the bed hanging onto the stand with all her energy.

The first thing that struck me about the unit was the cleanliness compared to Ward 11, everything was clean. The staff smiled, they looked clean and they were kind, you could hear genuine concern in their voices. Everything is explained to us and Mum is reassured, I see hope in her eyes. She laughs with the nurses, she's looking much brighter with the bit of kindness she is shown. I can see that she trusts them and that's the difference from Ward 11. I sit and take advantage of the calm of the unit I relax and catch up on some celebrity gossip from their up to date magazines.

It all happens very quickly. Mum is wheeled out of theatre and is in the recovery position. I want to go to her but I can see she is still and so peaceful. I stay seated as I'm not sure I'm allowed to go over to her, I suspect not and decide to wait until I am told that I can. I put down the magazine and watch her sleeping form and remember how much she loves her bed. She hardly needed any sleep when she was younger but as she got older she could sleep for England.

My thoughts are broken when the doctor calls me over and tells me that he has bad news. For some reason my mind has shut down and all I can think about is his first few words, "Poor prognosis". There are many things that people said to me during those eight weeks that I can repeat word for word but I only heard two words come out of his mouth, "Poor prognosis." He shows me the problem on a picture of Mum's oesophagus and it's not a pretty sight. The hiatus hernia has grown since her last visit and the hernia is restricting her swallowing. This is the reason why she has been unable to keep any of her food down. With this he is gone, I presume back into theatre as I stand reeling from the news. My legs feel as if they are going to buckle underneath me and I can feel the tears hot on my face, they just flow. I try to force myself to stop and to focus on something else. The room starts to become a blur and although I can hear voices they are distorted. I go over to Mum who is still sleeping but not as soundly as she was. I can't stay here, I can't let her see me crying and I can't stop, I try to bite my lip and focus on how peaceful she looks but his words keep returning in my head. "Poor prognosis". I push them out of my thoughts and know I just need to get outside away from everyone.

Yes that's what I will do, I must get outside, I need to be on my own and sit down before my legs give way. I ask the HCA to tell Mum I have gone for a cup of tea and I will meet her back on the ward, she looks concerned for me and asks if I am alright, what a sweet thing. I must play this down but what am I going to tell Mum? Let me just get out of here and I will be able to think. I'll talk to Sam.

I can't get out the door quick enough, I don't see or hear anything I just see bodies which I must avoid, the tears are flowing all I can think about is, "Poor prognosis". Before I am out of the door I am in floods of tears and wailing. I can hear my sobs and the strange noises that I am making. I don't remember ever crying in this way. I sob and sob, my stomach aches, I feel sick. The thought of being sick in front of everyone jolts me back and I find myself outside the hospital surrounded by people coming into the hospital.

I take deep breaths but the tears continue to flow but at least I'm now aware of the people around me. I begin to focus on what I need to do, I can't let Mum see me this way. She will know that something is wrong and she will want to know.

Samantha is Mum's oldest granddaughter and has always been close to her Nan. I ring her, her voice is a comfort and within minutes, she is on her way to the hospital. She has been working away in London and had only returned the previous night. She hadn't yet had chance to visit her Nan in hospital. The plan is that Sam will come to the hospital and I will compose myself. That way Mum won't see that I have been crying and that is as far as my thoughts extend. Sam and I haven't time to discuss what we will tell Mum, although I know we will have to tell her at some point. Please, just let us get through the next few hours.

Sam arrives and is her usual organised self, she has always had a way of calming any situation. She meets me outside the hospital and holds me for a moment, I draw strength from her embrace. She doesn't cry, she knows what she has to do and she knows she can't do it with smudged make up and red eyes. I move to the side of the hospital as Sam goes up to meet her Nan. I'm aware that the people going into the hospital are aware of me, I can feel eyes staring but the tears continue to flow. At the side of the hospital is a smoking shelter I decide to stand at the back hopefully so no one will see me. But the smell from the smoke wafts around the shelter and into my nostrils, I begin to retch. It's a blessing really because it shakes me out of my misery and I'm now focused on finding somewhere more private. It's now been around forty five minutes since I left Sam, I can feel myself calming now, I have got strength from somewhere, I breathe in the September air deeply.

Just as I'm thinking about going back into the hospital to wash my face and get a drink my phone rings. I practically have to empty my bag again to find it. It's Sam. The knot in my stomach is back but this time much tighter, as I race back through the hospital. I try to dodge people and push past others, I want to scream, "get out of my way! My Mother is dying". Sam has told me that my Mum is unconscious and she cannot find a nurse to help. I run up the three flights of stairs, oblivious to the four inch heels I am wearing. As I race along the corridor up to Ward 11, my phone goes off in my hand, I ignore it. I use the handrail to drag me faster up the stairs, as I run along the corridor the smell of the ward fails to hit me this time.

Sam is leaning over Mum, "Nan! Nan!" her voice is desperate and at the same time comforting to hear as it echoes through my ears. Mum is slumped in a chair at the other side of the room to her bed, someone else's chair. She looks unconscious, her head is tilted and she's dribbling.

"Julie, I've asked and asked them for help!" Sam is scream-ing at me. She had been asking them for over forty five minutes to help her Nan. She had been left there without any oxygen, the porter had told her the nursing staff would reconnect it but they hadn't. She had asked four different nurses for help, telling them her Nan needed reconnecting with her oxygen and then that her condition was deteriorating.

Within seconds of pressing the emergency bell, I see four doctors running towards me, I find myself on the main corridor shouting for help. The first thing the doctor says to me is, "Is she breathing?" Sam and I hold onto each other as Mum is put onto her bed and the curtains are closed as the doctors work on her. Ten minutes feel like hours suddenly the curtains are drawn and there's Mum with her eyes open, talking to us, she's groggy but she is alive.

Within seconds one of the doctors who had been working on Mum asks to speak with me in his office, alone. I look at Sam I know something is about to happen but what I do not know. The doctor walks me towards a room that I have seen the staff coming and going from. It's got about six tatty armchairs in its tiny, grubby and dirty cups litter the room. It must be their staff room. There're no windows as soon as I shut the door I feel claustrophobic and wish I hadn't.

The doctor's first language isn't English and I struggle to understand him but what he does say will live with me for the rest of my life. His words resound in my dreams often, although it has been played out in many different guises. Some nights I wake and I have answered him back, others I wake with my finger pointing back at him. I've recounted this meeting on several occasions, in public once when I gave evidence to the Independent Inquiry chaired by Robert Francis.

In the meeting he told me my Mother would die a painful death, before he had said that he had told me why in medical terms but I didn't hear that. At this point I had stopped listening, he also asked me to sign a do not resuscitate (DNR) form. He was stood opposite me probably only a yard away but it felt like he towered over my small frame. Then he showed me the DNR form. "Just sign this form," he said getting even closer to me now. I try to take a step back but an armchair hits the back of my leg. I realised I could not move away from him and that frightened me, I try to push the chair with my calf but the chair is too heavy.

I can feel his eyes as if boring into me, jet black matching his hair that was cut closely to his head. He shows no emotion at all when he speaks, it is all matter of fact.

"It will be a painful death and it is best if you leave her here with us." He speaks quietly, slowly but firmly and I strain to hear him because of his poor English.

He then moves his left hand in front of my face and he's that close I can smell his rancid breath. He puts his hand in front of my face and clicks his two fingers together, "She will die just like that". The noise of his fingers clicking together rings in my ear long after it has stopped. I don't know whether to look at him or his fingers, I feel mesmerised but I'm possibly in shock.

"Of course I'm not going to allow my Mum to die!" this statement comes out of my mouth without me being aware I am saying it.

At the time I had never heard of such a thing but now I usually hear from someone during my week that is being pressurised into signing one. It is a national problem within the NHS. Many people don't even know about the order and that one has been placed on them or their loved ones. I didn't want my Mum to suffer and if the conversation had gone differently, I may have been in agreement and signed the form. I wouldn't have wanted my Mum resuscitated, the damage that alone could have caused her would have been far too much for her frail body. She was eighty six and although she had had a hard life at eighty six she had had a good innings by anyone's standards.

What sort of a person was this man? Aren't doctors supposed to be mostly caring, considerate, helpful people? My body is shaking again. I'm going to be sick, I want to scream at him "shut up" I want to close my ears to what he is saying. I open the door and try to get away. I need Sam with me, he needs to be told he can't treat people in this way, he's a doctor. I need to get out of here. I can feel my stomach churning but as I open the door I see Sam walking along the ward. Seeing her gives me the strength I need and I call her into the room. I asked the doctor to repeat what he had just said and he does. He even clicks his fingers to emphasise that Mum will die a painful death and it will be quick.

This time I come back at him. I've had enough.

"Under no circumstances will I sign any form. You are neglecting my Mother to such an extent that you're actually trying to kill her. Sammy asked for nearly an hour for help and yet nobody came. Nobody even came and connected Mums oxygen! Why? Not one nurse came and helped her and isn't this supposed to be a hospital? Well I don't see much care going on around here. There are countless patients being neglected here, especially the elderly. We're not asking for special treatment, just basic care!"

I rant and I rave. Where it comes from I really don't know. Then I remember what he said about a painful death and it jars me back to what my priority must be.

"Right now my Mum needs painkillers. How long will it take for her to get them?" He mumbles something evasive about pain relief not being his remit and the pain manager will have to deal with that, which will just take a little more time that she hasn't got. I want to shout, 'So you can finish her off quicker!' but I don't I hold my tongue. The power this man has frightens me, I later find out he is only a junior doctor.

Before I leave the room I turn to him and say, "As long as my Mother is in this hospital she will have her family with her. I have no trust in you and my Mother is not safe under your care."

"This is the nurse's fault. Not mine, not the doctors." He is right but how could he be so callous, he's no different to the majority of the nurses, cold and uncaring.

When I leave the room I go to pieces, I'm shaking, my legs are like jelly. I really don't know where my strength came from to answer him back like that and to question him. I believe now that I am in shock because over the next seven weeks I don't challenge them again. I just sit and put up with it. We have the perception that doctors and nurses are like gods, they all have so much power over us but I was beginning to find out just how fallible they could be.

I stand outside the room, dizzy and my head aches. I just want to run away but I can't. I think of Mum and I know I need to be with her but at the same time I don't want to see her die a painful death. I must compose myself and get back onto the ward and get her pain relief, that's the priority now. I've wandered off the ward and I find myself slumped on the stairs. I look down and notice they are filthy and I am sitting in dust, with one foot resting on a banana skin. My legs won't carry me. At this moment Sam hands me a cup of tea, it's warm and weak but it does the trick. I feel it hit the pit of my stomach and slowly I feel I am focussing again.

I ring the family, Laura first, I don't tell her that her Nan is about to die, but I do tell her that I need her with me. Within the next few hours I have spoken to both children and Laura is on a train back from Swansea. My son, Martin, and his girl-friend, Sian, will leave Southampton and be with us around 11pm, I long for his support and his strength beside me. Laura will be different she will need my support, I dreaded ringing her. It took a lot of strength and skill trying to avoid what had actually happened that day but I managed to keep it brief and Laura just knew that something was wrong. I need to hold her in my arms and tell her the bad news. I know she will be devastated she adores her Nan and the feeling is mutual, they are so alike. It is hard to believe that there are so many years that separate them, yet they are so similar. It will hit her harder than anyone.

Nurse Ratchet and the Angels

That was the first night that I stayed by Mum's side, as I would do almost every night for the next seven weeks. I could no longer trust them to care for her. I had to be there to protect her. Laura arrives and spends that first night with me sitting on a hard plastic chair. It is agony, we ask in the middle of the night if there is a blanket available but there isn't and it's freezing. We don't want to sleep we want to spend what could be our last few hours with my Mum but it's so uncomfortable. Despite the discomfort I nod off and wake shivering when the nurse appears at my Mum's bed. This time it's a different nurse and she offers us a blanket, it's a relief. I spend the rest of the night planning what I need to make our stay more comfortable. Tomorrow I will bring blankets from home and a pillow.

My Mum drifts in and out of sleep, she looks so poorly and vulnerable, I daren't think about her condition and her painful death that could be any minute. Of course I haven't told her, how could I. It's not something one prepares for and I need time to think about how I can handle it. Mum still hasn't been given any pain relief, although her chest pain has eased and I think the chest infection is responding to the antibiotics. Each nurse we see I ask when Mum will get pain relief, but no one can tell me when. Although tonight she gets her medication on time, over the next seven weeks she rarely does and there are times she doesn't get it at all, other times I find it is signed for and yet it hasn't been administered.

During the night Martin, my son arrives and Mum greets him like nothing is wrong, she nods back off oblivious to what is about to occur. I hold her hand and hope above everything else that she dies during her sleep. The thought of her dying in pain, continually plays on my mind, she deserves better but once again I am powerless. Whilst Martin is there I take the opportunity and fetch myself a drink, it is only my second today. The thought of food doesn't enter my head but I return to Mum more refreshed.

Martin stands in silence holding her hand. The ward is so quiet you can hear a pin drop, which is very unusual on Ward 11. I can see the nurse in charge coming over.

"You need to go. You're disturbing the other patients."

She had earlier agreed to allow him to see his Nan for ten minutes and his time is up. Martin had stood in silence for the last thirty minutes, none of us had said a word. There are no words that we can say we're speechless, just watching her whilst she sleeps. His face tells me, he is thinking that this could be the last time that he sees his Nan. I want to keep him here with us but it is impossible. He hangs on as long as he can, cherishing every moment. Through the silence of the ward the nurse storms towards us again.

"I told you ten minutes, now you must go".

Martin is gone I hear his shoes leaving the ward I also hear the echo of her voice. Trying to find favour I apologise.

"I'm sorry. We just lost track of time. It could be the last time he sees her." I can tell from her face she didn't know Mum was that close to death but she doesn't apologise, she doesn't show any sympathy whatsoever. The briefest tinge of guilt makes her hesitate for a second before she walks away without eye contact, without a sound.

Within days of meeting this nurse we refer to her between ourselves as Nurse Ratchet, she's one of the nurses who shouldn't have been a nurse. The type, you wonder why they chose nursing as a profession. She's quite attractive medium build with strawberry blonde hair that she wears tied behind her back, held securely in a ponytail. Although attractive her features are sharp with a nose that is a bit large for her face. She always looks smartly turned out with clean sensible shoes and a clean outfit each day. I could easily imagine her as an old type Matron within a few years, at the moment she is too young probably in her late 20's. She looks everything a nurse should be that is until she opens her mouth when she thinks no one is around. These nurses lack any insight into the needs of others and their priority is more about their own needs. Nurse Ratchet is hard and callous but when anyone in authority is around she is different. When a doctor or anyone in a suit appears you would think she was a different person, instantly transforming into a model of care and professionalism.

But she's not the only nurse who behaves like this on this ward. There are more Nurse Ratchets than caring staff on Ward 11 and over the next seven weeks we lose our belief that most nurses are caring and compassionate towards others. Those that are, they are truly Angels trying to care for others in such an uncaring environment. Despite a chronic absence of leadership a few try to champion the cause of the patient. They fetch and carry and run around answering the buzzers, run off their feet but always with a smile on their face. They are real Angels.

The next day Sam arrives and we try to put a plan together where we don't leave Mum, alone on the ward, it simply isn't safe. Even if you are lucky enough to have good nurses working there are so few staff at any one time they can't provide anything near adequate care. We only considered the short term situation as that was all we thought we had. Luckily Sam was on holiday for the next two weeks and with Laura we would be able to ensure that she was never left alone. Martin was there too for the next few days and he would be able to spend some time with his Nan. He spends the following night sitting by her side whilst she sleeps. During the night he is disturbed by someone calling out for help, he searches without luck for a nurse. Eventually he opens the door to where the crying is coming from and finds a woman on the floor. During the next seven weeks we find several patients on the floor, they struggle to get out to the toilet after ringing their buzzers for so long. They give up on the nurse or they are frightened to ring the buzzer and try to manage themselves, unsuccessfully.

"There was just nobody around, Mum. Nobody!" He says to me, exasperated and sad.

It is now Monday and Mum is still alive. We did not expect this. The thought dawns on us… she could survive! The doctor had said she would die over the weekend. It's Monday and Mum, although weak, is looking better. She is talking with us and taking everything in. Although she is still being sick whenever she tries to swallow anything, the sustenance that is being given intravenously must be keeping her going. We haven't mentioned what I was told on Thursday, she has survived the weekend and so far she hasn't died the painful death that was predicted. What happens next? Could she get better?

An elderly man with long grey hair and a thick beard wanders into the bay, he's obviously confused but something he says makes me chuckle. "Where's she gone," he asks loudly but specifically to the woman in the opposite bed. She says nothing but just looks over at me for reassurance as I'm the only able body in the room.

"She's gone out and I've had no tea," I suspect he's talking about his wife. I don't consider that he probably hasn't had any tea.

I realise the knot in my stomach that I have had since Thursday, has eased without me realising. With that he wanders out the room his pyjama bottoms dragging under his bare feet. At this point I hadn't seen or heard much of the *Wanderers* but this would soon change as the lack of care increasingly forced elderly, confused patients from their beds.

We still haven't met the pain relief manager but Mum isn't in pain. The junior doctor had said she would be in pain when she dies but what does that mean? Will she be given strong painkillers ready for when she does die? Will we know then when she will die? I try to push my thoughts away, although I know I may have to face them.

I feel as if I had better eat something and I leave Sam with Mum and wander downstairs on the search for food. It's a standard NHS cafeteria — slide your tray on a rail past the fridges packed with day old salads and overpriced fizzy drinks, then onto the greasy hot plate, then the coffee machine designed by NASA before arriving at the till to pay motorway service station prices. Having said that, some of the food is actually not bad, especially the fresh hot food. I pick up a cheese sandwich and a cup of tea. The tea is good but the sandwich is a few hours past its glory. While I sit alone I try to plan in my head how we can get through the next few days. The priority now is to ensure that we stay with Mum. Working together we have been able to get the nutrition she needs and her painkillers, although not on time she has still had them in the end. Though we wait what seems like an age for the nurse to answer the buzzer, they do eventually. If Mum was here alone I am certain that she would be neglected. We have to stay with her, no matter what. That must be our priority.

I return back to the ward, the smell churns the cheese sandwich in my stomach and I swallow hard to keep it down. I return to Sam and in my absence Laura has arrived, looking shattered. We all discuss what we are seeing on the ward it really is a crying shame. But I tell them both that the priority has got to be that we stay with Mum.

"You've gotta remember that at any moment they can ask us to leave. We've got to stay on the right side of them. She's only survived cos we've been here, making sure she gets her fluids, making sure she gets her meds. So that's gotta be our No.1 priority, staying put. It doesn't matter what we see or what we hear we've gotta stay by her side. We don't give them any excuse to kick us out. We never raise our voice, we never question them, we don't give them as much as a funny look. Right?" They both nod in agreement.

I didn't realise at this point just how difficult it would be to sit and watch suffering and not be able to do anything about it. It really was torture during those seven weeks to watch those without relatives, or those that were confused, be fatally neglected.

During the eight weeks I spent at Stafford Hospital things happened that seem frozen in time. I can tell you exactly what was said and done, even what I was wearing, my thoughts are so vivid it often frightens me. Sometimes it's a comfort, I feel Mum is close to me. I can smell her, smell is the first sensation I usually feel. Sadly it's usually the ward that I smell, it's a relief when it's Mum that I can smell in the middle of the night.

It's the nights that are the worst on the ward, the buzzers just ring out, one after the other. I try to offer support to the few who are in the same bay as Mum. There are three other beds alongside Mum's and in each one there is someone in need. Ward 11 is supposed to be the Gastroenterology ward although the lady opposite to Mum has been admitted with asthma and often struggles to breathe. She's relatively young compared to the others on the ward she's probably only in her mid thirties. She's really tall but very, very thin. Her family are worried that she is barely eating any of the hospital food, but I'm not at all surprised. Asthma is new to her and at times she becomes really anxious, particularly at night. The nursing staff, have offered her little support but this could be that they have no knowledge of asthma. One morning she is told that when she reaches a certain peak flow she can go home. The nurse doesn't give her time to answer as she sweeps off out the door. She manages to laugh because she has no idea how to measure her peak flow. They have left her some sort of pipe to blow into but that is about it. She considers signing herself out of the hospital, but she is worried that they will not support her if she needs them in the future. She is discharged within the next few days but she feels she would have been better off at home with support from her surgery.

The woman in the bed next to Mum, Ethel, has lost one of her legs. It was removed in Stafford the year before. She suspects she will have to have the other one removed and she's awaiting tests. She is really sweet, a typical grandmother type. Grey hair with round spectacles that are often covered in fingerprints. She never asks you for anything but if you offer to help her she will always accept and thank you again and again afterwards. She expects nothing and every morning one of my first jobs was to help her with her headphones and put the radio on for her. She was really comical the way she would sit in her wheelchair with her headphones on tapping along to the hospital radio tunes. She's in her late seventies but I heard her singing along with the Bob Marley hit, "No woman, no cry" as her remaining one foot tapped against the pedal on her wheelchair.

Over the last few days we have got close to her and have helped her out, she has had no visitors at all. Although she is fiercely independent there are several things she just cannot manage and needs help with. At home she has carers three times a day, here she is lucky if she has help at all on the ward. Her buzzer often rings for over an hour and often when a nurse does come to her they turn it off and promise to return later.

We cannot believe Mum is still alive and we are so thankful for it. It is coming up to our second weekend on the ward and we have now met most of the staff. A few are truly wonderful and yet others simply dreadful, we try to avoid them but when Mum is so dependent it is difficult. This week has been a real battle to get the nursing care she needs. Whenever her cannula line needs replacing it is just impossible, the wait is endless. It's the same with her catheter it's practically overflowing before it is emptied, the bag looks as if it is about to burst. It's the same with the other patients they are neglected and wait much longer than Mum for attention. Thank God she has us here to bat for her.

Most of the nursing staff glare at us, you can just feel that they are desperate for us to put a foot wrong so they can ask us to leave. But we don't and we will make sure we don't. The kinder nurses, the *Angels*, tell us how grateful they are that we are able to stay and look after my Mum. It really is a shame for them, they try so hard to care and look after the patients but they are fighting a losing battle. It's really odd because alone they will speak to you but as soon as one of the Nurse Ratchets is around they clam up and hardly speak. You can see they are frightened of them and scurry off when a Nurse Ratchet appears.

We have identified several Nurse Ratchets, they bark at the patients particularly the confused ones. You can see they love the power they have over not only the patients but the relatives too. It's normally visiting time when you can hear certain nurses arguing with relatives. It's usually over a test result that they want chasing up but the nurses refuse to. Or they ask about their relatives care and they are mostly snapped at for asking. Tonight it's a familiar argument that I have heard between families and the staff. It's the male carer tonight who's probably in his mid forties. Average height and I suppose some would consider attractive being as he still has a full head of hair. Some days he styles it with gel, sticking up the front few pieces, a bit like Tin Tin.

"Why didn't you tell me he has become so ill" the poor woman looks in distress and stands motionless with her wet coat still dripping. I suspect she had come in at visiting time and found her loved one dying. She is fighting back tears as she wrestles for answers which I suspect she has no chance of getting.

"We rang you," he snaps defensively and then turns to go on his way.

"When? When did you ring?" She asks looking confused now.

He stops and you can see he is thinking on his feet now, "Dinner time, when the doctor saw him"

"But I rang at 3pm and was told he had had a comfortable night and was now sitting up in bed." She was almost shouting now and the distress in her voice was clear.

Flippantly and almost with arrogance in his voice he said, "You will have to ask staff" and turned, walked into our bay and unplugged Ethel's fan, taking it with him out the door.

The lady had already walked along the same corridor a few seconds before, no doubt about to search for the Staff Nurse for an explanation of why she had found her relative so ill when she had been told a couple of hours earlier he was so well.

Although we had discussed between us to keep our heads down and look after Mum the lack of care on the ward is frightening. It's now Thursday afternoon and Mum's buzzer has been ringing for over an hour. Her drip is blocked and the alarm on that is going off. It means that she is not getting her nutrition, you can see it blocking up inside the tube. I'd waited and waited trying not to disturb the staff and thinking it could wait until her medication was due. But it's now three hours late and she still hasn't had her lunchtime medication. The problem with antibiotics is they need to be given on a regular basis and they haven't been. The only time you see the nurses is when they have the drug trolley with them, but that isn't often.

The woman opposite had been discharged that morning and the bed had been empty all day. She had been on the ward before, she told me she didn't bother to use the buzzer, there was no point. She was hardened to the system, she answered the nurses back and challenged them when she had to. "I have been waiting for over an hour for the toilet. No, I cannot wait any longer," she told the HCA who tried to turn off her buzzer telling her she would return. We all knew she wouldn't, she'd done it before, but this woman has fallen for her promises once too often. I wish I had the courage to challenge like she does, the others in the bay are impressed too.

We had agreed that we wouldn't make a complaint until we had left the hospital, but I've had enough. All afternoon we have had to listen to the poor woman who had been admitted to the bed opposite. She looks pregnant but she looks too old to be pregnant. She screams out in pain. "Help me! Help me!" The nurses had come and put her into the bed about ten minutes ago, telling her they would be back with the doctor. At the time I thought, "I've heard that before". I didn't expect her to become so distressed so quickly. Mum wakes with the shouting and straight away tells me to go over to her. I do, but I don't want to and that plays on my mind. The problem is what can I do for her pain? The whole ward can hear her. I go over and there is nothing I can really say to her to help apart from pressing her buzzer. I feel helpless there is little else I can do for her. The poor woman is in agony, I return back to my seat but her screaming is chilling. The nurses must hear her, how they can allow this woman to be in so much pain is beyond me. I feel so angry sitting here and Mum is beside herself. She keeps saying, "Oh Jude, go and tell them", although I don't want to I can stand it no longer. From where I sit next to Mum's bed I can see the male ward opposite and two side rooms. I grab my chance when I see a nurse going into the male ward.

"Nurse, nurse." I call after her.

"We are waiting for the doctor." She barks back at me.

"Is there anything you can do to help her?" I ask.

"No. No, there's nothing we can do." She says dismissively.

The answer is no surprise to me. It's one of the Nurse Ratchets and I only approached her because Mum wanted me to. Deep down I knew the nurses wouldn't help her and all I have done is made the nurse angry towards me.

I go back and sit down, the frustration is almost unbearable but I am powerless to do anything to help. I feel myself sweating, it's agonising listening and watching someone in so much pain and yet not being able to do anything.

"Jude go and help her, the poor woman," Mum knocks me as she pleads for me to do something. I suddenly realise that Mum hasn't sussed yet that I have no power. Mum knocking me makes me realise that over the last few days our relationship has changed. I'm now the parent and she is the child. I want my Mum back, I don't want this change in our relationship. I haven't the strength to do this. No, Mum is the strong one, not me.

Just as I'm trying to muster up the courage to approach the staff again, a doctor arrives for the patient in pain. The poor woman has been screaming for over two hours and it continues on and off for the rest of the afternoon. Because of the size and nature of the room there is no privacy and everyone can hear what is said. It's a relief to hear that she will be able to have pain relief when it is needed.

During the afternoon and in between her screams she tells me that her name is Pat and she lives in the next town. She had been feeling rough for the last week but for the last three days she hasn't been able to pass water and this is why her stomach is so swollen. She isn't pregnant, she's too old, in her mid-fifties. Two nurses arrive to administer the morphine but I really don't know what all the fuss is about as the administration of the morphine seems to be no different from any other drug. The nurses chatter amongst themselves and it seems they are oblivious to the harm a mistake of the drug could cause. Pat is just so relieved, even her face relaxes and it makes her look younger. She lives in hope that her pain is over and she will now be pain free for the rest of the day.

However four hours later Pat hadn't had her pain relief and the battle begins again. I start by passing her the buzzer. She rings, we wait. She tries to talk to me during her discomfort but I'm not really listening all I can think about is her morphine. How long will she have to wait? Will she be screaming in pain again and will I have to call the nurses for her? This I dread, it's hard enough having to get their attention for my Mum. After forty minutes a HCA arrives and turns off the buzzer, saying he will get a nurse. She waits twenty minutes and I try not to look over at her, but I do. Our eyes meet and she asks me to pass her the buzzer again. That's a trick I have noticed, once the staff turn off the buzzer they put it out of reach of the patients. I go over and press the buzzer for her, it's the least I can do.

This goes on for the next day, Pat gets a different story from everyone she asks. One nurse says she can have morphine as often as she needs it, another says she can only have it every four hours, another every six hours. Eventually she is seen by a doctor, in general the doctors are more caring and sympathetic than the nurses and this doctor is a good example. He has fair hair and a thin face with kind eyes. He tells her to ring the buzzer if she needs anything.

I want to call him over and tell him about what is happening on the ward. I want to tell him that she has been screaming out all afternoon for help and no one has helped her. I want to tell him that we have heard a different story each time a nurse has come to her. I want to tell him that a nurse has told her that she shouldn't be in that much pain and not to disturb the other patients by screaming out. I want to tell him that morphine needs to be administered by two nurses and finding two nurses at the same time is nigh on impossible. I want to but I don't. I turn the page on my magazine not really reading but hoping to distract myself from my own cowardice. I'm ashamed of myself.

I try to only help the other patients when the staff cannot see me but sometimes it is difficult. It is hard to walk by the male bay opposite without one of them calling out for assistance. You can hear their buzzers sounding out and I try not to pass when it is sounding but it rings for so long sometimes it is impossible to wait. One man always calls out for a drink when I pass and I have stopped a few times and helped him. What has shocked me is the state of some of the patient's mouths, covered in a white film and bleeding. As I have passed them a drink I have had to turn away as the sight of their mouths has made me feel sick.

The Wanderers

Mum has still not been able to keep anything down and today we have waited for a doctor to change the line in her arm. Her arm looks so red and swollen. And then I notice. Oh my God, how did I miss that? Under her arm is an enormous lump which looks like fluid. From what I can see the fluid that should have been going into her body has been just laying at the top of her skin. I'm too frightened to touch it. It looks so sore, it looks like an enormous tennis ball under her skin.

"Mum, haven't you felt that, is it sore?" Mum was a hard woman and she would not complain lightly but I'm just amazed that she has something as large as that and she hasn't said a word. When I look closer though I can see the discomfort she has been in. With all that has been going on with the woman in agony, I haven't been keeping an eye on Mum. She tries to move her arm to look at it.

"Please don't move, Mum." I plead. I'm sure if she touches it, it will burst and half her arm will explode. Oh Christ, I ring the bell but how long will we have to wait? I can't wait, I will have to go to the nurses station and try and find someone. It's the second time today the first time I was prac- tically told to mind my own business, my stomach churns at the thought of having to bother the staff. Pat had been screaming out in agony and was rolling around the bed, I was sure she would fall out of it. In the end I had to go and face the wrath. It was the ward manager, I knew it would be. I was hoping I would see a nurse along the corridor before I reached the nurses' station but no such luck, it was a long straw anyway.

I knew she could see me but she didn't look up, she barely does when I speak. Today she has the same outfit on as every other day. It's easy to avoid her because you rarely see her beyond the nurses' station. If she is out, look out because it is usually to tell someone off. Before I had even approached the

53

nurses' station I had decided that it was too urgent to wait for them to look at me, I would have to disturb them.

"Can someone help Pat? She's in agony." I asked with urgency.

Nothing, she just sat there without even acknowledging me, her body still. She didn't move for what seemed like minutes but it was seconds really. Then she turned on her swivel chair, the wheels squeaking. There was no expression on her face but I could sense she was angry.

"What?" she snaps.

I tried again but this time I mentioned that Pat may have fallen out of her bed by now. She was on the edge when I had left the room.

"Can someone please come and help her?" I pleaded. I could feel the sweat on my brow, I could feel the pressure mounting.

It was her eyes that first told me that I was in trouble or about to be, I could see her looking down her nose at me at the same time as she said, "Is Pat your relative?"

"What?" I thought but dared not say, instead I stumbled a "No, No but..." I'd lost it, I was that weak person again who would be sent back without the help I needed, my tail between my legs.

"Pat is being dealt with, thank you." The wheels squeaked again as she turned back to the computer screen.

I slinked back down the corridor defeated, hoping I would see a nurse along the way. I didn't and I had to spend the afternoon in anguish practically on the edge of my seat. That is until I had to approach the same nurses' station again.

Its empty, Nurse Ratchet has gone, 'Phew!' I think. It's not unusual to find no one there but this is an emergency, I will have to go to the staff room. I knock on the door tentatively, I'm prepared for a row from them but there's nothing else I can do. No one answers I knock again and again but nothing. I'm beginning to panic what can I do, I ring Sam and tell her. I walk up and down the ward I want to cry out for help but there is no one to cry out to. It's like the Marie Celeste. I pass a couple of patients wandering the corridor, the confused. They seem to change daily always replaced by some other poor soul, who is lost in their own mind.

I know I keep saying it but it's true — the nights were the worst and I used to dread them. The confused patients, the

Wanderers appear to come alive at night and want to go home. During the day it seems the confused patients stay in bed asleep and come to life early evening. This is normally when they start to wander the wards, in and out of the rooms looking for a way to get home. At around 10.30pm, if they haven't done as they are told by the nursing staff, the porters are summoned to push them into their beds. Some nights it's a relief when you catch sight of the porters, at least you know there will be peace for a while. Some nights I feel so uncomfortable and guilt ridden as I watch the staff abuse the vulnerable patients. I try to look away but I know what's happening, I can hear the cries. I keep telling myself Mum is my priority, repeating it like a mantra in my head. It keeps me distracted but it can't absolve the guilt I feel as I allow it to happen.

I return to Mum. Pat is distressed again and in agony as she writhes in her bed. As I enter the bay I notice that behind me follows an elderly man. He's popped in and out all day obviously confused but cheerful, that is until now.

"Shut the fuck up" he shouts, I'm shocked at the anger in his voice and I try to block him getting at Pat.

"C'mon you, now. This way. This way." I stand in front of him and try and distract him by calling him back through the door. I'm acting firm but I'm scared and you can hear it in my voice. It distracts him and he moves across the room and over to the woman in the bed opposite Mum's. I press Pat's buzzer but why I don't know because Mum's has been going off for over thirty minutes now.

The woman had been admitted last night, we have had a chat earlier this morning but that was about it, as she was so poorly. The man grabs her toilet bag off the bed and starts to look inside it, the woman tries to reach out to snatch the bag back but she cannot reach.

"Leave it! Put that down!" She shouts at him.

"I want my fish," he says.

At this point I realise just how confused this man is and I wonder what I can do. It's too late because as I stand there wondering what I can do to calm the situation down, he runs over to the side of Mum's bed.

"Buggger off!" she tells him lurching forward in her bed, as if reaching out to him. I dread what he will do next and as I'm thinking she shouldn't have done it. He rushes back past me and back to the lady whose wash bag he'd taken, she's obviously an easier target than Mum. He reaches into her bedside cupboard.

"Go away, go away". She screams.

Trying to think rationally in this situation is difficult but somehow I do.

"Quick, quick, come with me," I call out loudly. And he does. I walk him out of the room and up the corridor. "I'm off to the shop now. You have a think what you want and I'll get it for you." I leave him thinking at the drinks machine after pouring him a cup of tea. He still has the poor woman's address book firmly in his hands but I'm not prepared to do battle for that.

I return back to the bay, I can hear Pat groaning in pain and to my surprise the new woman is now out of her bed. She has a small case on the bed and is getting clothes out of it. The next thing she is on the floor. She has collapsed, it all happens so quickly but there she is on the floor and I'm the only one who can help her. I help her back into bed but she is determined that she is going home.

"Please don't leave me." She sobs. "Please don't leave me. He'll come back, I know he will. Oh, I can't stay, I can't stay here." She is petrified.

"I've got to get a nurse. Listen, I'll just stand by the door, he won't get past me." I tell her.

She grabs at my hand. "I want to go home." I see the desperation in her eyes

"Have you got any family? Is anyone coming to visit you?" I'm clutching at straws but I just want to find her some hope.

Sam walks through the door and my face must be a picture of sheer stress, "What's been going on?" A look of disbelief and anger in her face.

"I've had enough, Sam. I've had e-bloody-nough." I hug her and sob on her shoulder, it's just got the better of me. I try to tell her what happened but I know I'm not making much sense. It's not till she sees Mum's arm that she understands. I can see the shock on her face.

"I'll get someone." She says but five minutes later she's back with no success.

We sit, waiting nervously. Where is everyone? Where are they? Pat is again in distress as she cries out in pain. Sam finds this too uncomfortable to sit through and goes off again to look for the staff. I sit back down and hold Mum's hand, this is agony for me and I dread to think how she is feeling. As I sit down I look out onto the corridor and see the amount of people who like me have been looking for a member of staff. The corridor seems crowded with people. It looks as if visiting time has started.

At this point the patients haven't had their tea, a drink or their medications, what on earth is happening. Just as Sam returns giving up her search again we both hear the wheels of the drug trolley and at the same time the food trolley.

Lyndsey is a Staff Nurse she's always scruffy looking, the opposite of Nurse Ratchet one of the other Staff Nurses on the ward. Her uniform is never ironed and she always looks unkempt. She always looks as if she has just got out of bed and come to work without checking herself over first. She was a little taller than I am with short straight blond hair and a spotty complexion.

She walks in to the bay as if without a care and begins to administer the drugs oblivious to the carnage that had just taken place. In a matter of fact way she tells us that she had to leave the ward unattended as they had to go and pick up a patient who had wandered off the ward.

"Oh Lyndsey we've had a terrible time up here. My Mum's arm's all swollen and Pat's been in terrible pain. And then a man came in from the other ward and started threatening us." I tried to put the last two hours into words but I waste the opportunity. I feel exhausted and my account doesn't give the scale of the problem I was left with. There's no apology, nothing, even Pat has to wait for her pain relief as there isn't another member of staff available to administer the controlled drug.

I appeal to her, I try to appeal to her as a nurse but it falls on deaf ears. The upshot is she will put a call in for the doctor to see my Mum's arm and as soon as there is another nurse available she will give Pat her drugs. As for her leaving the ward without any nursing cover at all she would do it again, if she had to. "It was nearly my tea break time anyway," she tells us dismissively.

With that she shuts the medication trolley sharply and pushes it briskly through the bay door.

I sit there for a few minutes in silence I can feel my heart racing because I have challenged her. Only briefly but it has

An Air Pressure Mattress and a Dirty Old Recliner

It's the usual start to the day at about six thirty the light is thrown on, never a *Good morning*, nothing just the stark, bleached-whiteness of the strip lighting, it often hit's me like a slap up my ear as it's usually very soon after I have nodded off. Then the curtains are thrown open, the noise often reverberates in my head. Observations are very often taken in silence. But there seems no consistency in who has their observations taken. Some days Mum has hers taken others she doesn't. Then nothing happens for another hour to an hour and a half, when the tea trolley is pushed in. The room is then left in silence, nothing just stillness and bright light. All we want is to go back to sleep as we are all knackered, the nights on the ward are the noisiest. Most of the staff seem oblivious to the fact it is night time in a hospital. They shout and giggle, ignorant that some patients are suffering or even dying around them

By the time the tea trolley is pushed in we have usually sat there for over an hour, the silence is often painful. It really isn't worth the wait, it's weak and it's warm. Most of the staff do not offer me a cup of tea it's the HCAs who serve the tea and it's usually the same miserable faces each day. I'm really fussy with my tea and I probably would have said no, but it would have been nice to have been offered. The shop downstairs that sells the tea doesn't open until eight o'clock and I'm usually the first customer.

I still to this day don't understand why they wake the patients up so early, there is no reason and it is often cruel to see. Observations and tea is normally given out in silence. This shocks me at first, as I would have thought the staff would be interested in how the patients are feeling after the night. But why would they? No, these staff know their place and are here

59

to carry out only the domestic tasks. The favoured appear to be given a step up the ladder and are assigned the role of taking observations, but it never seems to be the caring staff.

Most of the staff ignore me. I think they think if they acknowledge me I will be more likely to stay. It's odd but over the last week they seem to have accepted me being here. At first you could tell that that they were conscious of me being in the room but over the last week they've begun to no longer notice me so much. I'd estimate that twenty percent of the staff are lovely, absolute gems in this uncaring environment. Their very presence can light up the room, or should I say the ward, and they do. I've started to listen for their voices and I can recognise them as they come on duty, the cheerfulness warms me up inside and that's before I even see them. Over the seven weeks I realise that their presence calms the ward, even the confused patients are less agitated when they are on duty, they respond to their kindness. The problem is because there are three different shifts a day and very few caring staff, a kind word is rare. Each day there is unkindness because there are so many uncaring staff on this ward, the negativity feeding off itself and multiplying.

There appear to be two Sisters, both are moaners, not leaders. They don't inspire anybody and they certainly don't fill you with confidence. Anyway you rarely see them, they stand at the nurse's station but that's about it. There appeared to be two senior nurses the one we called Nurse Ratchet, the other we never gave a name but I will refer to her as Lyndsey. They really were like chalk and cheese, Nurse Ratchet is much more organised than Lyndsey. One afternoon no one got drugs because she had lost the keys to the drugs trolley, this seemed to happen on several occasions.

Lyndsey was an odd character some days pleasant other days it was as if she was in a trance. She always seemed to work in darkness and whenever she came into the room the first thing she would do was to turn the lights off. I was a bag of nerves when she gave the medication out as you could see she struggled to see the labels on the medication bottles holding them close to her eyes. She always seemed so low in mood too, her smile was always missing and she didn't get on with Nurse Ratchet. And of course we couldn't forget the nurse manager, the senior Nurse Ratchet, she is a dreadful woman and after eight weeks of observing her, I am convinced she should be in prison and not on a hospital ward.

Allowing the ward to be left without any cover at all was unforgivable to me and for Lyndsey to say she would do it again worries me. I struggle with what is the best way to handle the situation. The next day Sam and I mull it over, with the thought of the weekend coming up we know something has got to be done. The place is dangerous and it's not just down to a lack of nursing staff but the quality of those nursing staff.

It's not an easy decision, we think over the consequences and decide Mum has suffered enough. Laura stays with Mum and Sam and I enter the Patient Advice and Liaison Service (PALS) office. The PALS office is in the main entrance to the hospital and on the door it advertises if you had concerns to pop in. PALS, is supposed to be independent of the hospital and was established to answer concerns and inquiries about the NHS.

What we wanted was reassurance that the ward would be safer if we made a complaint. But the advisor isn't much help, she listens with obvious lack of interest. She's sitting at her computer screen as Sam and I enter the room and she acknowledges us with a reluctant smile. I sense we are disturbing whatever she was doing but she gets up from her chair, she's probably early thirties and quite tall with thin, mousy hair and a weak frame. As we tell her about the ward and what has been happening, she chews on the end of her pen. I sense her lack of interest as she looks around the room as we speak. The room isn't really an office it's just a cluttered room. There are boxes piled on top of what looks like a couple of tables. There's no sense of urgency from her, a ward full of ill patients being left without staff doesn't seem to have shocked her into action. She will take our number and with that we are seen out of the door, I sense she can't get us out quick enough.

Sister Leach is another Nurse Ratchet but older and more hardened to our concerns, I now know she had heard them many times before. After our complaint to PALS, I get a call on my phone. If we go back up to the ward the Matron is waiting to listen to our concerns. Sam and me look at each other and both hope that something positive will come from the meeting.

We enter the room and there are two Matrons wanting to listen, or that is what they tell us. Both Sam and I tell them both about what we have seen and heard over the last week.

"That is just dreadful!" Says Sister Leach with no sincerity at all.

The other Matron interjects, "That should never have happened." She's much younger than Sister Leach and has a kinder face. She very much lets Sister Leach lead and I suspect has been doing this sort of thing for less time. She seems the far more genuine of the two.

Their excuses are well rehearsed though. It's a busy time, they have lots of staff off sick and things will now improve. I throw in about the poor soul we had left behind on Ward 10. She even had an answer for that. Boy, this woman was good! But even at this time she didn't fool Sam and I, we both knew that she wasn't genuine. You see there was no concern when we told her about the suffering on the ward and the lack of caring staff. No shock, nothing just excuses that the ward has a lot of sickness. I later learn there is only one member of staff off sick and she returns in the last week of Mum's life.

"Go back to your Mum and things will be a lot better." She tries to reassure us but I'm not at all convinced.

"How? How will things be better?" I ask, I'm still frightened, they haven't convinced me that the care will be any better.

"We will get your Mother a pressure mattress immediately," the kinder Matron offers.

"A pressure mattress," I say to Sam on the walk back to the ward, "That will make a hell of a difference".

Sister Leach promises us everything and for the first few days things do improve, I learnt later that this was a standard response to complaints from the ward. But any improvements are not sustained.

Within a few hours of making the complaint an air pressure mattress arrived for Mum, I thought the woman in the next bed needed it more. Thinking I would strike while the iron was hot, I mentioned that the woman in the next bed needed one too. Nothing was too much trouble for this Matron and within a few hours another arrived. Although we waited all day for them to be put on the bed, the optimism that first night filled us all with hope that things would now improve.

The difference that night was striking Mum wasn't tossing and turning trying to get herself comfy. It felt so empowering because we didn't have to rely on the nursing staff to move her every few hours to avoid bed sores. It was one thing less to worry about as Mum was already, having to have a bed sore dressing on her bottom. Little did I realise though at this point the trouble the mattress would cause.

But that first night exposed just how mean those staff could be. I knew that night they were unhappy with me for complaining. I could tell by their faces and when I went to the toilet in the middle of the night and returned to Mum, my chair was gone. The chair we had washed down and moulded to my bottom had gone. They must have waited for me to go to the toilet. In the darkness I tried to find another one but apart from those next to the other patients' beds there was none. I wanted to cry but I couldn't I felt there were no more tears left. I sat on the end of Mum's bed trying desperately not to disturb her. With the pressure mattress it was almost impossible to perch but I tried to rest my bottom on the end of her bed.

To be honest it was a relief when one of the staff came and hauled the curtains open, the awful night was over. It was probably Mum's best night, because of her new mattress. Without warning a little later one of the *Angels* appears with a reclining chair. It was filthy and ragged but, oh my, what a treat! A recliner! I spend the day cleaning it and the Angel's kindness touches me deeply. Mum is over the moon too she has found it hard watching us suffer on a hard plastic chair with a tiny bit of foam that spills out at the sides. Cleaning the chair takes up the best part of the day. Sam is spending the night with Mum and the chair will be a real treat for her. It's one of her last as her two week holiday is over, I try to push the thought from my mind but I know from tonight things for us will get tougher. Sam has agreed to spend Saturday nights and I will stay the others. Laura will come in each day in the afternoon and stay until about 10pm. When she comes in I will go home, get washed and walk Jess and return to stay the night. I try to avoid Laura doing the nights alone but that changes as the time goes on and Mum's stay continues.

I don't really like having to leave Laura here alone but without her support, it would be impossible. When I returned yesterday after being away for a few hours, I returned and Mum had been put on a nebuliser. You might think, why didn't I ask why she had been put on the nebuliser. But who would I ask? No one seems to be in charge and no one seems to know why any decisions are taken. Laura and her Nan weren't given an explanation it was just left on the side, as if it was a postman delivering a letter. At the next drug round Mum was given two different types of drugs to go into it but the nurse just shrugged her shoulders, when I asked why.

The blue recliner is a blessing, Sam has made our little corner of the ward home from home, we now have cushions and a warm quilt. It's heaven compared to what we have had, but really the chair should have been condemned long ago. I try not to look down the cracks as after a day's cleaning it is nigh near impossible to scrape all the dry congealed food that lingers down the sides. There are parts that are torn where foam breaks out and the secret is, not to touch those parts. The recliner is actually broken as once extended, you have to climb out and collapse it manually but it's the best we are going to get and we are very grateful. It makes life better and the nights are easier to manage.

Although it was so uncomfortable for us all not once did Mum tell us to leave her and that was unusual. She was never one to put anyone out and you'd have expected her to have suggested we go, "go on, you get off. I'll be alright. I'm not going anywhere." But she never did. Every now and again she asked about me going to work but I dropped the subject quickly. Despite her strength before she encountered Ward 11, she obviously didn't feel safe to be left here alone which speaks volumes for a woman with her grit.

A Ray of Hope

Meeting Dr Hearing is like a breath of fresh air. Although I continually ask each doctor that has seen Mum we are given no idea of what is happening to her. The first thing Dr Hearing does is to introduce himself and that hasn't happened before during the last two weeks. Not one doctor has introduced themselves to any of the patients, they just appear. The contrast is shocking and Mum's face lights up and so does mine. He's so pleasant to us and it feels like we are in a different hospital. One thing that strikes me is there has rarely been a nurse on any of the ward rounds but today there is. It's the ward manager, Senior Nurse Ratchet herself, but she smiles today, we haven't seen that before. She still has on a badly fitting suit, but in a different colour. She tries to give the doctor the information he is asking but she is giving the wrong information on Mum. I interject when I have to but it is clear that the nurse manager hasn't a clue about the patients on the ward. With Mum she seems to be making it up as she goes along.

"Blood pressure is 120 over 80," she tells him after picking up Mum's charts from the edge of the bed.

"When was that?" Dr Hearing asks.

Dr Hearing was a very handsome man, he had a lovely smile that exposed his white teeth. He was always well dressed in an expensive suit and all the ladies on the ward liked him.

"This morning," says Nurse Ratchet.

Now I know this isn't correct as Mum hasn't had her blood pressure taken this morning. I sit there not knowing whether to say anything I choose not to until I have to.

"Have we altered the dose of Stemetil?" He asks with genuine concern. Stemetil is the anti-sickness drug.

"Not yet," she answers but with a puzzled look on her face.

I cannot avoid it I have to interject this time because she had a bad reaction to the Stemetil. I'm beginning to wonder how much harm Senior Nurse Ratchet has caused to other patients who have no relatives to speak up for them.

"I think that is the drug that Mum had a bad reaction to," I bravely say but I sit there afterwards hoping I haven't upset her.

"So let's look at your options..." Options? Options! We've never had options before! Hasn't the doctor noticed my Mum is elderly, the elderly don't get offered a choice on this ward. No, he means it, we have options and Mum's eyes light up once again. Mum has the most stunning eyes and she has the sort of face that hides nothing, you can always see what she is thinking and she's impressed. I begin to wonder if he has wandered onto the wrong ward and he's here by mistake. The contrast is striking. He's interested in our answers and her future plan of care. Christ! He's saying all the right things, we haven't heard of a *plan of care* before and we have been here for two weeks.

Mum agrees to a special feeding tube called a peg being fitted to bypass the hiatus hernia, and allow her to take nutrition directly to her stomach. There is a risk due to the anaesthetic but it's something for Mum to think about, if she needs to. Of course Mum doesn't need time to think about it and she tells him so. To be honest she doesn't really have an option but the doctor is too kind to tell her that. He's so positive he even tells her that she may not need the peg at times and she could just use it when her swallowing is restricted for the future. Future. It's a long time since I have heard that word.

After he has gone, with our mood lifted, for the first time we discuss the future. It has been so strange not being able to discuss anything any further than a few hours away. No, now there is tomorrow and the day after and we can look beyond the painful death that was imminent, only a few hours ago. It's Friday and Mum will be operated on next Thursday. We ring everyone with the good news and nothing will dampen our spirits tonight.

To keep ourselves going in such a hostile environment we have over the last few weeks given some of the staff nicknames, in private of course. Tonight to savour our good mood it's Amy Winehouse, a nurse that if you were ill you would want caring for you. She looks like Amy, very attractive and often wears her hair in a beehive. I only have to hear her voice and a sense of calm comes over not just me, but the ward. The fear that I constantly feel when I'm on the ward is eased when Amy is on duty. My fear is because you really don't know what is going to happen from one minute to the next. As Sammy says "Things can kick off at any minute," and they do.

In any one day there's usually around three confused patients wandering the ward. The majority of the staff don't seem to have any understanding of how to manage their behaviour. They seem to inflame the situation instead of calming it down. They continually tell them to go back to bed. Some of their responses are heartbreaking to sit and listen to.

"I've gotta get back. I'll get the sack."

"I've gotta be in Stone by three."

"I'm going for a smoke."

"I need to get to the shops."

"My Mum's waiting for me."

What strikes me as I sit listening and watching their faces is how determined they are. The more they are told the more desperate they become to get on with the task that is fixed in their heads.

Mum's bay is right at the bottom of a long corridor and at the end of the corridor is a locked door, there is a window between our bay and this door so we can see everything that happens outside it. The door seems to attract all of the confused patients and they think it is a way to get out. All they want to do is to go home or to the shop or for a cigarette, but they all want to get out of that door. They are all attracted to it, some just try the handle others rattle it and rattle it and rattle it. It's not easy to sit and listen to, but goodness knows what torture they must be going through in their heads. Next to the door are two single rooms, one I went into when the woman had fallen on the floor. They must also be used as isolation rooms as there is often a sign on the door saying so. Some staff before they go in apply an apron and put on gloves, others don't. Surprisingly to me it's the doctors that comply more than the nurses. The porters seem to be in and out but I haven't once seen any of them wear gloves or an apron before they enter.

More often than not, after the confused patients have realised that the door isn't going to open, they either wander into our bay, or into one of the two isolation rooms. What they are doing in there I cannot see but we often hear screams coming from the room and then the confused patients wander out but normally they are frustrated at this point and angry as

67

they haven't been able to get out of the door.

This man has returned to the door on and off all afternoon and has ended up in our room several times. A tall man, unkempt but pleasant and not at all aggressive, unlike some we have met during the last few weeks. One of the staff told us that many of the confused, particularly the violent ones, are coming off drink or drugs. It seems an odd thing to me to put someone violent on a ward with vulnerable patients. To add to this volatile cocktail is a lack of staff and very often the staff they have seem to antagonise those patients. The majority of the staff we have met seem poorly trained in just about everything. Even taking observations is difficult for some. As you can imagine this proves a real challenge to your care and very often the staff just write it down without a word to the patient. You don't expect it every time but a word of reassurance now and again would put our minds at rest.

But this man wanted a cigarette he'd asked on and off all afternoon, he didn't know who to ask and ended up asking everybody he came into contact with, myself included. He'd mithered all afternoon, everyone he saw he asked them to take him for a cigarette. I kept thinking if Sam had been here she would have taken him for one. A few days ago I had seen an elderly patient sitting behind the nurses' station smoking a cigarette. I thought I was seeing things as it was very early in the morning, perhaps 5am, and there he was as bold as brass. It made me smile because he looked so satisfied but oblivious to what he was doing. The station was deserted apart from him and as he smoked he shuffled with papers, "I hope it's not Mum's papers he's shuffling," I thought.

Mum has waited all afternoon for her cannula to be replaced in her arm but so far no one has arrived to do it. It seems odd to me but all of the doctors struggle to get blood or put in cannula's. The patients all look as if they have been a couple of rounds with Mike Tyson, particularly the elderly patients. Mum's arms are black and blue, the bruises are all at different stages. Some doctors give up and end up storming off unable to get blood. They always have trouble with her but funnily enough come the morning the haematology staff have no problems. They usually arrive about 10ish and they are a ray of sunshine, always pleasant to the patients and so efficient. They come and go within minutes but they are sometimes the only person that speaks to them kindly in a day if they have no visitors. That's another thing that surprises me the amount of patients that have no visitors at all. Always elderly and more often than not they have been admitted from nursing or residential care. It's a real struggle for the staff some days if they have come in the following morning from an evening shift and there is a different patient in the bed. One day one of the nursing staff nearly gave the wrong patient another woman's drugs. It was only by accident that it didn't happen as the poor woman in the bed had no idea who she was.

I spoke to one of the more approachable nursing staff after this incident. I mentioned that at other hospitals that Mum had been into the patients name is clearly marked above the bed.

"Oh we can't do that." She said looking at me with distaste at my suggestion.

"Why not?" I inquired, having no idea why my statement caused such a reaction.

"Patient confidentiality," she said unaware of how daft the statement was on this ward.

A new woman must have been admitted to the isolation room opposite overnight. She's elderly and mobile, perhaps too mobile. She's in and out of the room all day and several times I have passed her along the corridor. Every now and again a member of staff walks her back into the room, telling her to stop in there. She's obviously confused as no sooner have they put her back in than she is out again, pushing her Zimmer along with her. On one occasion a nurse catches her before she can leave the room and tells her to go back into the room. She's a tiny woman with silver grey hair but lots of it and some days she wears it in a hair net. From her manner you can sense that she is fiercely independent with a determined personality as she shuffles along with her Zimmer frame.

"No I'm not, I'm all alone in here," she tells her full of determination, as she tries pushing past the nurse once again.

"But you must, you are in an isolation room," the kind nurse tells her.

"But why am I in an isolation room?" the poor dear asks.

"It's for your own good", the nurse tells her "you have an infection".

"Well I never had an infection when I came in here, this hospital has given it to me." She bites back.

69

Eventually she does return to her room but I sit there admiring her challenge.

A Nurse Practitioner arrives, it's the first time we have met a Nurse Practitioner, she tells us how experienced she is and fills Mum with confidence. We tell her that she will be the third today to try and get blood. In the nursing hierarchy the Nurse Practitioners are above the Matrons. The Matrons are above the Ward Sisters. The Ward Sisters are above the Staff Nurses and the HCA. The student nurses are probably at the bottom of the hierarchy or they are, on this ward.

"Oh don't you worry. I'm a master at getting blood". The Nurse Practitioner tells us. "They call me when no-one else can do it." Despite her experience it all ends in disaster, for some reason Mum's blood ends up all over the bed, floor and nearly me. I hate the sight of blood and unexpectedly blood starts to pour out of Mum's arm and the nurse struggles to stop it. Eventually she does but there is a terrible mess and although the nurse is apologetic she walks away leaving the blood everywhere. I'm distracted all afternoon cleaning it up from the room and haven't really noticed that there is no sign of the man who had wanted a cigarette all afternoon.

The rest of the evening passes without any further incidents. I eventually clean all of Mum's blood apart from the curtain that runs alongside her bed. From our first week on the ward there has been blood up the window. The patient opposite's Mother had brought flowers in for her along with a pair of secateurs to cut the stems with but instead of cutting the stems she ended up practically taking her finger off. That was another fiasco as there didn't seem as if there was anyone on duty who could help her. In the end she went down to A&E and ended up having a few stitches in, but no one seemed to be trained in basic first aid on Ward 11.

Evenings are an odd time it's nice to see the other visitors as we have made friends with a couple of the patients and their relatives. We chat amongst ourselves and compare our concerns. The buzzers sound during visiting as the patients fancy their chances when their visitors are around. Or the families encourage them to ring their bells whilst they are with them to get information. The corridors are usually busy as some relatives stand along them waiting to find a nurse, some giving up on the call bell system. A strange thing about the call bell system is that the staff have no idea who has rung their bell first. What few staff there are before families arrive, as soon as it's visiting time they disappear. We are usually reminded it is the end of visiting time by a HCA walking up and down the corridor with a bell. Most relatives know their place and quickly leave when the bell is rung. Others brave it out and continue to line the corridor waiting to speak to a member of staff, but very often to no avail. All the staff usually disappear until about 10pm. Sometimes a hot drink arrives for the patients, other nights it's a HCA a little later collecting up the water jugs. Some staff make sure the water glasses for the patients are filled but some don't bother and leave the patients without any water to drink through the night.

One night the poor lady who is in the infection room comes out of her room and drinks out of one of the dirty flower vases that are lined up along the corridor, waiting to be emptied. I want to race over and get her a drink but it is too late, before I have chance to put on my shoes, she's off along the corridor again. In the years since this happened I have recounted this event many times and it's often repeated by the press, a headline writer's dream. Many people have had the nerve to tell me that this didn't happen, that I imagined it. I can tell you now it did happen, I saw it with my own eyes. The sad thing is this was not the only time I would see it.

I want to tell the staff, I want to tell them just what is happening on this ward but I don't. I just sit and watch, my priority has got to be to get Mum out of here and that is all that is important. I've just got to get through this. "Stay positive, stay positive." I keep telling myself.

I normally fetch the patients a hot drink from a drinks trolley just outside the bay. If I have been home I sometimes bring a flask of milk and share it with a couple of the patients. What I have noticed is the lack of any nutrition from the hospital food that the patients get. I wish Mum could have some of the hot milk but she is still needing to be fed through a tube and being sick, although I still try and test her each day. Before Mum came into hospital she had been on a soft diet. Since she has been in here I try to give her a few spoonfuls of porridge, each morning. It looks very unappetising, grey gunk, obviously made without milk and filled right to the top of the container. This makes it really difficult to thin it down as there is nothing to tip some out into to add the milk. The milk I had to purchase from the shop downstairs but I learnt it soon curdled and now I try to remember to bring a small amount from home. The soup is the same as the porridge, from a packet and made with water.

Mum loved Heinz chicken soup at home. I used to try to make her nice homemade soup but she just loved Heinz chicken soup. On her locker stand four cans which I'm hoping will tempt her into wanting to eat something, although so far she has been unable to keep anything down, despite my daily attempts with the porridge.

Not long now till Thursday and we know there will be risks with the operation but it is Mum's only chance now. Trying to get fluids into her is proving very difficult, what with the lack of staff but also the difficulty in getting lines into Mum's body. Her arms are looking terrible and the next step is to get a line in her neck. I know Mum hasn't the luxury to be fussy but the thought turns my stomach.

I try to settle down for the night, I now have my own little routine and it starts with a trek out onto the main corridor. The nearest toilet is about fifty yards down the corridor where I am able to strip off and put on something that resembles pyjamas. Not really pyjamas but something comfortable to try and get to sleep in. Both taps in the toilet only give out scalding hot water, which makes it difficult to wash with because it is so hot and there's no cold water to cool it with. Some days I remember and bring a bottle of cold water from home, but I often forget and try and wash in the scalding water.

I race back as quickly as possible as always in my mind is that anything could be happening to Mum. Usually I will shower in the late afternoon when I get home, It doesn't take me long to get home wash and return. There are days I try to go to bed for a few hours but it doesn't work. The most I can manage is to get home and walk the dog, I wish I could forget what is going on at the hospital but I can't. Some days I feel I'm going mad I can think of nothing else. Everything needs to be checked on because it's likely something has been forgotten. For everything there is a battle, whether that be medication, pain relief, a clean bed, getting Mum turned, just about everything. I'm not alone it's the same for everyone, or those with relatives anyway. Those who are alone and have few visitors are neglected and get attention after those who have shouted the loudest, if at all.

"Something's going on, Jude." Mum says to me as I come back from my wash. She nods her head. She's noticed there are lots of staff in the corridor, all rushing around. Usually we only see two staff at night, one a nurse who gives out the medicines and a HCA who tries to make the patients comfy, empty catheters and take away water jugs. Tonight there are at least three more members of staff wandering around and then they are gone. The lights are turned out and I try to watch a bit of television. I put on the headphones and with one eye on Mum and the other on the TV, I try to relax enough to spend another night in the reclining chair.

To try to protect ourselves during the night I established a little routine, it involved pulling the curtains all around the bed and securing them with the bedside table, the bed and my chair. I did this because on several occasions I woke up with a man standing over me, a vulnerable, confused man but it was still enough to frighten me. One night I was awoken by screaming coming from the next bay, the male bay. By the time I had come to my senses and got to the bay door I wasn't alone. Two elderly ladies stood at the door, one with a Zimmer frame, shouting at a man in the corner of the room. I try shouting to distract him as in front of him is Nurse Ratchet herself and he has her pushed into a corner. She is shouting at him too and the next thing two porters arrive along with what looks like a male doctor. The crowd is dispersed and we are ushered off back to bed, the man's shouts and screams last for a while after I have returned to Mum. I try to shut out the man's cries, in my head. I know beyond a doubt that Nurse Ratchet will be responsible for inflaming the situation. Funnily we haven't seen him earlier wandering the ward as we usually did. That poor woman on the Zimmer, where did she come from? All these thoughts whirl around in my head.

Once I have managed to secure the curtains around the bed I usually manage to nod off for a few hours. Mum's the same, because of her discomforts she ends up tossing and turning. Some nights I hold her hand, most nights we don't talk, once the lights are off, we don't want to disturb the others. Because Mum was hard of hearing it is difficult to have a conversation, if we have to I make sure she can see my mouth, other times words aren't needed, I know what she is thinking.

73

We must have both nodded off as I wake and hear voices, male voices. As I'm struggling to open my eyes I see a bright light shining and it looks like it's under Mum's bed. I try to prize my eyes to wake but before I have, the lights and the male voices have gone. Was I dreaming, I wonder? Was I asleep, but no I'm awake. I sit there for a while puzzled. What on earth was that?

The next morning I find out what had been happening the previous evening and during the night. The male patient who wanted the cigarette has gone missing and it was the police who were on the ward during the night. They were searching the ward and were using a torch shining it under the beds. The man had gone missing in the afternoon and it was hours later that the police had started their search.

The majority of the staff carry on as if nothing has happened while an elderly, vulnerable man is out there alone. I ask one of the nurses, another Nurse Ratchet. She has very poor English and struggles to be pleasant to anybody. I don't think she has spoken to me once, despite me being on the ward so much. As she arrives with the drug trolley a helicopter hovers over the hospital.

"Have they found him?" I ask.

"Who?" She answers.

It says it all to me. I feel sick that the man is missing and I could possibly have done something about it and yet here is a nurse who was on duty yesterday and she asks me, "Who!" Her lack of interest is astonishing and Mum and I just look at each other. Mum doesn't say much she doesn't have to, I can see what she is thinking and she is disgusted.

Over the weekend we hear and see the police helicopter as it goes back and forward, sometimes coming really close to the bay window. The noise is deafening and each time we hear it, it reminds us of that poor man. The weekend goes without anything else happening but he's on our minds all weekend. On the Monday, it is on the front page of the Express and Star (E&S), with a picture of the man who has gone missing, he is named as a Mr Baseley. "Friends in search for missing man" the headline said. It's chilling seeing him knowing the circumstances as to why he left the ward and a real worry as to where he could now be.

The next few days are hard to get through. Mum is still unable to swallow anything. But she is anxious now for

Thursday to come, just the thought that she could get out of this awful place. She telephones her Sister in Law, my Aunty Freda, on the Tuesday evening. The conversation still haunts me to this day as it is the first time that my Mum spoke about her possible death.

"Hiya, Freed. Yeah, it's Bella... There're gonna put a peg in my belly... It's the only chance I've got, I can't keep anything down and the lines in my arm keep going bad... It's not very nice, Freed. They aren't very nice at all. There's some poor souls here. I just wanna go 'ome, that's all, Freed. So I've gotta do it."

It's the fear in her voice that I haven't heard before or perhaps I haven't wanted to. She hands the phone to me and I say my goodbyes. That was be the last time she would ever speak to Freda and the next time I do, it is at my Mum's funeral.

Tuesday goes quickly, surprisingly. Very little happens, although Ethel is discharged home. Yesterday a doctor had appeared who I had never seen before and he tried to speak to her. There are no pleasantries with him, no introduction, nothing. He's a very small Asian man with a well defined moustache and small framed glasses. He too seems young, perhaps mid twenties at the most.

"You are being discharged."

"Pardon?"

"Good news. You're being discharged."

"Pardon?"

"We're letting you go!" You can sense the irritation in his voice.

"Pardon?"

At this he tuts and leaves the room. She was left not knowing what he had said or that a decision had been taken to send her home. Ethel had told us a few days before that a nurse had put her hearing aid into her pocket and taken it home with her. She had asked a few of the nurses when the nurse would be back on duty and she was told in three days time. That was now over a week ago and it doesn't look like Ethel will be getting her hearing aid back.

Ethel is left shaking her head as the doctor leaves and we all look on wondering who will now tell her. I decide to wait to see if the night staff tell her but they don't. I decide to sleep on it and I'm glad I did because the following morning, when I do

75

mention it, she is full of questions, questions that I cannot answer.

"But I can't go home. Who will help me?" and "Who'll get my shopping? How will I eat? Who'll put my heating on?"

She has many concerns. The first nurse that she saw happened to be a student nurse, a very kind student nurse but without a clue what Ethel was talking about. I explain about the doctor the day before and she goes off to find out what is happening. Ethel doesn't see her again and nothing more is said about her discharge until that evening when she is moved out and into the discharge unit, to await discharge. She looks terrified when the discharge manager tells her she is being sent home as she piles all of Ethel's belongings into a black bag. Within minutes of being told Ethel is gone, I worry all night as to what she has gone home to. She will have to come back into hospital later in the year to have her leg removed. We will all miss her and luckily we had exchanged phone numbers, promising to see her again. Although she was a quiet woman during the evening I miss her, the place feels odd without her. But at the same time it is one less to worry about and have to look out for. Hopefully the new patient that will be admitted to her bed will be more able.

Later in the day, Mum has swabs taken, something to do with checking for infection before her operation. I'm expecting it to be cancelled all day but so far we are still on for Thursday. One of the HCAs tells us that very often the results come back positive and if they do the operation will have to be cancelled. We hadn't considered the operation being cancelled but we worry all afternoon, that there may be a delay.

There's really nothing to distract us, each day I go down and fetch the daily papers. I even read the Daily Mail and the Daily Mirror because they're easy for me to read out to Mum. Though she doesn't always listen, she often seems miles away, and today is one of those days. The cleaner arrives late morning and mops the middle of the room and disappears as she does most days. As time goes on I build up a bit of a relationship with her and I move my chair out while she mops under it for me, with a filthy black mop. She uses the same cloth to clean the sink and table tops but all the same I am grateful. After she is gone I wipe the table tops with baby wipes that Sam brings in. In fact Sam does more of the cleaning than the cleaner and does more than anyone for infection control for the patients. I have never seen the ward cleaned properly, the only time we have seen anything you would consider a clean was oddly one Sunday afternoon.

It was visiting time around 4pm and in walks Nurse Ratchet herself and one of the Sisters, both carrying buckets of water. As I have said earlier to get two trained nurses in the same bay together was very rare, but today here they are to clean. It was unusual for both Sam and I to be on the ward together too, but Sam had stopped the Saturday night as usual and I was taking over from her. They asked all the relatives if they could leave whilst they cleaned. They went from bed to bed cleaning locker, bed, tables - with the same bucket and cloth, of course. But all the same it was the first time I had ever seen it done. Mum's was spotless already, Sam had made sure of that but the other patients didn't have a Sam to look after them. The first thing Sam said as they both walked out of the door was that an inspection was due and she was right. The following day a group of people in suits were seen walking along the corridor. They appeared outside the door of Mum's room, it was Mum that first spotted them and said "Look, Sam was right". Looking back now, I wonder why I didn't approach them. I could have stopped the suffering, or could I? No, I wasn't brave enough for that, I'd stuck my neck out now on three occasions and nothing had come of it, other than hostility from the staff.

After my visit to PALS and my interview with the two Matrons I also hand delivered a letter to the Chief Executive's office. It was after another bad weekend where patient's lives were put at risk because of the lack of staff and a lack of leadership on the ward. Another confused patient was wandering around and becoming aggressive towards the patients and staff. I'd come back from walking the dog and as I walked down the corridor the male HCA was stood in my way, arms folded shouting at an elderly man who probably was totally oblivious to what he wanted him to do.

"Get back into your bed!"

Another scuffle while he tried to drag him back to his bed. Within minutes he's back up. This time shouting and even striking out at another male patient who happened to be walking along the corridor at the same time. I pressed the buzzer as I saw him coming into our bay but nobody came in time to help. Without any warning he threw one of the tables across the room and began shouting at Lillian for no reason whatsoever. Lillian had been admitted into Ethel's bed and was probably less able and very poorly.

"Get out of my bed!" he shouted at Lillian.

My priority has got to be Mum but at the same time I have to protect Lillian, she's practically bed-bound. I knew he smoked, Sam had said she had seen him outside smoking, I was terrified but I knew I would have to do something. I thought it was worth a try although I could see he was so angry and would need some distracting.

"Come on. Let's go for a smoke. I wonder... where can we go for a smoke?"

Eventually he did come with me it must have been the hope of getting a cigarette, that swung it. Once out on the corridor with him, I could feel myself shaking inside and I was wondering, "How am I gonna get out of this one?" I carry on walking along the corridor, walking slowly trying to convince him I am looking for somewhere to go and smoke.

"Gotta be somewhere we can have a fag."

Inside I am praying that a nurse will appear but there is no one in sight. I can hear several other alarms going off as I pass the nurses' station. I reach the end of the long corridor, my time is up and there is no one to help.

I'd spent most of my career working with people with dementia. As a social worker most of my cases involved someone who was confused and I also had a lot of experience of residential care for people with dementia type illnesses. I'd always been good at distracting and today was no different.

"Have you got a lighter"?

"No".

"Then go and find your lighter. We can't have a fag without a light, can we?"

The male carer had just fuelled his aggression by standing there shouting at him and then dragging him to his bed. Now the male carer was nowhere to be seen although part of me doesn't want to find him as he was likely to inflame him again. As I'm just about to go off Ward 11 and onto Ward 12, a senior nurse from Ward 12 appears. The relief at seeing her must have been evident, I nearly cry, in fact I have to try and control myself but I can hear the fear myself in my voice.

"You need to wedge a chair up against the door to stop him getting in", she tells me.

"What good will that do? He'll just break in again. Where are the staff? We need more staff. There's nobody here, nobody to help him. Something must be done, the management need to know." My voice full of helplessness.

"If you contact management you'll just get us into trouble and that won't help anybody." She tells me.

I go back to Mum dejected. What can I do now? At first I do as I am told. I put the table in front of the door and try to wedge it to stop it opening, but it doesn't work. Within minutes he is in again. He's not aggressive now, but for how long? You know he's like a volcano ready to erupt at any minute.

We're not complainers, in fact I am aware that making a complaint is likely to make things worse. I mull it over all afternoon but I feel I have no alternative when I look at the risks involved. In my bag I find out a scrap of paper and a pen and I make the decision to write to Martin Yeates, the Chief Executive of the hospital. I decided he needed to know before anyone else got hurt within his hospital. I wrote the letter whilst leaning on my Mum's legs with her contributions. I thought within a few hours I would be interviewed by someone from the management team. Since we had first noticed that something was wrong on the ward I had tried to keep a record of what was happening. I got all my notes ready to use in an interview but we didn't even get a response, even though I had hand delivered the complaint to the top floor where the management had a suite of offices. We waited and were expecting a backlash the next day from the staff but we don't really notice any difference.

The following day the thought of another weekend on the ward prompts us to call the local newspaper, *The Staffordshire Newsletter*. Sam & I sit in the car and phone them, I speak but Sam is behind me all the way. The call is very brief and within seconds we are left without hope that anyone cares and will help us.

"Nah, we've run plenty of stories on the Hospital, staff shortages and what-have-you." I try to tell him about the way the elderly are being treated, I tell him unless elderly patients have families to look after them they will be neglected and some are being abused. But he doesn't want to hear,

"Nah. Newsletter readers aren't interested in that type of stuff."

Around 2pm I go and fetch the evening paper, it's now a ritual but today we are wondering if there is any news about the missing man. The woman in the bed opposite Mum's, who had collapsed on the floor when she had been frightened into going home, has taken to buying me cream cakes and chocolate, each day. At this rate I will be a size of a bus when I get Mum home, what with sitting all day too.

I'd managed to groom a few dogs that day, those that had been booked in before Mum came into hospital. When Laura had arrived in the afternoon, I'd managed to race to the salon and get a dog done. Normally a dog takes two hours but if they sense your mind isn't on the job it can take much longer. But I am only doing dogs that I must do, during the day the grooming salon stays shut. The dogs I do manage to groom I fit in the afternoon, I get to the salon around 3pm and I get home for 6pm. A quick walk for my dog, a shower and I'm back on the ward for about 9ish. Laura often stays for an hour and then spends the rest of the evening with her friends, trying to get over what she has seen on the ward.

The following day Mum gets her results from the swabs and they are negative, we breathe a sigh of relief. Without the operation it is very unlikely that Mum will survive much longer, getting the cannula into her arm is proving really difficult and that's all that is keeping her alive. The doctors just don't seem to be able to insert one and, to make matters worse, whenever they do manage to insert it into Mum's arm it seems very soon that her body reacts to it and rejects it. It is so nerve wracking because we know that once her body rejects it there's the wait to get it removed and in the meantime the swelling and pain Mum has to put up with. But then there is the wait to get a doctor to try to insert another line because all the time Mum isn't getting the nutrition she should. She has lost so much weight, I daren't even think about it.

In the Soup

Sam's suspicion of hospital acquired infections and all the cleaning she has done has paid off. Mum is free from infection and the operation will go ahead, it's now late morning and we wait and worry. Pat waits with me until she comes out of theatre, he's as nervous as me, worried about his Mum. The anaesthetic will be dangerous and the risks are high because of her chest problems. Dr Hearing has explained this all to us and despite the risks Mum has to go ahead with the operation.

Laura has arrived too and we all wait outside the unit for news that the operation is over. We try to talk and keep each other upbeat but it is difficult when we are so anxious. Then a nurse calls me over to speak to Dr Hearing. He looks different in his surgical scrubs but I can immediately see the smile on his face.

"I'm pleased to tell you that the operation was a complete success." I feel my whole body burn with relief, I could kiss him. "But the next few hours will be critical."

Once Mum is back on the ward, we find that there have been some changes since we have been away with two new patients. Mum spends the rest of the evening in and out of sleep, with us sitting anxiously by her side. That night she is given her first feed through the tube and the nurse tells us she has forgotten how to manage a peg feed. I wish she hadn't shared that with us but the woman in the next bed who has just moved to the ward has also had a peg fitted I'm hoping that will help them remember how to do it.

That first night it's one of the bank nurses who tries to set up the feed. It seems to take an age and the first problem is that she is unable to find a stand to attach the feed to. She then has to hunt for one for the woman in the next bed, which takes more of her time. She's an elderly woman too but has dark dyed hair with tight curls. She has no teeth in at the moment and that makes her face look much older. She looks as if she could only be in her seventies but her lack of teeth make her look older. She smiles every now and again acknowledging the stress the nurse must be under but she seems too shy to speak to us just yet.

It's now nearly 12.30am and the other patients on the ward are getting anxious. You can feel the tension in the air and the stress coming from the nurse as she tries to hunt down the stands. What an impossible situation for the poor woman, she decides to leave us. She will give out the drugs to the other patients and return. I'm relieved the tension in the air is beginning to frighten me. Some of the patients have been shouting out for help and within minutes of the nurse leaving us they become quieter. Although the trained nurse tonight doesn't fill you with confidence, she's kind and that will help. Above anything, we avoid calling for the nurse during the night as we know how busy they are, but it's nice to know that if we have to, someone kind will try to help us.

It's morning and Mum has survived the night. I've not managed a wink of sleep, watching her like a hawk for the first sign of trouble. It's a huge relief though because she has survived, the anaesthetic, the fitting of the peg, her first feed and the night. Things are really looking up until we hear Nurse Ratchet's voice down the corridor, just hearing her voice ruins our optimistic mood. She's barking at a man for something. I can't quite hear what she is complaining about but it is something that he wants and something she is not prepared to give him.

Enid has slept less than Mum and as soon as she is hauled out of bed she is sick, violently everywhere. Luckily the HCA is still around and helps clean her up but she's what Mum calls one of the *rough ones*. It transpires that most of the HCAs who work the early shift are unable to work the afternoon shifts. We are later told by the kinder HCA that they mostly work the afternoon shifts as some staff are allowed to choose what shifts they work and they mostly choose the early shifts. So that must be why the "rough ones" are together during the early shift.

Mum calls them the *rough ones* as they handle the patients roughly when they wash them and she complains that they leave her wet. I would wash her myself but with all the equipment around and on her I'm nervous I will pull something out and hurt her. Her face drops when she sees them coming towards her but she puts up with it all the same. She has no choice, she needs washing and they are the only ones who can do it.

Over the next couple of days Mum goes from strength to strength, she's even walked out of bed and down to the toilet. The physiotherapist is pleased with her progress and we are over the moon. There are a couple of different physiotherapists that are assigned to the ward and they are all very friendly and professional. Mum has a real fighting spirit and it shines through as she encourages herself to recover. Daily now she is able to walk up and down the corridor, she has now mastered walking with her own Zimmer frame. Enid is the opposite and looks very poorly, each morning she has been hauled out of bed and been sick as she has got up. Nobody passes this information onto the doctor and he is oblivious to her lack of nutrition.

Her daughter visits daily but she seems needy herself, she's recently lost her husband and the pain is still evident in her face. Her Mum is very poorly and barely talks during the evening visit. Enid hasn't been out of bed yet and it's now been several days since her peg fitting. I found out from her daughter that Enid had been having trouble with burping and that was all that was wrong with her. She'd visited her GP and an appointment had been made for a endoscopy. The morning of the appointment Enid had been shopping and fully expected to walk home from her appointment. She hadn't and now she lay extremely poorly in the next bed to Mum's. We find out the camera had perforated her oesophagus and she had nearly lost her life. Over the next few days she continues to fight for it and there are several occasions when I believe she will die.

The fight in Enid is remarkable and I awake each morning surprised she is alive. One of the nights I was so concerned for her, I went and sat with her for a little while. I didn't want her to die alone but it was also through guilt that I sat in the dark, cold, trying to comfort her.

After her operation she had never started her recovery like Mum had, but then Mum hadn't had her throat damaged. For the last few nights Enid had coughed continually throughout the night, together with both Mum's and Enid's buzzer going off incessantly, sleep was impossible. The day was hard to get through but seeing Mum getting better was a real tonic, seeing her so positive gave me energy. It was difficult trying to spend so much time at the hospital and sleeping in the chair but under no circumstances was Mum safe here alone.

Each morning Enid has been hauled out of bed at about 7ish despite her not sleeping all night as she had spent it coughing. As soon as the HCA put her in the chair Enid was sick everywhere. Yesterday the HCA had the good sense to pass her a sick bowl as she did this morning. But yesterday the carer had waited until Enid had finished and she took the bowl away. Today a different HCA left her with a bowl full of sick, with nowhere to put it. I had no option I had to go over and help her, the bowl was full of steaming sick! I have a really delicate stomach when it comes to vomit and this morning is worse than ever. With the lack of sleep and nothing in my stomach it churns my guts. I race to the sink and wretch into the basin to make matters worse I have Enid's sick bowl still in my hands, with nowhere to put it and seeing it makes me sick again.

Enid spends the day shuffling in the chair trying to get herself, comfortable. I suspect she has sores on her bottom and I hunt for a footstool for her to put her feet up. She just looks so uncomfortable as she tries to nod off in the chair. There's no point asking the morning staff to put her back into bed. For a start they would say it was none of my business, so I wait and hope that one of the caring staff will come on duty in the afternoon. They do and they put Enid back into bed, she can't thank them enough as she stretches out her legs. I just dread to think what her bottom is like because as she moves she cries out with the pain. I also suspect she has a chest infection coming, I recognise the signs from caring for Mum.

The night is no different to the last, both Mum and Enid have their feed attached at night and the buzzer sounds on average every hour. The alarms are so sensitive and once they go off the feed stops going through. It's agony sitting there because you know it's not an emergency but at the same time if the nurse doesn't attend to it, no feed will go through. So I usually sit and wait until I see a nurse come past the window. Although you know they can hear the buzzer you also know that they know it is only the feed that has stopped. They have so many other things to do and I understand they have to prioritise. It also doesn't help that the bay is the furthest away for the staff and they have to pass more needy patients on the way.

Tonight Enid coughs and coughs and between her coughing

and the two buzzers going off, I want to scream. Luckily Enid and Mum are hard of hearing and the other two patients sleep soundly, but they both have sleeping tablets. I wish they'd give me something to sleep. I'm exhausted. Enid wakes and rings her call bell, now we have three alarms going off. The HCA arrives, probably one of the worst HCAs you could ever wish to meet. Whatever possessed her to go into a caring profession I will never know. Not only have I never heard her be kind to a patient I have never even heard her speak to a patient. Enid braves it and asks her for a drink of water, her annoyance is written all over her face. I can just see her in the dim light, return to the sink and top up her glass with water. She's like an ogre I feel as if I despise the woman and yet I barely know her. The thought makes me feel guilty that I could dislike someone so much. She's a large woman with fair greasy straight hair similar to a younger version of Hattie Jacques. Not only is she well-built, she's tall with it and she seems to walk slowly without purpose.

Getting a drink during the night for the patients is difficult as it's part of the HCA routine to take away the water jugs before lights out. I learnt to keep a bottle of water in Mum's cupboard but the first time I asked for more was like something from *Oliver Twist*. I tried to get some sense from the HCA telling her that a glass of water often isn't enough for the patients overnight, particularly those patients that come alive at night. That includes most of the confused patients.

"No."

The HCA tells me she couldn't possibly leave the water jugs out, as they have to be sterilised overnight. With that she rushes out of the door and continues doing what she thinks her job is. Just another example of how the ward routine is inflexible, how the daily routine is for the staff's benefit and not the patients. Even the caring staff refused to leave the water jugs out for the patients, despite me telling them that the patients need more than a small cup during the night. As I said, the woman in the isolation room wasn't the only patient I saw drinking out of the flower vases that were piled up along the main corridor. What a state of affairs I thought, they have to remove the jugs because of health and safety Yet the patients can drink dirty water from a flower vase. The place has gone mad!

To fill my day part of my daily routine was to rinse out the flower vases. It was something I would normally do at home to keep the flowers fresher for longer. On Ward 11 it was to help keep the patients hydrated with as clean water as possible.

The carer has turned off Enid's buzzer but Mum's is still ringing, she puts the glass onto the table at the foot of Enid's bed and walks out the door. She might as well have put it on the moon, there's no way Enid can reach it. Enid is normally as quiet and timid as a mouse, a lady, but the inhumanity of the situation just gets to her.

"You stupid girl!" she calls out in desperation.

I can hear footsteps getting faster, closer on the corridor. There's no mistaking them, it's Nurse Ratchet. She storms over to her and with her face nearly pressing into hers, she spits, "Don't... You... Ever... Speak to my staff like that again." She resets Mum's button and strides out of the room.

Enid is humiliated, treated like a child. No, treated like an animal. To this day I regret not challenging her for being so nasty towards an ill, elderly woman who had waited hours for a drink. She should have been shouting at the HCA for putting the drink out of her reach. She knew Enid was bed-bound! I hear Enid crying and I have to bite my lip to avoid doing the same. I don't bother to put on my slippers as I prise myself out of the plastic chair and pass Enid her water. I say nothing, I can't bring myself to for fear of crying, I don't want her to see me cry. I want to comfort her and to be strong. I'm just so relieved she is still alive but all the time that I try to comfort her I keep one eye on the corridor to make sure Nurse Ratchet doesn't catch me, coward that I am now.

The night before last I really thought she had died and I stayed awake all night thinking we would lose her before morning. There was no coughing just moaning every now and again. I must have nodded off because the curtains being pulled around her bed woke me. I learnt that once the curtains are pulled around the bed it's a sign that someone is likely to die. But she didn't, she's still with us. How I don't know, because it's such a hostile place patients are likely to give up surrounded by such bitterness and abuse.

From what I have seen very few staff are concerned about the patients, most seem to go around as if there are no patients, particularly the senior staff. The Sisters on the ward are rarely seen and the caring, qualified staff, are so few in numbers. Amy has worked on the ward for several years but we need more like her. The other two senior nurses or who appear to be senior nurses are Nurse Ratchet and Lyndsey, they seem to be on duty the most.

It's apparent that Lyndsey and Nurse Ratchet don't get along, I suspect she is bullied by her. She contradicts everything that Nurse Ratchet says. The dressing that Nurse Ratchet put on Mum's backside Lyndsey said was the wrong dressing. The catheter Nurse Ratchet fitted had to come out as it was the wrong size, or that is what Lyndsey said, although Nurse Ratchet said the same, fitting another in a matter of hours. Practically everything Nurse Ratchet had said, Lyndsey contradicted. As you can imagine this was very confusing because it wasn't just Mum it was for all of the patients. Lyndsey always seemed in competition with Nurse Ratchet. How reassuring for elderly and confused patients, to have two nurses constantly giving two different stories!

Lyndsey's a nice girl but another that shouldn't be in nursing. She doesn't speak either she just gives out the drugs in silence and in the dark, for some reason. It's only later when she returns with the afternoon drugs that you see her again and she has a bit more life about her but in the light you then notice the dog hairs that cover her uniform. She told me once that she walks her dogs before she comes to work and her shoes are always covered in mud. She is pleasant but downtrodden, she's given up, thrown in the towel. She tells everyone she will, "be back in a minute," and I'm sure at the time she believes she will but she never is. We have now all learnt that when she says in a minute, it usually means you won't see her again for that shift. It's odd but the next day she says nothing, not an apology or any explanation. It's like it never happened.

Since Mum has had the peg fitted the difference in her is amazing, she's got a glint back in here eye. She must have put on weight I can see it in her face, but as yet she hasn't been weighed. Things have become a lot easier since Laura and I have been trained with Mum's peg. It was nerve wracking at first but a few nurses supervised us until I felt confident enough to connect the feed and her drugs myself, although we still have to wait for the drugs/food to be given out we have a bit more control.

Pat is still poorly and remains in bed but she isn't taking the morphine anymore and this takes a lot of the pressure off. As I said to administer morphine two qualified staff are needed, you hardly ever see two qualified staff together on the ward. You do at the nurses station but not on the ward. The doctors think she has cancer although they can't seem to make their minds up *where* she has cancer. The first day, it's one of the senior doctors and a posse of what must be junior doctors.

"You have cancer of the ovaries."

No warning, nothing. And this was in front of everyone. Despite the shock of it all, Pat fought back.

"I don't have any ovaries." She said, bewildered and angry.

"Oh. Err, let me see," He flicks through her notes, playing for time.

"Well we'll just have to check a few things."

And with that they are gone, scurrying out of the door with their tails between their legs. Her family arrived later that evening and complained about the way she had been told and how she had been left not knowing.

The ward manager came and apologised to Pat and her family, although her insincerity shone through. She told them it wouldn't happen again. But it did, the very next day. It's hard to believe, I know, but I was there and heard it. The same conversation took place but it was a different doctor today.

"You have cancer of the ovaries."

"What? I told them yesterday, I don't have any ovaries." Disbelief in her voice.

"Oh. Oh." The same performance as yesterday, a fumble through the notes, playing for time but this doctor won't leave until he's done. "Oh well then, it must be cancer in the womb." He doesn't even look up from the notes.

Pat's family complained again and insisted that whenever Pat was given any diagnoses from a doctor they were informed beforehand so they could be present. On the third day the same thing happened, a different doctor but this time Pat did have cancer, it was likely it was in her stomach but they were waiting for more test results.

Pat spent the afternoon in floods of tears and to make matters worse her family were unavailable. She had a lovely supportive family but they were working today and couldn't be reached. Pat kept ringing and ringing them between her sobs.

A student nurse who up until now had been relatively caring towards the patients, heard her cries and asked her what was wrong. Between her sobs Pat told her what she had just been told. Whether the student nurse thought she was saying the right thing I really don't know but telling Pat she was crying for nothing until she got the results back was not what Pat needed to hear.

Her family were furious when they visited later and heard that despite the reassurances that it wouldn't happen again it had.

Meanwhile Mum was going from strength to strength now she had her peg and we were getting food into her. Dr Hearing had told us that Mum may not need her peg as her hernia may shrink and she could eat normally again. But we didn't expect it to happen so soon. Remember, it was only a month ago that she was going to die a painful death and we had expected her to die over that first weekend.

It had been a miserable day outside but Amy had been on the morning shift and she really did create calm on the ward. There was no crying out or shouting and you hardly heard the sound of a buzzer going off. What was different when Amy was on duty was you would see her walking the ward and you could talk to her for either reassurance or advice. There were a few other qualified staff who were kind and caring but they were recently qualified and weren't as skilled as Amy.

I spent the afternoon as usual reading the news out to Mum, until the peace was broken. Each weekday afternoon a young woman arrives with the tea trolley to give the patients a hot drink. The first thing you hear is her voice, she was very loud and you could see the patients faces when her voice was heard. Like her voice she was tall around five feet eight inches and she was overweight. Each morning it looked as if she had prized her large body into this tight mauve overall. She always wore her long hair loose and it was always greasy as it swung around her neck. She wasn't really safe to be on the ward herself, she had a learning disability and I suspect should have had supervision whilst she worked but she worked alone and slopped over the floor, beds and even patients, the hot tea that the patients wanted. She would walk by several of the patients missing them out completely and the single isolation rooms never got a look in.

I always ask Mum if she wants a cup of tea, she used to love her tea and was known to drink a pot to herself before she went off to work each morning. Over the years she fancied a cup less and less and for the last few years would ask for, "half a cup," when you offered her one. Whether it's the smell of the tea I don't know or something else but suddenly Mum announces, "Jude, I'm hungry". You can tell that she is shocked herself and we laugh as we both listen to her stomach rumbling. I'm over the moon because it's a step nearer to getting her home and confirmation she is on the road to recovery.

Mum decides she will have soup at tea time, when the evening meal is brought. We spend the afternoon in great anticipation of her first meal and if she will be able to keep it down. It's a huge disappointment when the tea trolley arrives and I ask the HCA if Mum could have some soup, from the trolley. There's the usual palaver about not ordering a meal, although we have this every day as the patients are supposed to fill in a form each evening to indicate what they want to eat the following day. It's a great idea, that is if you are not confused or too ill to know that you need to fill the form in.

Some of the staff go out of their way to help the patients at meal times, where others do nothing. They know as they leave the trays of food on the patients' tables that they will be taking those trays away uneaten. They also know that given help the patients would have eaten the food. It's a crying shame but our priority has got to be Mum and getting her better to get out of here. When the staff have gone out of the room I sneak round and help the few patients, making sure the staff don't see. My priority has got to be not to upset the staff and to be able to stay with Mum.

Eventually the HCA returns with a bowl of soup, although Mum is very grateful to the HCA we both know as soon as we see the label that Mum will be unable to eat it. We both read the label at the same time *Spicy Mexican Tomato Soup*. Of course she can't eat it, not with a hiatus hernia. She hasn't had anything spicy for years (and she never really liked spice anyway, not many of her generation do) but also for the last few years she has had to avoid tomato. The disappointment on her face tells me she was looking forward to her first meal in weeks.

"Don't worry, Mum." I tell her, "I'll go and heat one up in the microwave." We still had the cans of soup but I'd moved them into her locker, I never thought she'd eat again. Nothing can dampen our mood today, not even Spicy Mexican Tomato Soup. She gives a lovely, warm smile at the thought of food. I leave her in her chair positioned ready to eat, with her table pushed in front of her. As I go out the bay door, she lifts her soup spoon to me in jest, to say she is ready and waiting. Pat shouts after me, "You'd better hurry up, Julie, or she'll eat the table leg!"

I don't have to walk very far, the kitchen is only a few yards away and Nurse Ratchet is in there getting something out the fridge. "I can't believe it," I tell her, finding it hard to control my excitement. I tell her about Mum's hunger and her stomach rumblings and her disappointment when she saw the *Spicy Mexican Tomato Soup.*

"Could I just pop this chicken soup in the microwave?"

"I'm afraid that due to health and safety regulations I'm unable to allow you to use the microwave."

Part of me expected this, she's so predictable. I don't tell her that the rest of the staff allow me to warm milk each evening in that same microwave. I don't want to get anyone into trouble and I don't want to cut off my nose to spite my face.

"I understand" I tell her, "I'll just nip it down to the microwave in the cafeteria."

"Oh I can't possibly let you do that." She throws at me as I'm walking out of the door.

"Why is that then?" I ask. I can feel myself getting angry, boiling up inside.

"That would also breach health and safety." She sounds so pleased with herself.

"Then I'll have to warm it at home and bring it in a flask."

"No. health and safety regulations won't allow that either."

"Health and safety regulations? How?"

It's really bubbling up now. Forget what she's saying, the smug way she says it is enough to rile me. All I can see is Mum sitting, spoon in hand, waiting for her soup. The food she has been waiting weeks to eat. Like Dr Hearing had said her hernia may reduce in size and allow her to eat again.

"You could make it too hot and scald her."

"What" I say in shock rather than anger. "I've cared for my Mum for the best part of three years and I've managed to avoid scalding her all that time."

"I'm sorry but under no circumstances can I allow you to heat that soup."

She doesn't even look at me. I can swear her mouth is on the verge of a smile. I can feel my face getting redder as I get angry, I know I've watched this woman for nearly five weeks now and she wants me to bite. She wants a reaction. I have heard the way she speaks to patients and relatives. She tries to goad them into a reaction and then like pack animals, the other staff get involved and the relative is then asked to leave. The first time I heard it happen was when I heard a relative asking why her husband's medication had been stopped on admission. Nothing more, just concern from a relative, the next thing she is accused of raising her voice, which she certainly hadn't done. Within minutes Nurse Ratchet has inflamed the situation and before long the relative is escorted off the ward by two porters. I can't allow that, that would be the last thing we need, not at this stage when we have come so far.

I say nothing but my anger is evident, of course I am angry what else could I be. My dear Mum hasn't eaten in weeks and now she wants to eat but Nurse Ratchet is standing in the way of that. I walk out onto the main corridor, my blood is boiling, I pace up and down trying to absorb what has just happened. What harm would I cause my Mum? Why isn't she pleased that Mum is ready to eat again? Nurse Ratchet made a point of telling me the first time we met her that she was an experienced nurse, whatever that means, and she has years of experience in gastro problems. The woman loves the power, that's what it is. My mind is racing with anger towards her, but I know it is wrong.

I ring Sam, she is due in shortly and she will bring in a flask of warm Heinz chicken soup. I want to cry out to Sam, I want to give in here and now, I've had enough, I don't know how long I can survive in here. I suppose I'm tired but the environment is wearing me down, the hostility. I sense it's what they want, they want one of us to snap at the staff and that way they can make us leave.

I want to cry but I won't, my priority must be to get back to Mum, anything could be happening back on the ward. To get to Ward 11 you have to walk through Ward 12 which is the respiratory ward. Separating the wards is the nurses' station and at the side of the station is a row of toilets. As I walk through I notice that the door is open and a man is standing at the toilet passing urine. As I walk past trying not to look at the man out of decency I can see that the door is actually missing.

92

Nurse Ratchet is giving out the drugs in Mum's bay when I return.

"I bet you think we are being awkward, don't you?" she says.

I can't help myself as I'm still stinging from her denying Mum her soup for what I consider idiotic reasons. I feel I must say something but I must be careful with what I do say. Other nurses on this ward would be pleased that Mum fancied food but not her. They let me use the microwave. It's the way she says *we*, who is *we* I wonder?

"No" I say, "I don't think it's anybody else but you that is being awkward."

I don't wait for a reply but I can see by Mum's face that she is pleased that I am standing up to her. I walk back off the ward and down to the shop and give myself time to cool off, once again. I feel so empowered challenging her for the first time after all I have seen and heard her do, it feels so rewarding. When I walk back onto the ward she has gone and then I have to tell Mum she will have to wait for Sam to arrive. Mum doesn't see or hear a lot, I try to shield her from what is going on. Her deafness is a blessing more than a hindrance but I tell her what has happened over the soup.

But it isn't long before Sam sneaks in the hot soup, hiding it so Nurse Ratchet doesn't see it. That would be the last thing we need because I'm sure if she found out what we had done she would confiscate it. Even so we both feel silly having to hide the soup, like it's contraband. It's not something I would ever have imagined having to do.

Mum loves it and licks her lips in fun, it cheers both Sam and I, to see her so happy and we all forget the fuss we have had to get her the hot soup. Distracted we don't see Nurse Ratchet come back into the room and start walking towards us. Sam doesn't miss a thing and quickly pushes the flask back into her bag and Mum holds the cup close to her chest. We're all partners now in this crime and I stand over her to try to hide the cup. Nurse Ratchet had no reason to come back into the room and it is obvious she guessed what we have done. But without asking us outright, she will never know for definite that we have brought in a flask of Heinz chicken soup for Mum, who hadn't eaten anything for over a month.

Two days later I find out the extent to which this woman will go to discredit me. Stirling Moss takes us down to the X-ray department again, for an X-ray on Mum's chest. As we are waiting, I start to leaf through Mum's notes. For some reason I don't really think I should be looking at them and I make sure I look while no one is watching me. I feel sick when I read what Nurse Ratchet has written about the Heinz chicken soup incident.

"Patient's daughter has accused all the staff of being awkward."

That's precisely what I didn't say and I made sure that she understood that I thought it was just her that was being awkward. She also wrote that she had told me that I couldn't use the ward's microwave but she had offered to fetch me soup from the kitchen instead. She never told me that at all. She also hadn't recorded that she had told me that I couldn't use the microwave that is for the public to use in the canteen or that I wasn't allowed to bring Mum soup in from home. She also didn't mention that she had told me that I couldn't give Mum soup, as I might scald her.

I feel physically sick and Mum can see by my face I am reading something I'm not happy with.

"What? What is it?" she asks, fearing it is something to do with her health.

I honestly can't believe that she has written the very opposite of what I had said. I explain what she's written in the notes, to Mum. I can see the disappointment on her face, we are both shocked. This woman who was not willing to turn a blind eye to a minor breach of health and safety for the benefit of a starving patient was prepared to falsify patient documents and lie about the behaviour of relatives to protect her own reputation. I still find it hard to believe.

It was only a few days earlier that Mum had asked me to buy a dozen bath bombs for the nursing staff. She had given Nurse Ratchet one too, she thought it might soften her up. It obviously hadn't and I can tell by Mum's face that she's annoyed that she gave her one. At the time I resented Mum giving to her but she couldn't do anything else, she wouldn't give to one without giving to the other and she felt so sorry for some of the staff. The Angels were trying to do an impossible task. What had prompted her giving the gift to the staff was one of the HCAs coming to us and telling us what bullies some of the staff were. In the end she was crying, real tears, sobbing because she hadn't yet had a break and wasn't likely to get one either. She told us it was common that those in favour always got their breaks and always got their requested days off, those that weren't in favour did not. The favoured also opted for the early shift refusing to work nights, the afternoon shift or weekends. Of course Nurse Ratchet was in the thick of it, I'd seen it myself with her. The way she spoke to some of the patients, let alone the staff was shameful. On this ward it seems really odd but the caring staff appear to be the ones that are thought of the least.

Mavis

That night I cried while Mum slept, in the early hours while patients cried out for assistance. What Nurse Ratchet had done had really hit a nerve. It was the realisation now, that we were alone, she had sunk so low as to write lies about me, I had no trust at all in her. I was also frightened of what she was capable of and the power she had over us all. What sort of a person would do something like that? And a nurse too. The previous evening she had been sharp with the woman who had been admitted in the bed opposite to Mum's. She was a young woman who obviously had mental health problems, her lower arms were covered in scars, where she had self-harmed. She told me she had been an inpatient in the local psychiatric hospital on several occasions and had found most of the staff at Mid Staffs hospital unsympathetic whenever she was admitted after harming herself. Sarah was only on the ward for a couple of days but I witnessed the staff being unprofessional towards her on a numerous occasions. They just didn't seem to care who they upset, it was as if they were unrestrained. Two incidents with Sarah stand out in my memory. The first time was from one of the student nurses, it was a comment she made as she had walked out of the door.

"You claim you're religious and then you do that to yourself." I was really shocked to hear her say this and in front of everyone on the ward.

I hadn't seen a vicar on the ward until this woman was admitted and he gave me a bit of a fright. It was early afternoon, Mum had nodded off and I must have too because I opened my eyes and there was this large, round black man in a black long cassock with a large cross round his neck, standing in the doorway. He came in and spoke to no one apart from the woman opposite, who received Holy Communion. I was dreading Mum waking up half way through it, because I had to rub my eyes and orientate myself, before I realised what was happening. What struck me though was his presence on the ward, odd that he didn't acknowledge anyone when he entered the bay or when he left. I think Enid was shocked too that he didn't even acknowledge her.

I was at home when Mavis was admitted, she should have filled the bed opposite Mum's, but Pat had negotiated the bed with one of the caring staff. We had laughed as Pat had offered money to move next to the window. Ruth, a kind HCA, had transferred the beds over and settled Pat in. By the time I got back to the ward it was around 10pm and it was bedlam already. There were two patients tonight pulling at the bottom doors and they both wanted a cigarette. It didn't take long before they were fighting between themselves and not a member of staff in sight. Here we go again I thought but tonight was different as I hadn't considered Mavis and her needs.

She was so unsteady on her feet and each time she got out of her bed, I held my breath as I was convinced she was going to fall. Back and forward she went to the toilet all night, or that's what she tried to do. After the first couple of visit's the urine was all over her trousers, having run down her legs. You could see the wet stain down her trousers, along both legs. I was dreading her getting caught up with the two men who continued to rattle at the door, she was so vulnerable. She was a tall woman but so thin and gaunt looking. Nearly as soon as she sat back down onto her bed, she's off again to the toilet. I see her through the window stagger past and back again. I'm wondering if she has a urine infection and that is why she is back and forward to the toilet. Lights are out and she still goes back and forward, past the one confused man that continues to rattle at the door.

After around 11pm, the one man slopes off and we don't see him again for that night but the other man is more persistent and he continues to rattle and bang at the door. Suddenly he is distracted and leaves the door but then enters one of the two isolation rooms. He continues to focus his attention between the locked door and the isolation room. It's all going on tonight because of Mavis and this man and Mum has her eyes fixed on them both. Usually I can distract her because of her deafness, she doesn't hear a lot and if I'm sitting down her eyes are towards me and not the door. Tonight it's different.

Luckily Mavis is seated on the bed looking bewildered when

it all kicks off. I try to will Mavis to stay on her bed and even start talking loud enough for her to hear in the hope it will distract her. Mum has a ring side seat and it's the noise that first alerts her to the scene. At first it starts relatively harmlessly and not dissimilar to other nights, the porter arrives and tries to get the confused patient back to bed.

"Come on. Back to bed." It's the short porter, he's about five feet four, small for a security guard but there is something menacing about him. I'd noticed it before but nothing like tonight. He begins by trying to frogmarch him back to bed and at first he is successful. Before long though the man is back at the door and the next time he tries to enter the isolation room, the guard grabs him and Mum can hear the commotion from her bed.

"Get back ter yer fuckin bed," he snarls as he tries to force him along the corridor.

The frail man tries to break from his grip. "Leave me, leave me," he cries.

The guard twists the man's arm up behind his back, forcing him along the corridor.

"Ahhhh!"

The frail patient screeches at the same time trying to break free.

"Yer fuckin bastard get down there!"

His face now contorted with anger, saliva comes out of mouth as he barks his commands.

The noise the man makes is shocking to hear and gives us an idea of the pain he must be in. He tries to struggle but the porter is too strong during the day he is a porter but I have noticed that the fittest porters double up as security guards for the night shifts.

The guard forces him back to bed but this time he makes sure he stays there. His aggression frightens me and you can see how angry the porter is, with his teeth clenched he has clearly lost his temper. There's one point as he forces the man's arm further up his back that our eyes meet, just for a brief second and then the moment is gone. That moment hasn't lost its significance and continues to haunt me, to this day.

"Julie, Julie, call the police", I just look in desperation at Mum. "What's happening?" She can hear him but now he is out of her sight. I stand up to see what his fate is. His bed is in the bay opposite Mum's. I stand and watch the abuse continue. The guard is now kneeling on top of him pinning him to the bed face down, as he struggles and tries to get up.

"Help, help!" He pleads, "Ger off me."

They are joined by another man who I can only presume is a doctor. It looks as if he has rushed here as his shirt is partly undone, hanging out of his trousers. It looks like he is trying to get a needle into him. Within minutes the man stops struggling and the porter gets off his back, pushing him aggressively into bed. He lays there uncovered still, both men stand and look for a few seconds and then they go off, out of the ward. I stand shocked, I don't know what to do and neither does Mum. I can tell she is as frightened as me, we both know what has happened is wrong. We discuss it for a little while and I convince Mum that he will be safe now, as he will sleep. I convince her that the best thing for us to do is to try and help the patients as best as we can but our priority must be to get on with the staff and not to upset them. No, our priority must be to stay there on the ward with her. I cry again that night. I cry for me, for Mum and for the coward that I have become.

If I thought things couldn't get any worse then I was wrong as the next weekend is one of the worst. Poor Mavis remains in the same clothes all over that first weekend and by the Saturday afternoon I can smell her. At one point I have to go over and help her as she falls to the floor between her bed and chair. She has now been here two days and apart from being given a meal tray at the end of her bed no one has been anywhere near her. The smell hits me before anything else and the first thing I think is that I need gloves to handle her. She's scrambling to get up and I have no option but to help her. The dried faeces over her hands makes me want to wretch and then I see it is all over her feet and slippers. I try to get her to wait on the floor until I get assistance but I realise she is too confused to understand what I am saying. I help her to her feet and sit her on the bed, she isn't hurt but I want the nurses to attend to her to check her over. I try the usual hunt but I have found from experience a hunt for assistance at the weekend isn't worth it and today is no different. Poor Mavis stays that way, covered in faeces until the Tuesday morning when she is seen for the first time by a doctor.

It was one of the worst weekends because we had to watch

her be so terribly neglected and we were unable to do a damn thing about it. The man who had been assaulted the previous evening spent the whole weekend asleep in his bed. Each time I passed his bay I tried to see if he had woken but he hadn't. If I stood next to Mum's bed I could see into his bay and I could see the man's still body. It was awful watching and thinking, "Will he die? Could I have done something about it?" I don't know what happened to him, one minute he was there the next he was gone and another man was in the bed.

Mavis spent the weekend wandering the ward at night and mostly asleep during the day. On the Saturday night after I had picked her off the floor I woke to find her leaning over me, calling out what I later learnt was her son's name. The ward was a creepy place anyway and I always made sure that I secured the curtains but she must have got through my barriers. I tried to help her back to bed but night was day to her just as it was to most of the confused patients. She ate nothing over the weekend, each time the meal trays were left I would sneak over and take off the wrapping and encourage her to eat, she was painfully thin. At one point I gave her a bowl to put her hands into and she did willingly, the site of the faeces that clung to the side of the bowl made me physically sick though when I had to empty it. She hardly spoke she was lost in her own world but her accent suggested a well-to-do background, a lady. It didn't make any difference to me what class she was but the way she was neglected that weekend still brings tears to my eyes when I think of it.

Normally there would be at least one caring member of staff on duty over the weekend that you could rely on to help you, but this weekend there wasn't one. Every other weekend there was one particular senior nurse who normally worked in A&E. But for some reason she would work on Ward 11 every other Sunday. It was an odd shift too because you didn't just have her for the early shift she would often stay for the afternoon shift too. She was a real treasure and I missed her terribly this weekend because I knew if she had been here she would have helped us.

Over the weekend we bring in socks, cardigans and even my Mum's old coats to put over Mavis as she is freezing all the time. It doesn't help that she is out of bed all night roaming the corridor and back and forward to the toilet. I daren't ask for blankets for her but when I do pluck up the courage to ask one of the least nasty staff they haven't any. I'd asked for Mum several weeks ago and they didn't have any then. They didn't have pillows either, we had bought them in from home. In fact they didn't have anything, there are no footstools, drip stands, towels, soap, everything, seemed to be in short supply. One night I end up having to beg the male HCA to fill up the soap in my Mum's bay. Posters everywhere about infection control and no soap in the gastro ward. You couldn't make it up!

It's Monday morning and we have survived the weekend but this morning I realise something that hadn't occurred to me before. It's the usual morning routine, lights on, curtains yanked open, observations taken but this morning all of the patients have their temperature and blood pressure taken. Enid is hauled out the bed, washed and placed in her chair. I wash Mum now so they don't have her to wash. I sigh, a sigh of relief when I see them filling a bowl for Mavis and they start to hunt for clothes in her cupboard. She hasn't any so off they go looking, as the bowl of hot water sits on the side going cold. Before long a HCA is back with a nightgown and she is just trying to wake Mavis when one of the nurses appear and says something to her. Mavis is oblivious to all this as she is still asleep, she has been awake literally all night and has only settled within the last few hours. Without further ado the bowl is emptied and Mavis hasn't had a wash since at least Thursday, despite being covered in faeces. I'm surprised because they must have smelt her, as we have, all weekend.

What dawns on me today that I hadn't realised before is that patients are guaranteed a wash and having their observations taken when particular doctors do the ward round. It is also the same with a nurse accompanying the ward round, only when certain doctors are doing that ward round. The junior doctors never get assistance from a nurse when they are responsible for the ward round and that is more often than not. We only see the Consultant on average once a week, although it is difficult to know who anyone is as they hardly ever introduce themselves. We haven't seen Dr Hearing now for a few weeks and we never see him on the ward again.

It appears today that the Consultant who should have been doing the ward round has cancelled (this is what the senior nurse must have told the HCA) so Mavis doesn't need cleaning up today as she will not be seen by a doctor until tomorrow. Tomorrow is a different story and the day begins as usual but Mavis is scrubbed to remove the dried faeces from her body. It's obviously painful for her and it would have been much easier for the HCA to put her in the bath but she doesn't as they will lose the race.

This is another thing that I didn't realise was happening until the last few weeks of Mum's life. A few of the morning staff, the favoured who get to choose which shifts they work, have a race between wards to get the patients up, washed and the beds made. The first person to run to the phone wins the race. I wouldn't have believed this happened but one of the carers had told me themselves. They thought it was fun. They also played practical jokes on each other, totally oblivious to the harm it was causing patients. To be honest you would think the patients weren't there at all sometimes. Looking at it from their perspective it allowed them to get through the shift with as much fun as possible. Can you imagine playing practical jokes to the sounds of call buzzers going off, one after another?

No sooner had the HCA started to wash Mavis than the male carer, who was a terror, disturbed her.

"There's someone on the phone for ya. Quick, they need to speak to ya." A thin smile on his face.

There wasn't, he was playing a joke on her, she chased him down the corridor, laughing and giggling promising she will get him back for this. It's not even funny as Mavis sits in the chair half-dressed behind the curtain, alone.

Suddenly Mavis gets the attention she should have had all weekend. Two nurses appear and fuss around her both trying to get her to drink a protein drink from a carton. They take her blood pressure and temperature on several occasions and one practically sits with her all morning.

She is seen by the doctor on the ward round and because of her low temperature she has to spend the next few days wrapped in a heated blanket. Before his visit Mavis had been washed and had her clothes changed, she was now in a hospital gown with her rear end showing for all to see. The clothes she has had on for the last five days are sitting in a black bag in her locker.

Despite the heated blanket she continues to go up and down along the corridor, back and forward to the toilet. Each time she gets up it's like listening to a large crisp packet, sleep will be impossible tonight. I'm convinced she has a urine infection because in the last four days she has drunk hardly anything. She may just have forgotten that she had just been to the toilet because of her confusion. Also there is a really strong smell from her, I thought it was the faeces but she has now been washed and there is still this pungent smell that fills the room. It makes you feel sick and it certainly puts me off eating anything.

One evening Mavis has a friend visit her and she tells me that Mavis has come from a local nursing home and that she has a son. Mum is over the moon that Mavis has a visitor and encourages me to go over and tell her about the way that she is being treated. I'm very careful with what I am saying and I make sure that I do not mention staff individually. I feel I have no alternative, she has suffered enough and I can see that the friend is shocked to find her looking so unkempt. The friend tells me that Mavis had servants in her past life and now she is reduced to this. She has no dignity now, they have stripped her of that as she walks up and down the corridor exposing herself to all, oblivious.

Mum has gone from strength to strength and is eating the ready brek that I make her for breakfast. If I have to I make it with cold milk and then sneak off down to the canteen to warm it. Most of the day staff wouldn't agree for me to use the ward microwave but it's different with the afternoon staff and I'm usually able to use it for Mum's soup at tea time. She's putting on loads of weight and although I am pleased I'm not sure she should be putting on so much. She has always been petite and is under, 5ft tall and usually weighs around 8 stone. I ask if she could be weighed, they had guessed her weight when she had her peg fitted as they told us the scales were broken, apparently they still are. We have no idea how much she weighs but I do know she needs a larger size in her nightdresses. What with me encouraging her to eat and the feed that is going through her peg, I'm not sure that she isn't getting too much nutrition now.

Going Home

Mum has been given good news today, we have been told that they are starting to plan for her discharge. I hug her tightly, we have nearly made it out of here! Apart from practical things to put in place she is fit for discharge. The doctor tells her this on the morning ward round and as I have said they don't happen each morning and there's no pattern to when they occur. Some days they don't, other days they do. Sometimes they are in the morning, sometimes in the afternoon. They are never on a Friday, weekend or a Monday which makes the four days a long time before you see a doctor.

It's excellent news, Mum is going home! I ask about her medication that she was taking before admission. It isn't the first time I have asked, I continually asked when Mum was first admitted. You see, Mum was on Warfarin and her Consultant had told me that she would always have to be on Warfarin. This was in 2000 when she had had a stroke and we didn't for one minute expect her to recover. But she did, to everyone's amazement she regained her speech and the strength in the left side of her body. As I said earlier Mum was a real fighter, she had spent her life working and that's what she did following her stroke, she went to work on herself to recover.

"Well what drugs was she on?" the doctor asks. I'd brought in at least three of Mum's drug sheets surely there must be one in the file? I try to recall what she had been taking on admission and when I mention Warfarin, he looks shocked. They had done the same with the other patients, they were all taken off the drugs that they normally took. I could understand that initially it would be beneficial to assess medication on admission but it seemed they were just forgotten about, as Mum's Warfarin had been.

Enid was taking Frusemide before admission and her legs were filled with fluid, each morning I tried to put them up on a footstool for her. Finding a footstool had been a real challenge and I had ended up bringing one from home in the end. Her legs were huge and lifting them some days was a real struggle. I mentioned it to one of the physiotherapists one day and I told her that she had been coughing all night, too. I didn't want to say anything as I didn't want to stick my neck out at all. It would have been easy for the staff to say I was a nuisance and I would be made to leave. I didn't feel I could have told most of the nurses, their response would have been different. It paid off as Enid was put back onto her Frusemide and she got antibiotics prescribed for a chest infection. I thanked the physiotherapist but at the same time did so reluctantly as I didn't want her to know that I was looking out for Enid. I had noticed though that the physiotherapists didn't seem to have a good relationship with the nurses, they were different. They seemed far more interested in the patients but you didn't see them often enough.

Before Mum could be given Warfarin she would need her INR (Blood Coagulation) levels taken, the doctor said he would ensure it was done immediately. It was and that very night she was given her first dose of Warfarin for five weeks. Normally Mum took 1mg to 3mg of Warfarin, that first night she took 21mg the following night 13mg. It seemed an awful lot to me but at least she was back on it and that was a huge relief and something less to think and worry about. We were told that a referral would be made to the Social Work team for help for when Mum was discharged.

We have already planned her discharge between ourselves and we are excited that we can now put it into place. Laura has agreed that she will delay going to university for as long as she has to. She will care for her Nan during the day and I will take over when I return from work. When we do get to meet the social worker she convinces us to have a six week home support package to help us at the start. We agree and a hospital bed will be delivered along with everything we will need for the peg feed.

Discharge will be on Friday, only four days away! Only four days to wait, four days to survive this place. Mum continues to improve she is laughing and joking but still aware that Enid hasn't made the same progress that she has.

Her daughter visits each evening and I can hear that Enid is still the Mother. Her daughter chats away about her own problems, trying to keep Enid engaged. When she does visit she fills in Enid's menu form and I am so tempted to say something but I don't. Her daughter is oblivious to her Mum's limitations and marks her up for a ham salad and fruit for her next meal. Enid can't eat either of those things and needs something mushy like Mum but she pretends to her daughter that she is better than she really is. The following day her meal will sit there untouched as there is nothing on her meal tray that she can eat. Today is no different and her friends arrive before the meal tray is taken away.

They have visited before and they are friends from the same church, a Father and daughter who were shocked at Enid's condition when they last visited. Today they ring the buzzer as Enid asks to use the commode. She waits and waits, they are not happy with this but we are well used to it. When Enid is desperate, I will fetch the commode from the sluice and help her onto it. Pat's daughter is a home carer and she will always help. She will also help me with Mum. Mavis will sometimes use the commode if you help her and it saves her staggering up the corridor with the fear of her falling.

Enid's buzzer has now sounded for nearly an hour and you can see she is getting desperate, the small talk is over. Enid's friend says she will go and get a nurse, Enid has waited long enough. She has but she usually does and very often she has to do it in the bed. Before we can warn her she is gone and I expect will not find a nurse to toilet Enid. I stay seated in the hope she will find a nurse.

It's like a thunderbolt has come through the door but it isn't, it's the ward manager. Before we have chance to take stock she has literally pulled Enid out of the bed and she's now in a sitting position. She walks over to Mum's bed and grabs her Zimmer frame stands it in front of Enid and pulls her up. Without further ado Enid is being marched along the corridor holding onto my Mother's Zimmer frame for dear life.

We look on in disbelief. Enid hasn't been out of the bed in at least three weeks and now she has just charged up the corridor. Fifteen minutes later Enid is charged back down the corridor, she looks grey, exhausted and collapses back onto her bed.

"You won't have to ring your buzzer again will you? Because you can take yourself to the toilet next time".

There is venom and spite in her voice as she hisses at Enid. She leaves her terrified, terrified of ever ringing for the toilet again.

106

We are all so shocked, words fail us. Enid hadn't even had a physiotherapist assessment because she had been so poorly. Yet she was dragged out of her bed and along the corridor and back again. Her friends pull the bed clothes over her and she closes her eyes. Before her friends leave they tell me they are going to complain about her treatment. I want to tell them about Nurse Ratchet but I don't, the coward that I am. I'm frightened they will mention me in their complaint. When they have gone I can hear Enid crying under her covers, making sure we cannot see her. I never see Enid out of her bed again and I certainly don't see her use the buzzer again.

Mavis was oblivious to the lack of care she was getting and she was certainly oblivious to the fact half of her backside was showing as she went up and down the corridor. To add to her lack of dignity she seemed to always use the toilet with the door missing. The door was still missing the day I left the ward, it had been missing for at least three weeks and yet it was right next to the nurses' station.

One night I was returning from the toilet walking back along the corridor. Mavis was sitting on the toilet exposed while the nurses were on the internet looking at something on eBay. I had to ask them for gloves as we had run out of them in our bay, they barely lifted their eyes from the screen, telling me they would bring them later. You didn't argue with them you, or should I say I, just did as I was told, leaving Mavis in the cold exposed and returning to Mum with no gloves. But from that night I knew that when they were huddled around the nurses' station during the night, it was likely they were on eBay. You often saw them during the night huddled around the computer screen but I had thought they were working, tonight had been a revelation. No they were looking at items on eBay, I was disgusted but kept it to myself until Sam came the following day.

You rarely had eye contact with any of the staff, they could just walk straight past you, without any form of acknowledgement. You can stand at the nurses station for minutes without any of the staff even raising their eyes. It was really unnerving because you didn't want to disturb them. Now I knew I was only disturbing their entertainment which put a different light on it.

It was also on the final hurdle that I realised what was happening with the medication on the ward and how patients were unknowingly being denied them. Since the first week of Mum's stay we had ensured that she was never left alone on the ward. There were occasions when it was unavoidable but I had always asked one of the other patients or relatives to look out for her and they had. It was early afternoon and I asked Pat to keep an eye on Mum while I raced to the supermarket. She loved sucking on melon and Tesco's did a ready to eat packet. Mum's afternoon drugs were due, she was now on antibiotics for an infection in her peg site.

I must have been gone about forty five minutes but when I got back Pat was nowhere in sight. Mum loved her melon and she sucked on it as if there were no tomorrow. She even finished off a bit of an egg custard that I had left. After we had finished and as I did each day I started to fill in Mum's input chart from her notes. Just by chance I glanced over her drug chart and noticed the letter R, which had been recorded next to her lunch time medication for that day. I asked Mum if she had seen a nurse whilst I had been gone. Just as I was discussing it with Mum one of the kinder student nurses passed the bay door and I asked her what R meant on the drug chart.

"R? R means 'Refused'. We write it when a patient refuses to take their medication." She replied.

"Refused?" I ask Mum at the same time but she just looks at me unsure of what I am saying. I know Mum wouldn't refuse her medication, if a doctor or nurse gave her poison she would take it. The student has been on the ward a few weeks and knows Mum well enough to know that she wouldn't refuse her drugs. She knows the patients who consider themselves lucky to be administered drugs regardless of the time. I ask the student if she would check if Mavis has had her drugs. According to Mavis's chart she too had 'Refused' her medication. The student looks embarrassed and agrees to ask the qualified nurse on duty to come to speak to us. We wait and wait and wait all afternoon until the student nurse passes the bay.

"I've spoken to Staff and she says your Mum refused her drugs."

You can tell she is unsure herself of what she is saying. Just repeating what she's been told.

Now I know that this wouldn't have happened but at the same time I know that Mum had been left alone for a little while. I also know that the outcome needs to be that Mum gets her medication, regardless of what has really happened. At the same time as I am pondering how we get out of this one, Mum tells us that a nurse did come to her this morning. She didn't speak but had looked at her notes and then went away. I ask her if she had been to Mavis too but Mum wasn't sure and then she remembered she had. The nurse in charge of the ward today, had very poor English and this I thought could give us some mileage, a chance to claim a misunderstanding. The student goes to tell her that Mum had made a mistake and because of her hearing and the language difficulties Mum must have misheard her. I only hope it will work because Mum needs those antibiotics. We need her out of here.

The next thing I hear is what sounds like an army coming down the corridor and towards us. It's not only the nurse in charge of the shift but the ward manager is with her too and there are also a couple of doctors. I freeze. What the hell will I do and say now? I can feel myself sweating at the thought of having to manage this. Their faces tell me that they are not happy with what they have just been told.

The nurse in charge says nothing it's the ward manager doing all the talking. The nurse in charge of the shift just stands there scowling at us, towering over Mum.

"You need to make your mind up, now do you want your drugs or not". I apologise and tell them because of Mum's hearing she must have made a mistake and misheard what the nurse had said. Totally ignoring me she now shouts at Mum.

"Well do you?"

Mum doesn't know who to look at, she's confused as to what is going on and what she is now expected to do. Mum was eighty six, of an era that if you are prescribed medication you took it and were grateful for it. Why would she not want to? She just looks at her with bewilderment because she can't grasp what she is being asked.

"Well, well do you?" She repeats but much louder and firmer this time.

Mum grasps what is being asked of her and of course she wants her medication. They all storm off down the corridor after the nurse in charge has added

"Next time make your mind up".

The student nurse returns with Mums antibiotics, saying nothing at all. But we all knew that something very suspicious had happened, that dinnertime. Mavis slept through the whole scene and stayed asleep until the early evening going without her lunchtime medication.

Later in the afternoon Pat had returned to the ward and I explained what had happened. Pat had had no option than to leave the ward as the physiotherapist had come to take her on a stair assessment before she could be discharged. But as she had gone down the corridor she had seen the nurse in charge coming towards our bay but with no drug trolley. Later, after I had made sure that none of the staff were around, I checked Mavis's drug chart and I felt sick. What I had suspected was correct as most of the drugs that Mavis should have taken were recorded as refused. I knew this wasn't true and seeing the evidence rocked me, I felt sick. I hadn't heard Mavis refuse her medication once, not once! And everyday it had been recorded that she had refused her medication.

Suspiciously they were in the same handwriting and even the same pen as if they had all been filled in together, at the same time. After this incident I noticed that every night the night staff would collect every one's case notes up and take them with them along with the water jugs. They would be returned to the patients the following morning all filled in before they finished their shift. I was really shocked when I realised what they were doing, you just don't expect it from nurses. From Mum's records she had had all her observations taken since the day she came into the hospital! The patients' notes were nothing but a long list of lies.

That evening it was Nurse Ratchet and the male carer, the two biggest bullies on the ward. Both domineering and challenging whenever they were together and had contact with patients. I will never forget their faces one night when they were putting Mum back into bed. I usually waited outside the curtain while they helped her but they had pulled the curtains open. As she was being moved back into the bed she must have pulled her stomach and she cried out in pain. They both just looked at each other and then at Mum as they tutted at her. Mum was a strong woman, everyone had said that. She had had to be, her life had been a hard one. She never complained and we rarely heard her mention her illnesses. Her priority was always other people and never herself.

The look those two gave my Mum said it all, they didn't give a damn about her or the pain she was in. That look hurt me so much and the way it must have made my Mum feel. She just looked at them as if wanting their understanding and yet at the same time apologetic that she needed their help. They looked at her with such disgust, as if she had no need to wince with pain. Even today nearly five years later it is so vivid in my mind, I can see their eyes meeting and their facial expression and the hurt in Mum's eyes.

Dropped

It's Friday and I race back with Mum's clothes to take her home, the house is ready for her discharge and homecare will start this evening. We're all so excited there is a real buzz in the air at home even the dog has picked up on our good mood. But things don't run that smoothly, not at this hospital anyway. We are told that discharge must be delayed until after the weekend. We're all so disappointed but at the same time Mum needs a nebuliser, doesn't she? Optimist that Mum is she accepts without any moaning that she will be coming home on Monday now. I'm not as accepting as her and I continue to moan to Mum for the rest of the afternoon, I just want my life back and I want Mum out of here because it is a dangerous place. It means we are here for another weekend and that fills me with dread. My fear is who will be admitted, who wants to come off drugs or alcohol this weekend?

Arnie, one of the junior doctors reminds me of how dangerous the place is later in the afternoon. We named him Arnie because he reminded us of Arnold Schwarzenegger. He catches me while I am in the sluice getting a commode for Mum.

"You need to get your Mum out of the hospital before she comes to any harm".

I tell him that that is precisely what I am trying to do and he doesn't have to tell me how dangerous the place is. He's spent a bit of time with Mum now and built up a relationship, he laughs and jokes with her and he cares. Mum is the opposite of him, where he is large Mum is tiny. Her nickname once was Mother Teresa and that just about sums up her physical appearance. She has always been petite but as she has got older she has got a lot shorter and now she's tiny, perhaps four feet ten inches and with her wrinkles, she really does look like Mother Teresa. At the time I don't think about what he has said, as I am in a rush to get the commode back, but when I am sitting later in the day I think what an odd thing for him to say to me, a doctor warning me about his own hospital.

That evening it is one of the bank nurses who normally works on EAU, we met her on the ward when Mum first came into the hospital. She's very brusque and not very interested in the patients at all. You can tell this by the way she speaks to the patients or rather by the way that she doesn't speak to the patients. Very few of the staff even call my Mum her correct name, although it is clearly recorded in her file and that is after being on the ward for six weeks. There're no familiarities or niceties with this nurse, she is here to do a job and so is the assistant who is with her. You just dread these nights when there isn't one caring member of staff on the ward as you fear needing them. She hands me Mum's feed and I know straight away that it is the wrong one. Both Enid and Mum have different types of feed. One day I asked the dietician what the difference was and found out the feed is made up for the individual. Although the bag she hands to me looks very similar to Mum's it isn't hers, it's Enid's feed. I am on the point of giving up and accepting the wrong feed and if it had been any other time I probably would have done but Mum is going home in two days and I don't want anything to mess that up. She is now back to normal, her bowels are working and I don't want anything to delay her discharge again and I tell her this.

"I'm sorry but I don't think this is the right feed."

"Yes, it is." Is what she says, "Who do you think you are?!" is what she means.

"No, I think this is Enid's. Sorry, I don't mean to be awkward but I don't want anything to go wrong, she's being discharged."

"No it isn't," she tells me, "Both are the same feed." She towers over me as if threatening me.

I want to scream at her, "They're not, they're not." But I speak even lower than I normally do.

"It's hard to notice the difference but if you look closer they are a different colour."

It's not hard to see that they are a different colour but I will try this tack anyway. I show her the remnants of last night's feed and compare it with the bag she is trying to give me. I hold it out for her to see the difference but she barely looks.

Instead she shrugs her shoulders and says, "There's no difference anyway," she practically snarls at me but still giving me no indication she is prepared to look for Mum's feed.

But I knew differently because I had spoken at length to the dietician who told me that each feed is made up specifically for that person, I daren't risk upsetting Mum's stomach now.

I try again, "I just don't want to mess Mum's stomach up, would you please look for hers?"

Eventually she accepts what I'm saying and leaves to get the correct one. When she returns her face is like thunder and without saying anything she just throws the packet at Mum, it bounces off her leg and lands on the floor. From her expression I can see that she didn't mean for it to bounce off the bed but throwing it onto Mum was bad enough. I scramble on the floor between the recliner and Mum's locker and retrieve the packet as if it is something precious. Once she sees I have it safely in my hand she turns and walks back out the door. I just hope I don't have to see her for the rest of the night and I'm reluctant to even pass the nurses' station that night to go out to the toilet. I keep telling myself it's nearly over and I know as soon as we get out of this hospital I will tell everyone what is happening on this ward.

I barely sleep that night, I can usually manage a couple of hours but tonight the anger inside keeps me awake. My mind won't let me rest and I recite in my head over and over again what I will say to the nurse if she is rude to Mum again. She isn't. We don't see her again and I have avoided going to the toilet just so I don't have to see her, coward that I am.

The morning comes too soon and I feel as if I could sleep forever, but it's our last weekend and I can almost touch home. It's Saturday and Sam is stopping over tonight. In the week she gave us some news that she is pregnant but she is still prepared to stay over with her Nan, sleeping on the reclining chair. Well, trying to sleep in the reclining chair.

As Mum is so short she needs the assistance of someone both sides of her to get out of bed, not to mention the added height of the air mattress. Until now this hasn't been a problem because we have helped but tonight Sam won't be able to assist. Mum will have to wait until there are two carers to put her back into bed.

It doesn't work out like that though and the following day, when I get back to the hospital, I can see from Mum's face that something is seriously wrong.

"What's happened, Sam?"

"They dropped her, Julie." She replies.

During the night Mum had wanted the commode and it was while the young carer was trying to put her back to bed she had dropped her. Sam had nodded back off after calling for assistance and awoke to Mum's screams. Mum was lying across the bed half on and half off, with her head hanging over the side. As Mum's screams awoke Sam she then went quiet and still, Sam thought unconscious. Within seconds Mum was awake but fighting for her breath and that's how she was now. Sam had asked and asked all night for a doctor to check Mum over as she knew something had happened to her. Mum's back had hit the metal sides of the bed and she still hadn't been checked over by anyone for injury.

I tried all Sunday afternoon and night but I knew there were no doctors available over the weekend. That first night Mum just couldn't breathe and I was just beside myself trying to help her but not helping her at all. To make matters worse it was Nurse Ratchet that night and we had to call for assistance. It was probably one of the first times Mum had needed medical assistance during the night and the buzzer rang and rang. I thought Mum was going to die there and then with the buzzer sounding with me not knowing whether to go and get help. Not wanting to leave her. In the end I have to and all four of the staff are gathered around the computer. I don't know but the thought that they are looking at something on eBay gives me the strength to disturb them.

As I stand there not one of them raises their eyes to even acknowledge me but I'm too worried about Mum to wait there until they do.

"My Mum can't breathe. Please can you get a doctor?" I plead.

"I'll be with you in a minute," She says, not even looking up from the computer. *I'll be there in a minute...* It's like their catchphrase. I could see they weren't busy and Mum needed help and she needed it now.

"Please help!" I beg. I'm desperate they must come and see Mum before she dies. I'm speaking to all four of them in the hope that one of them will listen, but really I know its Nurse Ratchet who holds the power.

"She can't get her breath. She's only been like it since last night. Since she was dropped."

115

I see Nurse Ratchet look up. That's it. I can see straight away that I have hit a nerve. Now I have their attention. Nurse Ratchet comes from behind the station and follows me back down the corridor. Usually most of the staff walk so slowly on the ward, no sense of urgency at all. But not tonight, I'm practically running after her.

Mum is grey, ashen. Not the person she was yesterday, every now and again she gasps for air. Nurse Ratchet has kindness in her as she tries to comfort Mum with words.

"There, there," she says patting her hand, "Try to breathe slowly." She tells her. But then I realise her motives.

"You weren't dropped. You slipped from the bed didn't you, Isabella?" she tells her with such persuasion. Mum can barely talk but Nurse Ratchet insists that she answers her.

"I said you slipped, didn't you Isabella? You weren't dropped, were you?"

It dawns on me that the staff have obviously been talking about Mum being dropped for Nurse Ratchet to be so insistent with her now.

"You slipped, didn't you?"

My poor Mum, gasping for breath but Ratchet, in a horrific abuse of power, will do nothing for her until she agrees that she slipped, that nobody was at fault. Mum's not stupid, she knows unless she plays along with the lie she has no chance. She nods her head and makes what little noise she can come out of her mouth.

"Ok. I'll get some help." She walks out of the bay leaving us both feeling violated. What else could we do? I know she'll die unless someone sees her. It seems like an age before the Nurse Practitioner arrives and prescribes medication to go through the nebuliser and something to settle Mum. The night is a torture the nebuliser and the sedative don't seem to help at all and to be honest I think they makes things worse. I try all night to get Mum to try to breathe slowly, instead of panting but what I don't know at this point is that Mum has no option, it is out of her control.

Nurse Ratchet has moved Mavis, she has had a mattress placed along the corridor opposite the nurses station. Every time she gets out of bed she shouts at her, "Get back into bed!" you can hear her hollering all the way down the corridor. "Get back in your bed." We hear it all night because Mavis has short term memory problems and she hasn't remembered that she has just been told to get back to bed.

Mum clings to me all night and every time I try to move her grip tightens, she is terrified. I stand all night with her gripping my hand I try to calm her but every now and then she even forgets who I am, her breathing deteriorates and she pants for air. The morning staff have arrived and I can't wait to ask them to get a doctor, Mum desperately needs to see one, something is wrong with her. Whatever the Nurse Practitioner gave her last night hasn't helped, they have just made things worse in my opinion. It's Lyndsey, Lyndsey cares and that will help us but it's out of her hands. She will call for a doctor but it's unlikely that one will come soon, perhaps tonight.

"Lyndsey, Mum has been really poorly since she was dropped. Whatever the Nurse Practitioner gave her, hasn't helped. In fact I think it's made her worse. She said Mum was having a panic attack but I've worked with people having panic attacks and none of what I know applies to Mum. And her legs! Her legs are all swollen. That's not from a panic attack is it?" Lyndsey takes a look at Mum's legs and sees they are like a sumo wrestlers. You can see on her face she knows the Nurse Practitioner is wrong.

"I'll put a call out for a doctor." She says, but from experience I know that from Friday to Monday it is rare to see a doctor on the ward.

Later that morning Lyndsey brings me a large medical book for me to try to diagnose what is wrong with Mum. Looking back now I wonder at her logic but at the time she did it out of kindness and concern for Mum. It didn't take me long though to find out what I thought was wrong with her or what the book was telling me was wrong. It was Mum's heart that was the problem. Her heart must have been damaged by the fall the same heart that this time two weeks ago was fine. I tell Lyndsey what I have found and what the medical book has said is wrong with her, it took me minutes to find a diagnosis, they were classic symptoms of heart failure.

The next two weeks are hell, just sheer hell. If I thought things couldn't get much worse on this ward I didn't have a clue what lay ahead for us. Mum was later seen by another Consultant who said that a referral had been made for the respiratory specialist to see Mum. She was already under the respiratory doctor, Dr McLeod. She used to see him every few months for her breathing problems, he was an excellent doctor, not only clinically but also his people skills, which is more that we could say for the other respiratory Consultant.

Mum waited three days to see him and when I saw him coming along the corridor, I instantly thought of *Carry on Doctor*, a seaside postcard stereotype of a doctor. A tall, broad man wearing, a brown check wool suit and a dickey bow. He looked out of place on a hospital ward, like he was in fancy dress, especially on this ward with all its faults. There were no niceties with him, nothing.

"Out, out" he commanded, like a farmer to a collie, ushering me away from Mum's bed while he pulled the curtains around her. I was irritated by his manner but at the same time I was so relieved that he was going to examine Mum. I stand there biting my lip, hoping he can help her, something has gone terribly wrong. Within minutes he's pulling back the curtains and the wait is over, as I had suspected, it is Mum's heart and not her chest.

"Her chest is fine," he tells me dismissively as if we have wasted his time.

"Thank you," I say, for what I do not know but I thank him all the same.

"It's her heart not her chest that has a problem." He's practically at the door when he tells us this and with that he is gone.

Her chest is clear and probably better than it has been for a long time. I've known this all week but having it confirmed rocks me. I want to cry, I want to get down on my knees and bawl, but Mum's watching me. I can see the anguish on her face, the hope she once had of getting out of here has gone, I can now see fear on her face.

Over the Rainbow

Those last seven days of her life were a sheer misery, a torture, for Mum, for me, for Laura and for all the family. Every time a nurse came near to her, she was terrified, terrified of the very people who should have been there to care for her. She clung to me like a baby night and day and when the staff came near she would dig her nails into my hand in fear. She was put on Frusemide and managing the dose was like walking across a tightrope. A tightrope that you were always conscious of falling from or even that staying on the tightrope was completely out of your control.

Every time a dose was due, we sat there dreading a delay because as soon as it was due Mum was unable to breath. If Amy or one of the caring nurses were on duty it wasn't a problem as they understood and either left the drugs for me to administer or they were able to prioritise. Of course Nurse Ratchet made it as difficult as possible, or that's what it felt like. I'm sure I wasn't imagining it, she knew Mum wouldn't be able to breathe but instead she would choose to give out drugs in a different bay and leave ours till last. Some nights it would be gone midnight and she would still be waiting for her medication that was normally given at 10pm. For two hours she would have gasped for air. Her lungs filling with fluid all the time she waited, sweating and struggling, taking in any air available. It was torture.

I am now unable to help Mavis and Enid, they now have to survive alone and having to sit and watch is agonising. Each time Mavis stands she staggers as if she is going to fall and she lunges up the corridor, unsteadily. This time last week Mum would be concerned, as would I, as we watched and hoped she would come back unharmed. This week Mum's only priority is to stay alive and it is mine too.

One night Nurse Ratchet arrives with the drug trolley, I feel sick as Mum has struggled for breath for the last hour. I have tried to talk to her to get her to breathe slowly but it is no use. Just as she wheels in the drug trolley, I can see the relief on Mum's face as very soon she will breathe again. I sense even more that the nurses, or should I say most of the nurses, love the power they hold over the patients. Just as she opens the hatch opening up the drugs Mavis rises, she's off to the toilet again. She always struggles with the little bit between her table and the door as there is nothing for her to hold onto. Just as Nurse Ratchet is about to assist her, I offer to help instead.

"Don't worry. I'll take her." I can't let Mum wait any longer, she is now frantic for her Frusemide.

As I walk along the corridor with Mavis I can hear the others calling and crying out, the drugs are late tonight as Nurse Ratchet has started the drug round differently. Mavis is terribly thin and holding her hand along the corridor it's a shock to feel how thin she is. I try to steer her away from the toilet without a door which I do successfully but as Mavis steps into the next bathroom her feet go from underneath her, she has slipped on a pool of wet urine. Before she has even hit the floor she screams with the shock of falling.

I have to race back to Nurse Ratchet who patches her with a few bandages, Mavis carries on regardless, wandering all night. It delays Mum's medication though as she has to wait for Nurse Ratchet to finish with Mavis. When I return back to Mum she is crying, the tears are rolling from her eyes it's such a shock to see. I try to comfort her but I cry too, seeing Mum, my Mum who for the last forty odd years has been a tower of strength, has been reduced to tears. There is nothing I can do about it, nothing I can give her to ease her suffering. We just now have to wait for her drugs to start working.

I only find out by chance that Mum is still being given the Diazepam and I don't think this is helping her breathing either. It makes her confused too and at times during the night she is unable to recognise me. I ask why she is on the Diazepam.

"It's for her panic attacks."

But she isn't suffering with panic attacks! She has been seen by the Consultant and it's her heart. But it's given anyway despite me suggesting it might be making things worse for Mum.

The following morning after an awful night watching Mum suffer the nurse tries to give her another Diazepam. Again I question why and she suggests I talk to the Consultant as she agrees that Mum shouldn't be on the drug. Five minutes later I have spoken to him and she is off the drug. Luckily I had managed to catch him as he was walking along the corridor. Flippantly he tells me just to tell the nurse to take her off it, I do and surprisingly they listen and she is never given it again. I'm dreading telling the nurse that Mum can come off the Diazepam, I'm expecting her to say, "Who are you to tell us to take her off the Diazepam?" but she doesn't. Another thing that strikes me as odd happens that day and involves the same nurse. That evening she tells me that I can now qualify for a reduced parking ticket and where I need to go to apply for the reduction. After eight weeks of paying twelve pounds a day to park, I now qualify for a reduction. Parking has cost me a small fortune and I'm not going to complain at the reduction but why tell me today?

The following day the doctor arrives and tells Mum she needs a blood transfusion. He tells us there are risks but they will be well managed. I just look and say nothing but I suspect getting anything well managed on this ward is near impossible. I'm not wrong either the first hurdle for the next few days is getting the blood onto the ward. We are told for two days running that the blood transfusion will take place today but later the same day we are told it won't be going ahead as they haven't had staff available to fetch the blood. The Haematology nurses have taken blood every day from nearly all of the patients and yet until now we have never heard any of the results but now Mum needs this blood transfusion as she has reduced white blood cells.

On the third day we wait all day and later we are told perhaps tomorrow. I go home and walk the dog, I'm exhausted. I normally love a walk with the dog, I live a stone's throw from Cannock Chase with miles of outstanding beauty but today I'm exhausted. But it's while I'm out walking that I meet Jackie, another dog walker who I haven't seen for a while. Anyway tonight as we walk I mention that Mum is in the hospital and before I can say anymore. She says, "I hope she's not on the death ward." I can feel an instant chill through my body and I press her for more information. I gather that Ward 10 is known locally as the death ward, although she does then say that some are saying that it is spreading to other wards.

I race back home, shower and I'm practically just coming out the door when Sammy phones, she is sitting with Mum. She tells me that Mum is having her blood transfusion this minute. I race back to the hospital thinking there must be a mistake, why give her blood at night? But they are and they had promised that they would take their time and be careful with the transfusion. As I expected it doesn't happen like that.

The day before the Consultant, had told me that to eliminate some of the risks with a transfusion the blood is given really slowly and extra Frusemide would be given alongside the blood. At the same time as he was telling me this a junior doctor was recording what the Consultant was saying. Very soon after this conversation Judy, the student nurse, and Lyndsey came and virtually repeated what the Consultant had said. Judy also said that she was Mum's named nurse for the day. Now if you could have chosen a nurse for the day from Ward 11, Judy was one of them. She had a similar small frame as I have and long wavy blonde hair that I was envious of. She was mid twenties, attractive with a fair complexion. She was kind to everyone and she had a lovely smile that the confused patients responded to. I didn't say anything at the time but I did think this is odd as no one had said they were a named nurse to anybody, in the eight weeks I had been on the ward. Some of the staff were exceptional and Judy was one of them, she really did care and she tried to provide care for all the patients. Others you could tell just resented having to help people, you could tell that they saw it beneath them to help others. One night a student nurse told Mum that she hated working on the wards. Mum was speechless and didn't know how to answer her, but instead she just said "Poor dear".

We thought it was too good to be true, as instead of the transfusion going slowly it was rushed through. By the time I get to the hospital the blood has finished. Mum has had a blood transfusion in the past and it made such a difference for her. She hoped it would be the same this time and for the last two days she had been anxious for the blood transfusion in the hope it would help.

It's the ward Sister tonight and it's very unusual to see her on the ward, she normally stays at the nurse's station. She's just finished disconnecting the blood and I ask about Mum's extra Frusemide. I'm already worried, you see as I know that to

122

administer the drugs we need the drugs trolley and it is nowhere to be seen.

"I haven't had a tea break yet today," the Sister tells us. Of course we feel sorry for her but at the end of the day, Mum needs that tablet and it's only a matter of handing it to me and I can do the rest. She can see that Mum is struggling for air and her Frusemide will relieve it.

Three hours later and we are still waiting for the extra Frusemide and her next dose is now overdue. Mum is fraught and every second she is getting more and more distressed. Laura has joined me and it's a comfort to have her support but even between us I know things are going to be tough.

It's Nurse Ratchet again tonight and I believe if any other nurse had been on duty that night it wouldn't have been Mum's last. It was hard enough for Mum to have to wait in such a desperate state, gasping for air. What happened next was totally unexpected as by now I knew that Nurse Ratchet was uncaring but I never realised the extent to which she would go to demonstrate her power.

She stands there with her hands on her hips while Mum struggles for air, arguing. I try to reason with her.

"But isn't it normal that someone who has a blood transfusion has Frusemide alongside the blood? That's what the doctor, Lyndsey and the student nurse have been telling me for the last three days." Ahh I think, I have her there what could she possibly say to that."

"There's nothing in the file about extra Frusemide."

"You can see, she can't breathe. Please! The doctor prescribed it, I was there when he did it."

"There's nothing in the file about extra Frusemide." She is unmovable.

"But she's had a blood transfusion. Isn't it normal to give extra Frusemide?"

"There's nothing in the file about extra Frusemide." She can't even hear me. She neither sees nor feels nor cares.

"Then can you please call a doctor?" I beg, tears on my face, desperation in my voice.

"I'm in charge of this ward and I'll decide whether to get a doctor." As if I needed any reminder that she was in charge of the ward! Every day she asserts her authority with an iron fist, bullying, humiliating and tormenting the poor souls under her care.

She always seemed to be on the ward, much more than any other nurse. At first I thought her cruelty meant I noticed her more but Lyndsey told me once, that she took all the overtime as she was saving for a mortgage, being very friendly with the ward manager she was offered all the overtime she wanted.

"She needs it. Look at her."

"There's nothing in the file about extra Frusemide."

I want to scream at her, I want to ask her why she is so mean but I have learnt that some of the staff want to make you angry. I have realised that the staff want a reaction. I have seen it so many times over the last eight weeks, some of the staff try to instigate conflict. They love to use their power over you and I need to avoid that but it is so difficult now as I know how important the Frusemide is for Mum's survival.

Since Mum had been dropped there hadn't been one night where she was able to sleep. I have stood by the bed holding her hand trying to comfort her until her Frusemide is administered. She has clung to me desperately fighting for her life, while I stand by watching her suffer. I have been unable to leave her during the day as she has clung to me like a baby clings to a Mother. I'm that tired that when I walk I do it without thought and then all of a sudden I realise that I am walking. My head aches and all I want to do is to lie down and sleep knowing that we are all safe. I want a peaceful sleep that's all and it doesn't seem a lot to ask for but at this point I do not know that it will be a long time till I achieve that.

I must control myself, I want to pick up the table, that is all I can see is the table and I want to crash it over her head for the misery she has reaped on the patients, on Mum and me. I've fed Mum off it, I've leant and read off it but tonight all I want to do is to crash it over Nurse Ratchet's head. I've spent time washing the metal frame ensuring it is clean and free of infection the melamine tray that covers the top has been scrubbed by me but all I want to do is crash it over her head, over and over again. I'm not a violent person but I'm totally powerless, there is absolutely nothing I can do to get Mum her medication.

I can bear it no longer, I must leave here. If I don't leave here now I will do something stupid, I can feel it. I'm coming to my senses, the mist is clearing. I must leave. I turn and our eyes meet for the very last time. That look plays on my mind for years and haunts me, my Mum was petrified. I saw fear in her eyes like I had never seen before, not just in my Mum's eyes, I had never seen fear in anyone's eyes like that before. I never saw my Mum alive again and my last sight of her was in fear. They destroyed her. A strong, vibrant woman who they robbed of any dignity or self, left begging for her life.

I walk off the ward and stand outside, trying to think but at the same time knowing I am not able to think properly. I want to ring Sam but it is too late she will be in bed by now. I'm hoping that Nurse Ratchet will realise that she has made a mistake and with me out of the way it will be easier for her to acknowledge that with just Laura there.

I get home and wait for Laura to ring to tell me that Mum has her drugs and her breathing has improved but she doesn't. She doesn't ring until 7am the following morning.

"Mum. You'd better come. Come quick." She is crying on the phone to me. It's the call that nobody wants to hear and especially after what happened last night. I must have fallen asleep. I could kick myself! I'm on the sofa with my clothes on but I don't change. I must get to Mum and to Laura, I shouldn't have left either of them.

Mum was eighty six and everyone would say she had had a good innings and so would I if what had occurred over those eight weeks hadn't happened. We all expect to lose our parents, its normal, but it isn't normal to watch her waste away in such an uncaring, hostile place that we are led to believe is created to nourish and care. I had always believed that nurses cared and to this day I am still confused at what I saw on Ward 11.

I can do nothing but cry when I see Mum, she is in the final stages and I know that her life will come to an end very soon. I want to shout and scream at them but what is the point? The damage is done. One of the kinder nurses tries to help and gives her the drug she should have had last night, but it is too late, she is dying. Watching somebody die is torture but if it is your Mother it is even more so.

"Don't take her! Please, don't take her!" I don't know who I am talking to.

"Please help her," I beg the ward doctor. I recognise her as she has been around for the last few weeks. She was a slight Indian doctor older than most I had seen, in her late thirties. Why I am asking her for help I really do not know. Her English is very poor and she has done nothing to help anybody on the

125

ward over the last few weeks.

I soon realise that Mum is dying before my eyes and I begin to accept she is leaving us.

"Your dad's waiting for you. And your brothers, Tommy will be there." I try and comfort her as she leaves us.

The kind nurse offers her condolences she has been very kind not only to Mum but to the other patients too. But even at this stage as my Mum has just died there are nurses on the ward who walk by us without even eye contact. They can see us crying and yet not even a glance from them and yet they know what they have done. One of the nurses on duty this morning hasn't spoken once to us or to Mum. We haven't had much to do with her but one day I asked her if Mum could have a Paracetomol as she had a high temperature. She refused, saying she was too busy to get them. She said that if she had time she would get them later, she didn't and Mum suffered all day. That morning I could have quite easily challenged her, I wanted to remind her of her cruelty, but I didn't.

On the way out of the ward Arnie offers his condolences and I thank him for his kindness towards Mum and us. I also see the junior doctor who should have recorded the extra dose of Frusemide to go alongside the blood. I also see the Consultant, who tries to comfort me but instead of accepting, I snap at him.

"This hospital is killing people through neglect and my Mum was one of many". He tries to calm me by telling me that my Mum was old and I had done everything for her, I could do no more. Deep down I know that but I also know that it is the hospital that is responsible. My Mother was walking out of here two weeks ago, that was until she was dropped and then denied vital medication.

Sam, Laura and I leave the hospital. Though Mum is dead I don't want to leave her there in that chaos but I do, we have to. We sit in the church in shock, what the hell have we just witnessed? It is hard to believe what we have seen over the last eight weeks and I have stood by and let it happen. Not only that I have stood by and let others be abused thinking I would be able to save Mum but now I am left without her and without my pride. I am broken.

We go home in shock, driving in total silence each one of us with an aching head and heart from the sheer weight of what we had seen. Out of the November gloom suddenly ahead of us emerges the brightest rainbow I have ever seen. The colours are so bright and vivid, it lights up the road in front of us and we have to drive through it to get home. We like to think it's Mum. Her colour, her radiance, her Marvel.

I need to be alone. I need space to reflect on what has just happened. I feel a failure to everyone, everyone around me. As a Mother I have failed Laura by leaving her at the hospital to fight alone. As a daughter, I have failed my Mother by allowing her to suffer and to die in misery. But I have also failed myself. What sort of a person would sit and watch that abuse? I have sat and allowed others to be abused and I have said nothing. I have even spoken to those abusers as if nothing has happened. I had done it to save Mum but now she is dead. What sort of a person does that make me? What sort of a person have I become?

Alone I find no comfort only guilt. I get up from my bed and find myself pacing the room. Up and down I walk around the bedroom without stopping. The guilt absorbs me. I want to scream, I can smell the hospital all over me.

I bathe but find myself scrubbing at my arm with such force it frightens me into stopping. I cannot get rid of the smell but then I realise it is inside me, that's where the problem lies. The smell will never go until I do something about it and try to stop the abuse that is happening right now on Ward 11.

I still need to be alone and I get back into bed in the hope that sleep will come and I can forget what has just happened. But sleep doesn't come. All I can see is my Mum's eyes the evening before when I abandoned her, the fear. I sob uncontrollably, into my pillow trying to stifle the noise. And then without warning or any explanation I feel my Mum's arms around me, she pulls me tightly to her. The warmth absorbs me and I close my eyes and fall silent, my tears have gone. The feeling is so real I can even feel it now but I turn in the bed half expecting her to be next to me. She isn't and I close my eyes in disappointment but all I can see is a bright shining rainbow. I rise from the bed in an instant as I know I cannot change the past, my Mum is dead, but I can certainly help those that we have left behind. In the weeks ahead the memory of the rainbow gives me comfort and hope, hope that I have the strength to fight. I may have lost one battle but the next one is about to begin.

Part Two

Let the Battle Commence

Eating and sleeping is all too difficult. The only thing I can think about is the letter of complaint. What I need to put into it goes over and over in my head, I need to be careful that I don't leave anything out, I want it to be so strong they can't ignore it. It's odd but Mum had helped me write the complaint or at least part of it. One day as part of my usual routine I had read her out an article by Melanie Phillips from the *Daily Mail*. Melanie had lived through a similar experience with her Mother and was shocked at the state of nursing. "It's everywhere, Jude," Mum had said and that article stuck in my mind along with Mum's words.

Mum had said very little on the ward about the nurses, I could tell she was shocked at what she saw and yet at the same time she felt so sorry for the Angels who overstretched themselves on every shift. Mum was the type of person who was grateful for anything, if anyone helped her she appreciated it, but at the same time we knew all along that once Mum was home we would write a letter of complaint. Mum had encouraged me to write the letter, the one I had written to Martin Yeates, as she thought it might make things easier for the staff. We both knew the place was dangerous, out of control.

A couple of days after Mum's death, and before I had had chance to finish my complaint, I received a letter from the Director of Nursing (DoN), Helen Moss. It was out of the blue and it angered me but at the same time I saw it as hope, hope that today the suffering on Ward 11 would stop. Once I had simmered down I realised it was a standard letter that was sent out once someone had died in the hospital.

"Sorry for your loss and if you have any concerns about the standard of care, please contact me".

What had annoyed me was that I had already complained now on two occasions. The first was to PALS who had arranged for me

128

to meet the Matrons on the ward, the other to the Chief Executive Martin Yeates telling him how dangerous Ward 11 was. This letter remained unanswered and quite possibly unopened.

The only experience I had to go on was when I was a social worker and what happened when a complaint came into our social work department. If you were involved in that complaint it was handled with professionalism and impartiality. Case notes would be seized and statements taken immediately. The correct procedure was used and everything was audited afterwards. It was unheard of for someone from the same department to be involved in the investigation, unlike the NHS.

I didn't feel writing to me asking if I had concerns with my Mum's care was professional at all as they should have known I had concerns at this point. Although annoyed the letter did give a telephone number to contact if I had any concerns. 'Oh I've got concerns, alright,' I thought.

Within a few minutes I'm ringing the number. I have in front of me all the evidence I will be including in my letter of complaint. I have dates and times that incidents happened and names of the staff involved. I'd poured myself a cup of tea ready for this opportunity to tell someone who could do something about the abuse. Just the thought that things could improve today for the other patients lifted my mood and I had been able to eat a small breakfast as I waited for a reasonable time to call her.

After nearly an hour on the phone to this woman I find myself on my knees, in tears, begging her to help the patients on Ward 11. When I have finished talking to her and I have had time to reflect on the conversation I feel as if she has just accused me of lying about the standards, or lack of any standards on the ward. She tells me, "I walk the wards on a regular basis and I have never seen those things".

I had told her about the charade that goes on during the day shift where the staff manage to keep things under their control. I'm desperate to cry but I must control myself a lot is resting on this telephone call. I think of it as my one opportunity to tell someone independent about what I have seen. I know I have already spoken to the two Matrons but they were hardly independent. No, this Helen Moss is the DoN, she has no allegiance to the ward, she's a professional or that's what I think.

I bite my lip and continue "But the day staff bully the patients the vulnerable ones are terrified and few are brave enough to ring their buzzers for assistance". I swallow hard and continue, "Because of that they go without". I pause and wait for a response but she is quiet so I continue. "The staff walk by the patients and any new patients onto the ward soon learn that the staff are the ones in charge". I try not to think about what I am saying as I know the tears will flow and that will be the end.

"I just don't agree," she cuts in but I ignore her and continue this is too good an opportunity to waste.

"You don't agree? But the place is bedlam, complete and utter bedlam. Particularly the evenings and weekends, I saw it". Just talking I feel empowered

"I am often on the wards at those times" she tells me and I think but do not say it, 'Like hell you are.'

"But I never saw you once and I saw patients not given food, drinks or medication over eight weeks". That will shut her up I thought and I carry on, "patients are allowed to wander around without any care or attention". I pause but she says nothing in reply so I keep on. "The staff are always fighting with the patients, there was always violence and several of the patients were covered in bruising"

I am coming to the end as my mouth is drying up but I must tell her what has been going through my head constantly over the last few days.

Nights on the ward, particularly the male ward next door to Mum's, were awful, I can still hear the sound of men crying. Each night was the same as the last, it all begins when the first buzzer sounds, fifteen to twenty minutes later another starts. Then a male voice will start calling for the nurse, "Nurse, nurse". He will continue calling out, each time the desperation in his voice gets stronger. Then anger, "Nurse, nurse," with much more force than the last call and then sheer desperation and then silence, apart from the buzzers still sounding out. Then the sobs would begin, sitting listening to a man crying because he has wet the bed is torture. Torture I have to sit and listen to for eight weeks, eight very long weeks.

"It was just dreadful torture for them." I can feel my body tensing but I have got to stay strong and continue, this Helen Moss needs to know what is happening on Ward 11.

After the sobbing the man will call out "Nurse, nurse". But now with much more anger in their voices. Some nights at this point you would hear a crash to the floor and you presumed in anger the man had thrown something across the room. Other nights the other male patients on the ward would shout at the man to be quiet or some nights you would hear a scuffle break out. Some nights you would hear a fall to the floor as someone would have struggled to help themselves too desperate to wait or unwilling to wet the bed.

Some nights I would be brave and go and have a look other nights I wouldn't, those nights still played on my mind. Even today the guilt can consume me, taking away all of my strength. In my defence, what could I do to help them? Trying to get the nurses to come to their assistance was almost impossible. If you found a member of staff you then had to face their wrath. They wouldn't openly say anything no it would be the looks and the atmosphere they created. I soon learnt that it was better not to know or to pretend to yourself you didn't know about the suffering in the next bay.

"I walk the wards at nights too and I have never seen or heard anything like that". My sobs break through as I plead with her to listen and help the patients. I have lost it again and the tears are back uncontrollably.

I plead with her to listen but she isn't listening "But they need help, please help them" I think of the patients still left on the ward and I try not to give in but my sobs overpower me, they are out of my control. I bite my lip in between but I've lost it and I begin to cry unrestrained.

"Why don't you come and talk to the staff about your experience you could help with their training" she suggests her voice now quieter, calmer again.

"Training, training". What is this woman talking about? "You expect me to help train your nurses?" I wipe my eyes and hold the tissue to my nose I'm still crying but I'm back in control I'm angry.

"Yes, people often find it therapeutic and it is really good for the staff to get the patient experience."

"But you don't understand, I will probably never be able to go near your hospital again." I tell her.

"Well have a think about it, you will be very welcome and it will be so helpful for the staff"

"Please go onto the ward and you will see what the patients are suffering." Thoughts of Mum's suffering have filled my head and I'm crying again. This is going nowhere and she will not help the patients.

"I do regularly." she says confidently.

I feel as if I am talking to a robot, this woman has no feelings, I must end the call. I find out later that she has heard about this abuse before, I find out later that what I am telling her she has heard over and over again.

I put down the phone and find myself on the kitchen floor in the foetal position, sobbing. Again I feel in despair, powerless, and now there is nothing I can do about it. Who can help me now? All the suffering and the abuse I saw in those eight weeks are flashing through my mind. I hear the sound of the drugs trolley being pushed along the corridor and I can now see it clearly. I try to focus as I try to wipe the tears away from my eyes to clear my vision. It's Amy pushing the drugs trolley into the male bay and a feeling of relief comes over me. Relief because it's Amy and relief that it will be Mum's turn next to get her drugs. But just as quickly the vision has gone along with Mum, Amy and the drug trolley. I feel the tears flowing again as the conversation I have just had goes over and over in my head.

"I walk the wards on a regular basis and I get regular feedback from my nurse leaders".

I manage to get up from the floor but I continue to sob. I'm here alone and I need now to sit and think what I can do next. I dry my tears and trying to control my sobs I wonder what my next step must be, I now feel desperate.

I want to scream out, "Help me, someone, help me!" I'm in floods of tears again. I sit down on the sofa and sob, I cry for my Mum, I want her here with me. Over the last few days I have tried so hard not to think about her, I'm finding it too difficult. Whenever I lose control of my thoughts and my mind drifts to think of Mum, I find it unbearable. My whole body feels as if I have been cut open, it consumes me. I focus on the patients' suffering, it's an easier option than thinking about my own Mum's. It is what's driving me.

I often wake in a sweat thinking I am back on the ward but I have never experienced anything like that during the day before. I feel dizzy and nauseous and realise I have barely eaten or slept for days. I have no interest in either but I know I must otherwise I will not have the strength to continue. The dog sits down next to my side and tries to comfort me but I'm not interested, it seems nothing will take away the pain today, but after a little while she does manage to distract me and I find myself smoothing her.

I'm focusing again and I try and think who now could possibly help me. The DoN's response has shocked me. Why would she say that she knows what is happening on her wards? She clearly doesn't? I ponder this for a while and I find no explanation at all, she must be aware of what is going on but why would she deny the poor care and staffing levels on the ward? I come to the conclusion that she must know and if I cannot trust the DoN at the hospital who can I trust?

I suddenly feel enlightened. The light has been switched on and I can now see things more clearly. Today I realise I have a fight on my hands and what I thought would be easy will now need all of my resolution. The DoN's denial of a problem has been a real shock to me, even if she had said that she would have a look at what I was asking her to but the way she dismissed my concerns has opened my eyes because she is part of the problem, she is in denial for some reason.

I now realised that the problem was much more serious than I could possibly have imagined and I knew I would have to go above and beyond to get anything done about it. I started to trawl the internet looking for anyone who could help. I came across a group called *Action Against Elder Abuse*. They may be able to help me or know someone who will help me. I have no other alternative and I tell the person on the other end of the phone what I witnessed on the ward, once again.

"Patients are being abused on a daily basis by not only the nurses but the doctors too," I tell her with desperation in my voice, I can sense it myself.

"That is terrible," she says with genuine concern in her voice.

"I know it was absolutely awful but I'm frightened it's still happening," I'm so relieved that she is listening to me my stomach relaxes.

"We are an advice line," she adds and already I sense her defensiveness.

"Yes, yes, what can I do? I need your advice." The despair is back in my voice.

"We can send you out an advice pack." She tells me almost dismissively.

"But what will it tell me? Will you be able to help me?" I am pleading and I can sense my voice is raised a little.

"I will send you out our advice pack if you give me your details," she adds efficiently now and I can sense it's time for the call to end. Her job is to take my details and ensure an advice pack is sent to me but I push her for answers, I have to.

"But what will the advice pack tell me?" I ask impatiently, I can sense it myself my irritation is becoming hard to control.

"You can write about your experience at the hospital and return those details to us. We hold those details on our database until the press show an interest in that topic."

"But how long does that take?" I ask trying to control my voice now, I don't want to be rude but I want help.

"I will get it in the post today" she enthuses.

"No, no, until the press make contact?" I ask in all hopefulness.

"Oh I couldn't tell you that, we never know." She adds, as clearly I have misunderstood the purpose of the pack she is about to send me.

"But people are suffering now, as we speak. They are older people too," my voice is breaking and I know it is time to end the call as I am about to cry and then she will not be able to understand me at all.

Once again the call ends in disappointment. Once again I am left for the rest of the day walking up and down the living room, pacing. I can't sit and I can't stand and I'm certainly unable to lie down. I need to lie down, I need to sleep but can't. Each time I lie down the ward fills my head. Not only what I have seen and heard but also what might now be happening, how are the patients suffering today? What are they going through? Who will feed them? Who will open their food packets? Who will pass them the call bell and, most importantly, who is protecting them?

That evening we sit down together as a family and try to plan a way forward, we're all suffering and doing nothing isn't an option. I tell them about my day and the fact that nobody seems to believe me or even care.

I also find a website where you can tell about your hospital experiences but then I find out that you can only do that once you have exhausted the NHS complaints procedure. That's after I have written a page and a half of feedback about the abuse I have seen. No sooner do I press 'Send' than I receive a reply from the Chief Executive of the Patient Opinion website telling me it cannot be submitted until my complaint has been dealt with by the hospital.

At this point I have no idea that the NHS complaints proce-
dure consists of three stages, the hospital, the Health Care
Commission (HCC) and the Parliamentary Health Service
Ombudsman.

This has now all changed and only consists of two stages.
Much later I discover that they are all hopeless the process
leads to years of torture for many and very often at the end of
it you are no wiser as to why they failed your loved one. My
complaint has probably been one of the most high profile cases
of poor care within the NHS in recent years. To date I have no
answers as to why my Mother had to suffer so much and no one
has been held to account for those failings.

It's today that I have realised that alone nothing will
change but if others are saying the same thing they will have
to listen. I tell the family that the other relatives I have seen
on the ward must be feeling the same as me. Tonight the campaign cure the NHS is formed. We have no idea at this point
that the campaign will introduce me to three separate
Secretaries of State for Health over the next four years, not to
mention a Prime Minister. I have no idea that I will be
embroiled in trying to make not only MSFT Hospital a safer
place but the whole of the NHS.

My family are with me and this gives me the support, the
courage I need. My children, Martin and Laura, are here with
their partners, Sian and Dan. We sit down and it feels like a
meeting of minds we all feel the same about what we saw.
Together we come up with a way forward, a strategy. It's a long
night but by the early hours of the morning we have a plan, a
letter is written to our local newspaper, *The Staffordshire
Newsletter*, and a website is organised to launch our campaign.
Between us we agree that the launch of the campaign will be
the day after Mum's burial.

Help us cure the NHS

*I recently said a final goodbye to my Mother Bella Bailey on
ward 11 in Stafford General Hospital. Were it not for the 24-
hour care her family provided for almost eight weeks she would
surely have died of neglect.*

Many elderly patients were not so lucky.

We feel compelled to write this letter and launch this campaign as what we witnessed in those eight weeks returns to haunt us in our dreams.

We admit that staffing levels on the ward were very low through-out our stay but what we found was that the staff that were there were either uncomfortable with the care they tried to provide or others that didn't really want to care or even be there.

The ward relies heavily on health care assistants who are poorly trained and lacking in the skills needed. Their priority should be to meet basic needs instead the most vulnerable patients are left hungry, dirty and often in pain.

Meal trays were often brought and left without any interaction, trays were then returned unopened as the poor souls didn't know the food had been served. Others needing nourishment were too ill to reach their food and it was returned uneaten. The first time I saw this happen I complained to a senior nurse and was told it was an isolated incident and she would investigate. Sadly it happened time and time again depending on who was on duty.

We experienced at least four weekends where elderly confused men wandered the ward sometimes aggressively but mostly looking for care. It was during our stay one Saturday afternoon that one man from the Cannock area wandered so far looking for attention he ended up dead on the streets of Stafford. Not aggressive at any time but hopelessly lost.

Others searched for the lives that they had lost, the pleasantly confused. Nursing and care staff were oblivious to their needs and how to meet them. The security team who were often summoned were even less understanding.

Some readers will still believe that the Florence Nightingale principle of nursing still prevails, where patients are cared for and given respect in our local hospital. Yes, at times it does even on ward 11 but sadly not too often.

I believe that the nursing revolution during the eighties has created Nurse Ratchet clones who strive to reach their own potential. They are often seen ticking boxes and signing their name ensuring that they will be noticed with no urge to care for the vulnerable patients.

Other readers will have experienced the care provided during the 'honeymoon' period of weekday visiting hours, when the nurses are all smiles and efficiency, touting for the next management post.

After spending eight weeks on the ward we had to look beyond this facade and we found demoralised staff, some wanting and trying to care with others who would benefit the patients more by not being there.

Care in the NHS needs to change

We don't really know how to achieve this but what we do know is we need your help for change to happen. We cannot allow our most vulnerable members of society in Staffordshire to be treated this way in our local hospital

Can you help us?

If you have a similar story or if you want to stop this happening to others please contact me

Julie Bailey
32 Main Road
Milford
Stafford
Curethenhs@hotmail.co.uk
The Newsletter letters page, 20th December 2007)

We buried my Mum in Stafford cemetery on the 15th of November 2007, about fifty feet from my Father. The service was held at Stafford Spiritualist church, conducted with grace and sensitivity by Gerard Smith. She was a popular lady and this was reflected by a very high turnout, faces that I hadn't seen for years turned up to pay their respects. We marched her coffin to the grave singing *Who Let the Dogs Out?* by the Baha Men, surreal moment that many would have found baffling. She used to love that song and would have a good laugh singing it at home when it came on the telly or the radio. I even bought her a dog-figure treat tin that she kept her Rich Tea biscuits in which would play the song every time she opened it. It was a brief moment of levity that helped to get us through a very emotional day.

I try not to think of Mum and her sufferings all day and surprisingly I am able to get through her funeral and the day without tears until I am alone. Being alone still isn't a nice place for me. I find no comfort at all thinking about Mum, whenever I do I feel such unbearable pain. It's still like pouring vinegar in a cut and I have to quickly try to move my thoughts.

Very quickly I received a response to my letter of complaint which had really focused on the poor care that my Mother had received, although I did briefly mention that neglect on the ward was widespread. The response was from the hospital's *Champion for Older People,* Sister Leach, one of the Matrons I had met after my first complaint to PALS.

The first page of the response told me all about Sister Leach herself, her extensive qualifications and experience. It was comical that she was so proud of her title and yet she was openly allowing the elderly to suffer so much in her own hospital. She also told me about her own training record and all about the *Essence of Care*. Throughout the next year I would hear so much about the *Essence of Care*, practically every press release from the hospital mentioned it. My only wish was that they would implement it instead of talking about it.

To say I was unhappy with the hospital's response would have been an understatement. I was furious! Oh, they were sorry if I felt that my Mother had suffered in the hospital. If I *felt*! They were also sorry if I thought that the staff had been uncaring. They even tried to make me feel guilty by telling me that when the staff had heard about my complaint they were hurt as they thought we had a good relationship and they were very fond of my Mother. "Fond of her? After eight weeks many of them didn't even know her name!" I hear myself saying.

It was odd at first hearing the nurses call her Isabella and Mum thought it was odd too. At first, I mentioned to them that everyone knew her as Bella but in the end I gave up. A few of the staff did call her Bella but that was the *Angels*, for the others it was nice if they even spoke to her. There was nothing about the poor care, no acceptance that there was a problem, nothing at all. Nothing about Mum being dropped and Nurse Ratchet's refusal to give her the Frusemide.

I'm so angry and I spend the rest of the morning reading the letter over and over again. I can't believe how they have responded to my complaint. I have even put that I had independent witnesses who could verify my account, they haven't even acknowledged that. Reading the letter over only makes me angrier and I can feel my hands shaking as I read parts over and over again. "I'm sorry if you feel your Mother's care wasn't up to our usual high standard." Once again I'm alone and crying, which I can't stop.

I cry for my Mum and without thinking I go into her room to get a tissue from the bathroom. I freeze after I realise what I have done and on the bed I see Mum's slippers, her favourites. She had had them last Christmas from my brother, Pat. "Expensive ones they were, Jude." she had told me Christmas morning. They were those old lady slippers the ones with the Velcro fastenings in green tartan. I close my eyes and try and block out my thoughts. I can see her now lying in her bed with her big smile, quickly I try to clear that vision. I feel my stomach churning I'm going to be sick. I run out before I have chance to reach the tissue and hang my head over the kitchen sink as I am sick.

I try to push the thoughts of her out of my mind. I want her here I want her now, I hear myself saying while I sob "I'm sorry". I'm talking to Mum but she is not here and then my strength returns. My head clears and I can think again but then I realise that today is the first time I have been into Mum's room since she died.

Who Can Help?

Enraged, I write a letter to the local Labour MP, David Kidney, telling him of the harm that is going on in the hospital. I also send the letter we wrote together as a family to *The Staffordshire Newsletter*. I wash my face in the bathroom and try to conceal that I have been crying. The cold air hits me and I can feel my stomach settling but my hands are still shaking as I post the letters into the post box. I've never suffered with the shakes before but now it seems to be every day. On the way home I think about the reporter I had spoken to from the Newsletter when Sam and I had sat in the car outside the hospital. "We have heard about staffing problems before". I only hope that he doesn't get to choose which letters are printed.

However unlike my last contact with them they are now interested in what I am telling them is happening. They make contact immediately and say they want to come and take pictures and get a fuller story. I'm over the moon! I ring Sammy and tell her the good news. She is struggling too and the thought of the newspaper being interested helps us through the next few days.

Sleep doesn't come easy and most nights I lie awake in pain, pain for what has happened to my Mum and what could be happening to others. I try not to put my head on the pillow until the early hours. After spending the night trawling the internet for anyone who may be able to help me. Very often as soon as I have lay down I put on the radio and listen to anything that may distract me. It's early one morning far too early to get up I have had another sleepless night.

I turn on the radio and there's a debate from the previous day in the House of Lords. It's a Baroness Masham discussing her husband's care in her local hospital, she describes it as appalling. There are a few others joining in the debate but she is the stronger voice. I jump out of bed and hunt for a pen to be able to write down their names. It's pitch black still and I later find I have written what I thought was her name with an eye brow pencil but who cares. Later that day as I try to piece together my writing I search the website and find she is Baroness Masham of Ilton. Later that day I once again write and tell her about the suffering that is happening at Mid Staffs hospital. I write and ask her if she can help me, could she help me to stop the abuse?

I also contact all the local radio stations BBC Radio Stoke, Beacon Radio and Signal Radio telling them about the launch of the campaign *CTNHS*. It doesn't matter who I am speaking to but I tell them about the abuse on Ward 11 and the death of my Mother. They all tell me they will get back to me if the producer is interested. BBC Radio Stoke, ring me back a little later and ask if I will go to their studio to do an interview on the 2nd January 2008. "Of course," I agree without a thought. It is something I can think about later I'm just ecstatic that they are interested.

At this point I will do anything, just about anything, to get something done at the hospital and I am conscious that it is now in the hands of the MP.

Living in South Wales I had learnt that that was how you got things done, if you had a problem you contacted your MP who sorted it. Or that's what the MPs that I had encountered in South Wales did. That's not quite what happened with this MP, David Kidney the local Labour MP. It was Christmas Eve when I received a reply to my letter it wasn't a reply from David Kidney himself but a case worker working for him, a Vincent Brennan. It was such a relief to get this sort of response and on Christmas Eve too. It was going to be a difficult time, our first Christmas without Mum, but getting this response would make Christmas that little bit easier.

His reply said that I had, "Raised matters of very serious concern". As soon as Christmas was over I would get a full response from the MP. It was a huge relief as I thought the suffering would now stop, remembering it was now five weeks since I had lost my Mum and that amounted to a lot of suffering that had been allowed to continue.

The story made the front page of the Christmas edition of the *Staffordshire Newsletter* for December 2007 and there was a picture of both Sammy and myself holding a picture of Mum. The headline was "Horrified by care of OAPs." I thought with it

141

being the Christmas edition even more people would be reading it and I had added a comment, "I am determined to raise awareness of the problems we cannot allow some of the most vulnerable people to be treated this way." And I damn well was determined.

Helen Moss replied giving a comment saying, "I would like to express my sincere condolences to the family of Mrs Bailey. I can confirm the concerns of the family have been dealt with by the trust under our formal complaints procedure".

Well they hadn't. They had just said that they were sorry if I felt the care wasn't good enough. She had also said that the hospital would be increasing the number of nurses following a staffing review. This was the first good news we had had and it was something positive to hold onto. She also wrote that the hospital had received 160 complaints and they had all been acted upon. "Really?" I thought, "just as you claim mine had."

The *Staffordshire Newsletter* not only covered the story they also published the letter that we had written as a family. We were glad they had run the story, the publicity we earned really

"We can't allow some of the most vulnerable people to be treated like this". - Julie Bailey

HEALTH CAMPAIGN: Julie Bailey and her niece Samantha Round with a picture of Isabella Bailey.
Jon Thorne

Horrified by care of OAPs

helped to get the ball rolling for CTNHS, but we couldn't help shake the feeling that if they had acted when we had first brought our concerns to them then Mum, and countless others, might still be alive.

As soon as that newspaper went out the floodgates opened. I received several calls from relatives who had suffered at the hospital and it was that day that I realised that it was not just Ward 11 that abused patients at Mid Staffs Hospital. I wasn't really expecting to receive so many calls so soon. I wasn't really prepared but being a listener helped me through.

One woman told me that her Mother had been on Ward 8 in May a few months before Mum's stay, she had suffered at the hands of the staff. Her daughter had tried to alert the nurses that her Mother needed feeding but they had told her that her Mother could do it herself. Her Mother, like mine, had been a strong woman and they had left her in tears.

Like me she had tried to complain whilst her Mother was still alive. She had met with the Matrons and they had promised that things would improve. They didn't and she had died in pain robbed of any dignity she had. She had written a letter of complaint and as yet had heard nothing not even an acknowledgement to her letter. The calls continued and each one told me about more suffering, I could only listen and offer my condolences. After each call I would either visit them or take the details on the phone.

That evening I met a son who had spent six weeks at the hospital on Ward 10, the death ward. Originally from Wolverhampton he had moved to Stafford to care for his Mother and he lived with her in sheltered housing accommodation. It took me ages to find his flat it was pitch black and I drove around in the pouring rain looking for it. When I did eventually find it I was over half an hour late but he welcomed me in and didn't mention my timing.

Pictures of his Mother adorned the walls which felt as if it had been in a time warp due to the decor. Everything reminded me of the 1940s with its art deco fireplace and its elegant furnishings. I wonder if Ron is going out as he is wearing a suit, but then I realise he has dressed for our meeting. He offers me tea in a fine china cup which he has taken from a beautiful glass cabinet. He sits opposite me in his three piece suit and tries to sip from his cup. I can see by his body language that he feels awkward his hands shake as he tries to rest the cup back onto the saucer. His eyes glance over at me embarrassed and I feel the need to reassure him.

"I'm finding it difficult too." I say in the hope it will help to comfort him but it is also the truth.

He needs no further encouragement to talk and as soon as he starts he continues for over an hour. The tears flow throughout that hour each time he talks it is painful for him and he cries. I want to cry with him but I bite my lip, it is difficult as his experience is so similar to mine on Ward 11.

Again like me he had stayed at the hospital as he had been too frightened to leave his Mother in such an unsafe place. He had gone in early one day and caught one of the nursing staff shouting at his frail Mother for wetting her bed. He learnt that she had waited for nearly three hours for someone to help her.

His Mum had been in a single room as she had contracted a hospital acquired infection (HAI) but he had seen and heard as I had. He had sat and watched the suffering for those six weeks. Over that period he had sat and watched his Mother die before him, just as I had. Like me he had also sat and watched other patients suffering and like me he had done nothing about it. Like me he was now consumed with guilt for allowing others to suffer.

"I have no family you see, I was trying to care for her alone."

As I sit there listening I wonder how he managed to stay there for six weeks without leaving her, he must be exhausted. I struggled and I had help from Laura and Sammy, I shudder to think how I would have coped alone. I would have been in a mess.

He had no idea of the complaints procedure or even that he could complain. He told me about the way he had been treated by the hospital and whenever he had tried to tell the staff about his concerns they had turned on him. He told me about one male nurse a real bully who had instigated an altercation with him. Within minutes the rest of the staff were on him like pack animals. I had seen it myself on Ward 11 and knew exactly what he was describing.

Everything he told me was similar to what I had heard during my stay. "The staff were squealing during the night and running down the corridor while my Mother was so ill." He tells me and it all sounds so familiar to what happened on Ward 11. He described the staff chasing each other and playing games whilst the patients suffered.

Listening and trying to offer some comfort to him whilst he cried was probably one of the hardest things I have ever had to do. Before I even have chance to get to my car, I am in tears. I sob all the way home and long after reaching home. At times I even consider pulling the car over at the side of the road but it is dark and I struggle to see through my tears. Once home I try and make a hot drink to try and steady my nerves but it's hopeless, the tears continue. What strikes me are the similarities with Mum's care. His words go over and over in my head. His Mum suffered like mine.

Another call that week came from an ex member of what I later learn is the Patient and Public Involvement Forum (PPIF) from the hospital. I learnt that the PPIF had replaced Community Health Councils (CHC). CHC's were set up to represent patients, to be their voice. According to some people they did an excellent job. Some say that they represented the patient voice too well and Hazel Blears in 2001 was instrumental in replacing them with the PPIF. CHCs had a lot more teeth than the PPIF and some groups used those powers. From my research some areas had very good patient representation and others were less successful. In 2001 legislation was passed to abolish them and under Section 11 of the Health & Social Care Act 2001, PPIF's were established to replace the representative and inspection elements of the CHC work.

On the phone the former PPIF member tells me that she resigned along with several other members who complained about poor care and conditions. One man was even thrown off the hospital premises for complaining and told the police would be informed if he ever set foot within the hospital again.

I wondered if I was hearing things right as I was trying to groom a dog at the time and had the clippers on. I asked the woman to pass my number on to the others involved it was important that I spoke to them myself. Within the next few days I was contacted by five ex PPIF members, all having resigned as they hadn't been listened to when they raised concerns about the standards within the hospital. From what I learnt whenever anyone started to question the management or the board of directors they were ostracised. A picture was starting to emerge of a deep-rooted culture of silence where any dissenting voices were cruelly dealt with.

They also gave me a great insight into the management. Just

like the Nurse Ratchets it sounded like they should never have got the jobs in the first place, displaying a gross lack of professionalism and diligence throughout their tenure, especially the chief executive, Martin Yeates. At the same time that week I went delivering leaflets that I had made asking for people to contact me if they had concerns about the hospital. I had to I just couldn't settle doing nothing and the more people that were saying the same thing the more likely they are to believe me.

Each evening I would go out delivering in the hope that the more people that came forward the more chance we had of getting the hospital improved. Each night I would return home and stay up into the early hours printing and preparing more for the following day. Receiving David Kidney's response made me even more determined and I couldn't settle knowing what I did.

I held out such hope for the MP's response. We had always been a strong Labour family, I had been a trade union rep and party member and in her youth Mum had campaigned for Herbert Morrison in the run up to the Labour landslide of 1945, the election that heralded the formation of the National Health Service. I had brought my kids up to have a strong sense of social justice and a belief in the state as a force for good. As a 'Labour' family I did not expect any special treatment but I did expect a Labour MP to listen to the genuine concerns of his constituents. When I did get a reply from him a few days after Christmas it was such a shock after getting such a positive response from one of his agents before Christmas.

He told me in his letter "I visit the hospital often and meet staff and patients. I hold regular meetings with the senior management when I ask questions about issues like quality of care, infection control, hospital food and so on. I also seek independent verification of the information I receive from groups like trade unions, groups like Age Concern and the above mentioned PPIF. I also receive copies of Healthcare Commission reports and the reports of the Primary Care Trust (PCT) and the Strategic Health Authority (SHA) ".

He had included in his reply a recent copy of an inspection that the patient group had recently undertaken.

The inspection report was a joke and it made me so angry that he had even sent it to me. The only criticism was that they had gone into a fridge and found a lid off a jam jar! I wanted to scream, I think I did, I couldn't contain my anger. "Go and walk

146

on the ward, open the door to Ward 11 and you will smell it, Mr Kidney, look at the patients look at their mouths." I shouted but no one could hear me. That was all anybody needed to do, I suspected even the toilet door would still be missing and here was an inspection that had highlighted a lid missing off a jar of jam.

I was devastated and yet now so determined that my Mum didn't die in vain. No, I wouldn't let this get me down I have got to keep going, someone has got to listen. I was so angry with his response or should I say the lack of a response. Immediately I write to the Secretary of State (SoS) for Health to complain, it was Alan Johnson at the time.

I believed that the Labour Party would look after those who were unable to look after themselves. I trusted the Labour party. I suppose it had been part of my upbringing. That's what Mum had always instilled in me and that was why I had gone into social care and later social work.

As I got older I came to realise that no matter what a party tells you in opposition once elected it never materialises. It's all about power and looking after, their own and their cronies' interests. Blair's government had opened my eyes to that. I had had so much hope when he had been elected but his Government left me so disillusioned with politics. But writing to the Secretary of State for Health just seemed the most sensible thing to do as I was so unhappy with my MP's response. I knew Alan Johnson had a good reputation as a down-to-earth man of the people and I was certain he would listen to us.

I didn't realise when I received a reply back from him that a year later he would be visiting my cafe. Whilst he sat drinking my coffee and eating my homemade cake I challenged him on his response to me the year before. In the letter he had offered me condolences on the loss of my wife. I was shocked when I had received it, the fact that he had completely ignored the abuse I was telling him was happening and how he could address a letter to a Miss and offer condolences on the loss of my wife.

I can't remember how he responded, I vaguely remember him offering his apologies, but he didn't come over as a genuine guy anyway. He had visited the cafe a few days after the Health Care Commission Report was published, along with Christine Beasley, the CNO who had given evidence to the MSPI the day I began to write this book.

I suppose it was naive of me to think that the SoS would read a letter from a member of the public and respond but when that letter was telling him about widespread abuse in an NHS hospital alarm bells should have rung immediately. I had also enclosed the thirty letters I had received from other concerned relatives too with the same themes running through all of them, neglect and abuse of our loved ones particularly the vulnerable and the elderly.

Four years later I was contacted by a woman who had lost her Mother under appalling circumstances within an NHS hospital in London. She used to work in the complaints department within the DOH and handle letters similar to mine. She told me that they send out a set response to complainants and that is what I got. The letter suggested I took my complaint to the hospital's Chief Executive and Chair. But hadn't I already done that?

The woman was now going through the NHS complaints procedure herself. She had been employed as a temporary employee with the Department of Health (DoH) she was given no training and quickly left, like many others she told me. The Department had been poorly staffed and lacked any real structure or system to handle complaints about the NHS, in other words it was a mess.

After the response from the DoH, I stayed up and printed more leaflets and over the next few days spent all day delivering them, I was so angry. The only thing that was driving me now was the thought that I just needed to recruit more people. There was no plan at this stage, I just wanted more allies hoping that with more people we would have more power and something would get done.

I mainly targeted the older persons' housing as this is where I thought I would gather support. It was mainly the elderly that I had seen suffering and this proved to be a good way of contacting people with concerns. Usually after each day or evening delivering I would get at least two calls from people who had suffered or who had loved ones who had suffered. Each call I got about the hospital gave me the strength that I needed to keep going. Each call I got I would go out and see them and it really was difficult having to listen to their sufferings whilst inside me I was raw, mourning for my Mum.

Just like Ron, the first man I had gone out to see, everyone I spoke to had had the same concerns as their loved ones had suffered the same treatment. It also seemed that it didn't matter which ward the complaint was from, the staff had behaved the same way. Each time the relative was totally ignored despite very often being able to give valuable information. In each case I heard there were so many missed opportunities, if only they had listened but it didn't seem to matter. The staff made you aware that they were in charge and they knew best but in most cases it transpired they didn't.

Most relatives I spoke to had only visited at visiting times and had only become concerned when they realised that their loved one was deteriorating. This was because they had put their trust in the medical staff and many now lived consumed by guilt. Once they had recognised there was a problem getting any of the staff to do anything was difficult. For everyone I spoke to it was always too late and their loved one went on to die. It wasn't just the loss it was the way they had died, most had died in pain. Getting pain relief had been a huge problem on Ward 11 and, it seemed, on most of the wards.

Surprisingly my first live interview on BBC Radio Stoke went smoothly and much better than I had expected. I didn't know how to prepare because I didn't know what to expect. I had thought and worried about it for days but once over I wondered what all my worry had been about. I didn't need to prepare because it was all there in my head, I was reliving it every day and night. I had sat and watched not only eight weeks of my Mum suffering but eight weeks of a whole ward suffering. I didn't need to think about it at all my answers came from the heart and I felt as if I was giving those that had suffered a voice. I felt empowered for the first time in a long time and that was healing in itself. I have found that, though, with every interview I have given since, it's cathartic.

Driving home from the interview both Sam and I were relieved and in a good mood as we had nearly missed the interview. The only nerves were caused by trying to get in and out of the town as her Sat Nav had left us running through Stoke on a bitterly cold morning to get to the interview on time. It was 2nd January 2008 and luckily for us the roads were empty with everyone still being on holiday. It was my first time in a radio station studio and much quieter than I had anticipated. It was the first time I met Pete Morgan, the presenter, and the first time I met Chris King who is now our local reporter for the station.

It went much better than expected and on the way home we listened to a nurse who phoned in after my interview. She worked at the hospital and told the listeners that she witnessed what I was saying every day. She told us that she couldn't bear the suffering anymore and she was leaving nursing. As I suspected the caring staff would leave and the only nurses left would be the Nurse Ratchets, the bullies, those that didn't care about the patients.

The Chief Operating Officer, Karen Morrey, had been interviewed by the station in response to my interview. Sam pulled the car over and we listened to her response at the side of the road. It made me so mad to hear her denying everything saying that there was nothing wrong at the hospital. Listening to her excuses made me want to scream, her voice was so irritating. I normally like a Potteries accent but her's grates on me, it's got a whine to it.

"It had been a busy period during her Mother's stay and we only receive very few complaints about poor care." I later find out from the PI that this isn't true. The truth is they have so many complaints many are left unread due to a backlog, they simply can't handle the volume. One thing that did strike me though, was that she too sounded like a robot, automated with a set programme to say to the listeners, similar to the DoN when I had spoken to her. That night the website I had set up in November received over thirty responses from that one interview. It was only a few days to go before CTNHS first meeting at Breaks Cafe and I had invited and had confirmation from around twenty people that they were coming along. I also needed to get my finger out as I still had decorating to finish.

What I had heard in the last two weeks had filled me with dread, it wasn't just Ward 11 where the patients were suffering. The families who were contacting me had lost loved ones very recently and some were going back to 2006. One person who made contact had just come out of hospital following a hysterectomy. The day after she had been operated on she had to get out of bed to help the elderly and the vulnerable on Ward 8, otherwise they went without. Like me she was horrified about what she saw and vowed when she got out she would do something about it. Although she was still poorly she was determined to come along and I promised her a comfy chair as she still hadn't had her stitches removed.

Since the first coverage of our campaign in the press the hospital had issued a series of statements. Each one told us that, "The hospital had seen 30,000 patients in the last year and the majority were happy with their care." They did recognise though that there had been a shortfall in my Mum's care. This was due to it being an exceptionally busy period and to ensure it doesn't happen again they will put a new system in place.

They would now establish a nurse response team that would respond to shortages of staffing on the wards due to staff sickness. There was nothing about the standard of nursing or the quality of the nurses on the ward, nothing about the lack of basic equipment, but it was a start. At least they had acknowledged the poor care my Mother had received and that staff shortages were a problem. The DoN told us that there had been a staffing and skill mix review and it would shortly be going before the hospital board, this was January 2008. I thought this was odd as only a few weeks ago when I had spoken to her on the phone she hadn't mentioned staff shortages. She had told me that she walked the wards on a, "Regular basis," and she had always seen, "Plenty of staff."

Despite these promises though I was still hearing from families telling me that nothing had changed at the hospital and the wards were still desperately short of staff. But at this point I didn't realise that this was spin and there would be plenty more of it coming out of this hospital. In fact we heard during the MSPI that the staffing and skill mix review wasn't presented to the board until April, over five months since it had been completed saying the hospital was desperately in need of staff.

Listening to all of these families I was horrified and realised that the hospital was far worse than I had anticipated. I was determined to do all I could to stop this. I knew that getting together as a group was essential. In preparation for our first meeting I was up all night, not going over mortality statistics or press releases but stapling the upholstery to the seats in the café. It was a great distraction and I kept telling myself that every chair represented another member, another voice.

United We Stand

I had tried to go back to the grooming salon but I had just found it too difficult, there were too many memories. Some people take comfort being where their loved one had been when they have lost them. I felt differently, I couldn't bear to be in the grooming salon, I found it too painful. It was the same with my Mum's bedroom. I could still see, smell and hear Mum all over the house and it was the same with the grooming salon. I couldn't bear to go into her room as it was too painful for me, I just wasn't strong enough.

I knew it was the wrong time but I had seen the cafe lease come up and had discussed it with Mum when she had been alive. We had had a good laugh about it on the ward as Mum was going to be the "hostess with the mostess", or so she said. Mum had a fantastic sense of humour and I always thought she could have been on the stage. She had a knack of being able to make me laugh real belly laughs and sometimes I only had to look at her. I have many memories of times we were together and both of us couldn't control our laughter despite us needing to. That's another reason why the ward was so difficult, laughter was very far from our thoughts and something we couldn't do. Laughter had always been a coping mechanism for us and we felt a whole area of communication was taken away from us.

One afternoon I had popped down the town for her melon and I saw a sign up for the lease. Mum thought it would be a great investment and much easier than grooming dogs. Though losing Mum made it a lot harder it was an ideal distraction and after finding myself unable to return to the grooming salon, I knew I needed some income. I had now been off work for three months and I had spent a fortune at the hospital. Each day I had spent about twenty pounds on food and drinks and the parking was on top of that. I now needed to start earning some money before I ran out of what little savings I had. What I had left I would use to start up the cafe and it would also be good for a meeting place for the group.

Over the last couple of weeks I had heard about some dreadful cases and although it was hard to listen to what their loved ones had suffered, oddly it was a comfort to me. At first I had found this wrong that I could take comfort that others had suffered like Mum had. After giving it some thought though it meant that none of us were alone, we had found each other and although we were all different, we had something very important in common. Our loved ones who had been very precious to us had been harmed by the same people and that would prove to be a strong enduring bond.

I had decided that I would have to have a meeting to bring everyone together and getting the place ready was a real challenge. On the night of the meeting I had a rough agenda that I wanted to get through but it really was a new experience for me. I didn't at this stage know who was going to turn up or how many. People I had spoken to on the phone had told me they would try to come along but I had no confidence at this stage of who would attend.

I had spoken to a mixed group who said they were coming to the meeting. Some were patients others relatives some part of the monitoring of the hospital who had tried to do something about the standards but failed. Although I had spoken with these people on the telephone and heard some of what their loved ones had suffered. Hearing it from them and seeing how they were still suffering was so very difficult.

There was some at the meeting who could barely speak, Chris Dalziel was one of them. I had previously spoken to her daughter and tonight her son in law came along too to support them both. Chris tried to talk about the lack of care her husband had to suffer but her words would barely come out of her mouth. Her daughter, Alison tried to finish the sentence for her but she too was struggling when she tried to recall her Dad's suffering. Both were in tears sobbing and their pain was clear for all to see. The room was in silence and Pete, Alison's husband, spoke instead but words were difficult for him. It was clear that they were a close family and obvious the death had devastated them.

Chris was tiny, and her daughter Alison too, probably no bigger than my Mother at 5ft. Chris spoke with a strong brummie accent being from Birmingham originally but she now lived in Rugeley. Alison her daughter lived in Stafford and had been the apple of her Father's eye. Chris had a son too but he was far too upset to attend the meeting. I suspected that Chris was in her early 60s but it was difficult to judge because of her grief. She had the type of face that told you everything she was thinking and her daughter the same.

Alison had short blonde fine hair in a tidy bob. Her Mother had dark thick hair with tight curls that looked as if they had been secured with grips. Both were dressed well but they both wore really dark clothing which seemed to echo their sadness.

It was heartbreaking listening to what her husband of forty two years had suffered in the hospital. George had had major bowel surgery and spent the next three days begging for pain relief. The staff kept telling him he had had an epidural and he couldn't be in pain. Three days later they found it hadn't been put in correctly but it took three days before they had checked despite the family and George telling them he was in pain. But even then he suffered through lack of any care from the staff. George had gone into hospital a strong man and yet he ended up frightened of the staff the very people who should have been there to care for him.

Castell and her daughter Rebecca sat in the corner silent throughout the meeting. Rebecca was the more confident of the two, despite her young age which I would guess would be around twenty. Like Chris and Alison, Castell and Rebecca looked opposites in appearance too. Rebecca had long thick blond hair tidily plaited she too wore dark clothing but because of her pale skin it made her face look drawn, sad. Her Mother Castell was the opposite with a small frame. She had dark hair, thick and extremely curly she looked Mediterranean with dark skin and eyes where as Rebecca was very pale with bright green eyes. I found it really difficult to estimate Castell's age perhaps early fifties but like Chris her eyes were full of sorrow.

Castell and Rebecca are from Stafford. Many say that Stafford has no accent but it does, sandwiched between The Potteries and the Black Country the accent has elements of both. When they do speak their accents give them away as local, although they are also very well spoken. Castell barely says a word. She wants to, I can tell, but I think she is frightened her tears will flow and she won't be able to stop them.

Castell had trusted the staff and hadn't realised that her Mother wasn't in safe hands until it was too late.

I had spoken to Gill Peacham on the phone, she had lost her husband Arthur the previous year. Arthur had gone into hospital with pain in his back and ended up dying of a HAI. Everyone I had spoken to had commented on how filthy the hospital was. Arthur had only just retired after working hard all his life. Now it was time for them to start enjoying their retirement together. The hospital had ruined everything and Gill was now left alone. It later transpired Arthur had only been suffering with arthritis and nothing more serious until he became unwell with C.Difficile.

Gill was the opposite of the others she really was a feisty character and was determined to get answers to her husband's death. Although she was retired she looked much younger than retirement age. Being blonde and dressing stylishly took years off her.

It would have been easy to spend the evening just listening to their experiences but at the same time I needed to achieve something more from the meeting. It would have been easy to have spent the evening as a counselling session for the bereaved but I needed to create a balance and try to listen to everyone that had attended. Most people came from the area but others travelled a long distance just to attend the meeting.

A few had come along who had been involved in the hospital and from what they told me the management really did sound a nasty bunch of people. One man had been involved with infection control and had been so concerned about the high rate of HAI that he had tried to affect some changes at the hospital as early as 2004. It seemed to me that the PPIF had been captured by the management and he wasn't prepared to be captured too. He wasn't alone, that night there were four other former members of the PPIF at the meeting and they had all been involved at different times. Much later all four would give evidence to the MSPI, in one form or another.

One previous member of the PPIF had stopped attending their meetings as she felt she wasn't achieving anything. She attended the first CTNHS meeting as she wanted improvements at the hospital before she or her husband needed their help. Unfortunately three years later she was devastated when she lost her husband at the hospital. As soon as he had died she had contacted the police as she felt his death was so suspicious. The police weren't interested as it was concluded that his death had been natural. To this day this woman continues to seek answers as to why her husband lost his life so hastily.

Little did I know at the time that most of the people in this room would share the next five years of my life, some of them would become like family to me and to my children. In that room that first night were people that would become great friends and we would share a very close bond that I am sure we will share forever.

There were about twenty people at that first meeting and Sam was there helping me to make drinks and settle everyone down. Although I had spoken to most of the people on the phone putting faces to names took up a lot of my time.

There were no nerves as I stand in front of them there's too much to say and do to be nervous. I can be a shy person but it's now too late for that, I must change quickly and I do. I know whatever I say I must get them to trust me as an important job has got to be done.

The words just come out I have prepared nothing but the next minute I am telling them why I had written my appeal letter to the newspaper.

"During those eight weeks my Mother was neglected and I saw patients being neglected every day," although I feel nervous my voice, surprisingly, is confident but calm.

"I saw it too, something has got to be done" one male called out his face full of sorrow.

"What I have heard over the last few weeks has horrified me and we here tonight have got to do something about it". I felt there was no alternative it was now in our hands. I paused and waited for a response there was none.

I continued, holding my hands tightly together to stop them from shaking, "This is something I have never done but I will lead and I will not let you down as this job has got to be done. It is too important as our loved ones didn't die in vain, I will make sure of that".

"Thank you." Several in the room said in unison, so I continued.

I really don't know where it comes from my mouth just opened and the words came easily and I keep my word. Over that year and for the next four years not a day goes by where the campaign is not my focus, my everything.

Seeing everyone there had left me feeling I had done the right thing. As I spoke I could feel myself shaking but at the same time it felt the most natural thing to do. I suppose it was because it was the only sensible thing to do.

At that first meeting I covered basic ground rules or those that I thought we would need for the meeting and for our campaign. I told them that if we shouted and were unreasonable we would lose our case and nobody would listen, we had to earn respect.

"It's important that we act professionally at all times as we need to gain support, we want others to join us." I could feel my hands shaking as I spoke but I had to continue. I'd stood in front of the main door hoping I could get a clear view of everyone. As I spoke I moved to the centre of the room as I thought this would be a better position. Now I could hear the raw emotions, the tears, but I could also feel the anger inside some.

"We will get nowhere if we shout and bawl." I look around the room and everyone is still listening intently, some wiped their tears as they listened. This was important and I was not the type to argue and make a show of myself, it would be the last thing we needed.

"Because of the way the hospital has treated us it is important that we respect each other and give each other support when it is needed". I could feel everyone's eyes on me, all focused and hanging on my every word. It felt so sad seeing so many people so vulnerable through grief but I could also feel the power in the room, the shared voices and experiences.

I tried to give everyone an opportunity to talk, some chose to tell us about the harm their loved ones had suffered, others chose to sit in silence, too raw to talk. I had to be careful that I didn't allow one person to hog the meeting and at times I found that difficult. We all introduced ourselves and although I didn't get chance to speak to everyone I could see they were all talking to each other afterwards and that was a relief.

That night we heard some dreadful cases and all were at different stages of the complaints procedure. Ron was an older man who had lost his partner in 2006 he was still awaiting the inquest for her death. It had been a dreadful case but I had heard of many similar deaths. What was different about this death was an inquest was pending and the family had evidence of the failings. Like many others I had spoken to Ron had been

Gill's main carer and until she had gone into the hospital she had been safer than she was in the hospital.

What had been different about Gill's death was that Ron had caught the hospital out. They couldn't deny the neglect that Gill had suffered because Ron had gone in and found her unconscious. Like many others who hadn't been given their medication Gill paid the consequences with her life.

Ron had a background in social care and knew what he was talking about and what he was looking for. He happened to overhear the doctor telling the nurse that Gill's insulin had not been administered for days. Sadly Gill never regained consciousness but Ron overhearing that conversation was evidence that couldn't be hidden.

I believe Gill didn't die in vain as our legal team during the MSPI was able to use her case as an example of the sheer neglect that I suspect many had suffered. Because at the time the police were still involved with Gill's death and the inquest was outstanding Ron had to be cautious about getting involved. The case had gone to the Crown Prosecution Service and the Health and Safety Executive were still considering the case.

"I will help as much as I can but I need to very careful," Ron added his voice quiet but at the same time determined

I fed back my response from the MP David Kidney and from the DoH. Suggesting that as a group we attended the MP's next surgery to tell him he needed to take action as people were suffering. I was so angry at his dismissive response and if he could hear the concerns from us all it may push him into doing something.

"That's his job," Pete called out, "He should be helping us." he added

They all agreed but I felt that they would have agreed with anything I would have suggested. Some of them were so desperate, desperate that others didn't suffer as their loved ones had. I suggested we each prepared a banner and they were full of ideas of what we needed to write on them.

"Protect the patients!" A male voice called out

"Nurses that care needed!" Another man who had travelled from Lincoln called out. He had lost his Mother the previous year, another older woman who had suffered on Ward 11.

A former PPIF member who had attended knew a local solicitor and suggested I took advantage of a free thirty minute consultation with him to get some legal advice. I could see straight away that he was a knowledgeable man and he told me his background was in quality and safety systems. He was one of three men that night who had worn a suit and on the night I was impressed with his knowledge of the NHS. I couldn't quite place where his accent was from, perhaps down South somewhere. He told us he had been involved in the hospital for a few years and had been trying to identify areas for improvement.

Another former PPIF member had been consulting the HCC asking their advice on infection control matters and he asked if he could come along with me to meet the solicitor. He sounded as if he knew what he was talking about and his efforts for improvements at the hospital were encouraging. Robin had been involved with the hospital for some time following some treatment his daughter had received, thinking he could help the hospital by offering his time and skills. He quickly realised that something was not quite right and started to probe further. He was a tall, thin, bearded man with greying hair. Robin was obviously well-educated, you could tell by the way he spoke with his Shropshire accent. He was probably in his early sixties but looked older because of his white beard, I found out he had been a university lecturer.

The following week we both went along to meet the recommended solicitor in his office in Stoke. It was a gorgeous day and the sun shining had lifted my mood as we were shown into the waiting area. Both of us had spoken on the way over and agreed I would do most of the talking describing what I had done up to this point. It was a really swanky solicitors and I was glad that we were not paying for the consultation, I imagine it would be quite expensive.

The seats are very plush and I'm reluctant to even sit down. I've rushed out of work and I can smell the chip fat on my clothing, I regret not spraying myself with freshener before I left. "Take a seat" the receptionist tells us, so I do. My feet are dropping off, I have been on them since early morning in the cafe. Both Robin and I sit in silence, I'm parched and wondering in this decadence whether we might be offered a cup of tea. I've shut the cafe early to get to the appointment on time and didn't have time to change my clothes. It never occurred to me before that working in a cafe I would end up smelling like a chip and

I am only just noticing it. The cafe is going really well and I am far busier than I could have expected after only being open a few weeks.

We are escorted into the solicitor's room by the young receptionist who has made us a lovely cup of tea. She tells us she had worked in the office since leaving school and would like to train as a solicitor one day. I'm tempted to take the tea in with me but I leave it hoping that it will have cooled by the time I come out.

The solicitor is a pleasant man, very tall and handsome with a strong Potteries accent. He introduces himself and both Robin and I begin by telling him our experiences.

I tell him about my eight weeks on Ward 11 and the suffering I saw. I try not to mention Mum as I do not want him to think that this is an individual complaint. I tell him that I have lost, I cannot change that, but people are still suffering. I tell him about my contact with my MP David Kidney and his reluctance to accept there is a problem. He has done nothing to help so I then wrote to Alan Johnson and he too has done nothing despite me enclosing over 30 letters all with the same complaints.

Robin tells him that he has been concerned for a while about the cleanliness within the hospital and the amount of HAI. All the time his eyes are focused on Robin as he speaks, he just listens intently. As Robin talks I listen intently too as some of what he is saying I haven't heard before. It seems he tried to get information on complaints when he was on the PPIF but at the last stage his efforts were blocked by the Complaints Manager.

The solicitor gives us practical advice that is all that he can do as there is no legal route to go down. I ask about challenging the SoS and my MP and add, "They have done nothing to stop the suffering and it is still going on". I had been contacted that very morning by another family who had suffered at the hospital. I can see by his facial expression that he finds my comment comical, smiling he tells me that that is impossible. Nobody challenges the SoS or an MP, it's just something that you don't do. If they don't do what you want them to do or you think they should do you just don't vote for them at the next election.

I feel so naive and wish I hadn't said anything now. I suddenly get a whiff of chips from my clothing and hope he hasn't. Feeling self-conscious now I just want to leave as I was hoping today the suffering would end for those in the hospital or about to go into the hospital.

I'm still listening but my disappointment is obvious as he tells me to contact the HCC as they are one of many that should be monitoring the hospital. The HCC are the regulators and they should be inspecting the hospital on a regular basis or at least receiving regular feedback from them. He tells us that the HCC is made up of several different departments and it is likely that the local team would be visiting regularly.

We shake hands and I am out the door, I don't even try and retrieve my cup of tea. I race home hoping I will get there before the HCC shuts as I plan to ring them as soon as I get in. After dropping Robin off I get home and ring the number the solicitor has kindly given to me but there is no answer. I lay awake all night again disappointed that the harm is continuing and also too frightened to sleep about what will fill my dreams. I eventually nod off but I am up at the crack of dawn far too early to ring them but I go over in my head what I will say.

***

At the same time as I had written to the SoS I had also written to the Overview and Scrutiny Committee (OSC), which was made up of borough councillors. I told each individual councillor (there were about fifteen of them, from different political parties) what I had witnessed at the hospital and how people were suffering. I had found them on the internet and found that they had a responsibility to scrutinise the hospital. I wasn't quite sure how they did this but I thought they would be very interested in my evidence.

My evenings were now spent delivering leaflets and meeting relatives but during the early hours I scanned the internet for anyone who could help. I was frightened to close my eyes as each time I did the horrors I had seen continued to fill my thoughts, so I worked through the nights getting any information I could. The cafe was now open for business and that was keeping me occupied during the day.

I soon received a reply back from OSC and like the rest they weren't interested. In fact I received a letter from their solicitor telling me not to contact them again. His letter told me:

"I wish to advise you that it is not the role of the Health

161

Scrutiny Committee to pursue individual cases from members of the public in relation to health related matters, particularly given the prevalence of other agencies such as PALS that are able to provide you with support of this nature". Ironically his letter continued and told me,

"Moreover the role of the Health Scrutiny Committee is to review and scrutinise matters relating to the health service in the councils area in accordance with the Regulations under the Health and Social Care Act 2001 and assist in the reduction of health inequalities in the local area".

It didn't put me off although it was a shock to receive it, I just couldn't understand why they would complain at being told that people were suffering. It just made me more determined and I wrote back immediately telling him that instead of trying to frighten me into silence he should be more interested as a solicitor in protecting the vulnerable at his local hospital.

I was beginning to realise that there was something wrong here as those that should have been concerned were not. Along with that was a campaign of positive stories in all of the local papers. One was even from Ward 11 and it was from a family whose Mother had been so well cared for on the ward they had donated £200. The headline was, "Allowed to die with dignity" and the story told us how Lyndsey had cared for their Mother so well during her final hours. The problem was I was still hearing from many who weren't dying with dignity, I was hearing from many *robbed* of their dignity. I suspected this was an orchestrated campaign and it was likely that the OSC were involved, or that's what I suspected.

I found out from the MSPI that a few months later the OSC had met with the hospital management and tested the food that was given to patients. I had never mentioned that I was concerned with the standard of the food, the problem was getting the vulnerable fed with it.

During their visit they failed to check on any of the patients, they didn't meet with any, only the management. Odd behaviour, I know but I later found out that most of them were very friendly with the management team at the hospital. I also found out later that the OSC had played a part in a comprehensive assessment that the hospital had recently completed and they had commented that they had no concerns about the standards of care.

The scrutiny committee was a cross party group of borough councillors and following my letter one of the Tory councillors contacted me one evening. She was very charming and it sounded like I had found an ally. She even had a neighbour who was in the hospital now and was also being neglected. I should have asked what she was doing about it but I was seduced by her offer to help.

The management from the hospital met with the scrutiny committee around six times a year and they are allowed to question the management about their performance. She asked me if I wanted to put forward three questions to be asked at their next meeting but I had to think of them now, immediately. I wished I could have had more time but from the top of my head I asked about the feeding and fluids for vulnerable patients, staffing levels and the training of staff. These were the three main issues from memory but I could have thought of hundreds more with more time.

During my time on Ward 11 I am sure that some patients died through lack of nourishment and fluids. I had tried to feed those I could but the last two weeks of Mum's life I was unable to help any of them. Sitting watching them claw at their food trays was heartbreaking and still is today as I recall those times. The ward was so starved of staff it was impossible for them to manage a ward and care for all of those patients. I wanted to ask about the training of staff to manage confused patients. Listening to the confused and the way some of the staff handled them on the ward was heartbreaking too.

It was common to hear the staff telling the confused patients to stop being silly as the loved one that they were calling for was now dead. Many called for their Mothers and would be left in despair as the nurse had told them they were dead. "Dead! Dead? My Mother isn't dead," they would often say and then spend the next few minutes in what would seem like shock as they stood still, silent. The nurse long gone down the corridor to reap more grief on other vulnerable patients, like demanding they got into their beds which to them, in the middle of the day and with no recollection of the bed, seemed silly but they continued, oblivious to the time they were wasting shouting at the poor patients to, "Get back into your bed". Those words echoed down the corridor, particularly at nights, and now into my dreams.

Following the meeting with the local solicitor, I took his advice and contacted the HCC. He told me that they were an independent body that monitored the hospital. At the time I thought, "Well they're not doing a very good job at the moment," but there was nothing else to do but contact them, I was running out of options.

The following day I contacted the HCC as the solicitor had advised. Though the advisor was very friendly and sympathetic I didn't really sense any urgency. She suggested that I write a report of my concerns. I mentioned all the letters of complaints I had now received from others and she suggested I include those in my report. "What? I need to write a report?" I ask her in hope that she will say no, but she doesn't.

I started by laying out on my living room floor all of the letters I had received. Some were the same letters I had sent to the SoS, others I had received afterwards. People had also sent me the responses they had received from the hospital. What struck me immediately were the similarities, not only what our loved ones had suffered but the response from the hospital.

It was obvious that the hospital had cut and pasted letters to relatives even pasting the wrong name onto one of the letters I had read. I was horrified at what I saw, the letters were practically identical with the same excuses for the lack of care. All the letters started with "I'm sorry if you feel… ". I also had several action plans that families had been sent. I was shocked at the standard of the plans, very basic and there was never a date when the action should be completed by. It was always marked 'Ongoing' which was an odd thing to see, especially as it was for most of the improvements. Finding the same complaint over and over again was heartbreaking as I knew that it meant more suffering for another patient some time later and no lessons had been learnt. I was so shocked as it dawned on me that if I had seen a pattern whoever was dealing with complaints at the hospital must have realised that things weren't improving.

I was working on the report each evening but I wasn't really sure what I was supposed to be doing. What I felt was important was that I included all of the points that people had sent to me. I decided to write a covering letter and then write out the things that we had all experienced as bullet points.

I lay all of the letters I had received from relatives on my living room floor along with the matching action plans. Reading through them over and over I can identify the same problems over and over again. I also witnessed it over those eight weeks, all of the things that these people are saying. Even one letter taken alone is enough to identify there is a problem to whoever is reading it but looking at all those cases together it was clear the problems were endemic. You see it's the nature of them, the extent of the failings. They either mention the lack of very basic care, the suffering, the lack of care from the staff and the fight to keep their loved ones alive. That night I realise that something very bad was going on at that hospital. Who is reading these complaints and why isn't anybody doing anything about it?

It is hard to finish as I know I have found something out tonight that I didn't think could be possible happening within our NHS. I stay up until the early hours and finish the report. Since Mum's death whenever I have thought I can take it no more and I despair I seem to get strength from somewhere and tonight although it is Mum's birthday I feel her close to me. Some moments I forget she has died and I am about to speak to her before I realise she has gone and grief consumes me once again. Again it feels like yesterday that I lost her but today on her first birthday all I have done is to concentrate on getting this report finished and the distraction has helped.

I send the report to the HCC and label it *The 66 Points*

1. Patients not fed or given fluids, meal trays left on tables where patients are unable to reach.
2. No assistance with feeding — packets hard to open
3. If the menu the previous day is not completed patients are left without food the following day — confused patients are unaware they have to fill in a menu
4. Patients left lying down when meal tray is brought to them — they are unable to sit themselves up
5. Lack of concern by nursing staff when families have told them of their concerns over lack of nourishment
6. No monitoring of nourishment no accurate monitoring of input/output intake
7. Patient weight not monitored — even when concerns have been raised
8. Haphazard monitoring of bowels/urine
9. Buzzers left out of reach for patients to use

10. A long wait for the buzzer to be answered even longer at night
11. Staff are unable to assess the urgency of the call — often respond to a patient who has rang later and another patient has been waiting longer.
12. Patients having to wet themselves or to soil their beds due to waiting so long for a response
13. Patients left in soiled wet beds — often overnight
14. Patients not helped to the toilet — but told they must use the bed pan (staff too busy)
15. Over use of catheters — no explanation of why they are being used
16. Catheters not emptied often enough and left to overfill
17. Patients not helped to wash or those needing total care not washed at all.
18. When the staff have time to wash patients they are always put in hospital gowns which exposes them at the back, despite them asking to be put into their own nightwear
19. Dentures and hearing aids not given — dentures often left in mouths for days
20. Frail patients left sitting in chairs from very early in the morning, (7.30) until late at night when the night staff have time to put them into bed.
21. Confused patients allowed to roam the wards exposed wandering into male/female wards and staff ignoring them
22. Staff unable to manage confused patients
23. Confused patients fighting and arguing with other patients due to boredom
24. Staff shouting and pushing confused patients — ordering them back to their bed
25. Patients hitting out at nursing staff who have shouted at them.
26. Overuse of medication to control anger in a confused patient who the staff have upset
27. Patients calling out to staff and being ignored
28. Staff shouting, squealing and laughing through-out the night disturbing patients
29. Patients left without pain relief as two trained staff are rarely available to administer controlled drugs
30. Medication not given on time
31. Medication not monitored for side affects

32. All medication stopped on admission and often not restarted — despite patients being on the medication for years — no monitoring
33. Lack of general pain relief
34. Drugs required often not on the drug trolley — patients often told nurse will return with the required medications but often not given as nurse forgets to return as she is too busy
35. Wound dressings not changed or even checked by staff
36. Immobile patients not turned for pressure relief
37. Over use of health carers — often new to the ward and not told what they need to do — No guidance given by more senior staff
38. Observations not taken on a regular basis — machine often broken — or health carer hasn't been trained to take, read or respond to the results.
39. Staff not washing hands when it is required
40. Lack of hand wash and towels to wash hands
41. Lack of cleaning of equipment (tables, chairs, beds)
42. Isolation rooms often not cleaned after a patient has left(staff too busy) and another patients admitted
43. Lack of information around infection — not told or tested for MRSA, C Diff
44. Patients discharged without tests for the above but then readmitted a few days later — tested with a positive result but recorded as contracted at home
45. No compliance with manual handling — staff unaware of correct handling procedures
46. Lack of risk assessments
47. Patients often lifted by staff/patients dragged up the bed and left in pain
48. Patients put and left on commodes for long periods — often fall trying to get themselves back to bed
49. Staff roughly handling patients
50. Patients found on the floor not checked for injury by staff
51. Staff often rude to patients and families
52. Lack of consultation with family/carers
53. Family rarely told of diagnosis or medical opinions, test results
54. lack of communication between doctors and nursing staff
55. Lack of communication between confused patients, doctors

and nursing staff

56. All charts collected and filled in by staff at night — oblivious to what has happened during the day — often incorrect
57. Staff often in tears — telling relatives to complain on their behalf
58. Long periods where relatives search for staff to assist them with their relative.
59. Patients notes left lying around — often going missing when required
60. Staff lack skills to help relatives to deal with death — very little comfort from staff
61. Lack of training for staff which covers — basic needs, confused patients, handling aggression, risk assessment, manual handling how to take and respond to observations, medication, basic communication, dealing with death, wound dressings, nutrition, discharge planning, working in partnership
62. Complaints not being dealt with — issues overlooked
63. Notes/records distorted and altered
64. Discouraged from making official complaint as told to discuss with the ward staff
65. PALS found to be ineffective
66. PPIF found to be ineffective

Because this is what all of our loved ones had suffered on those wards. I thought it was significant that I told them what we had all experienced and not just what my Mum had suffered. That way I felt it would help to ensure that they did something as it wasn't just me saying that something was wrong at the hospital. I still felt I needed to prove my case or that I was determined that they had to believe what I was saying. I could feel the desperation inside me sometimes, other days I was more positive and knew I had the evidence now that was needed.

Unexpectedly I received a telephone call from someone from the HCC helpline who I had been in communication with. She told me that the HCC investigating team were having a meeting on Wednesday regarding the mortality at the hospital. Would I be able to send my report into them by then? I managed to finish it on Mum's birthday, the first birthday without her, 16th February 2008. I sent it recorded delivery and stood in the post office with hope that it would lead to something positive. It was odd standing there in the middle of the village post office as people passed me not realising the significance of what I was about to do.

The following week I was contacted by the same worker and it did lead to something positive as I had hoped. "We have inspected the hospital overnight and found many of the 66 points, you told us about," she tells me in a strong southern accent.

I felt sick. It was early in the morning and I was on my way to work, I pulled the car over and took the call. I could tell by her tone that the investigating team were very concerned about what they had found at the hospital. Sitting alone in the car I cried tears of relief, relief that someone believed me and relief that the suffering would come to an end. Perhaps I would soon be able to sleep. As soon as my head touched the pillow, I was back on the ward and sleep was proving to be impossible.

Who Do You Think You Are Kidding Mr Kidney?

In the meantime I had reluctantly agreed to meet with the management, I had felt a little railroaded into it. The former PPIF members had wanted to set up their own monitoring group and had mentioned this when we had met the MP at his surgery.

This was our first protest and even today can be seen on the internet on You tube[1]. I'd worried all week that nobody would turn up but I needn't the turnout was far greater than I had expected. I had spent the night preparing a banner for myself and the rest of the night getting my evidence together for the meeting.

Everyone at our meeting was in favour of attending the MP's surgery, we all agreed that it is an MP's responsibility to be acting on our behalf and he should be protecting the vulnerable. I had arranged to meet everyone at the local supermarket car park and I really didn't know who was going to turn up. At the meeting I had encouraged people to come along but I didn't know these people and had no idea if I could rely on them. I worried all night thinking I would be the only one to turn up.

I had contacted all of the press I could think of and all of the local radio stations. That week I heard about some dreadful cases where people had died on different wards at the hospital. I just couldn't understand why people were still dying under the same circumstances as my Mum and now it was months later but it sure steeled my nerves and made me determined to protest.

---

[1]http://www.youtube.com/watch?v=VL_l8KWMxGg

I'd tried to sleep but it was impossible and I ended up getting up and getting myself ready far earlier than I needed to. I walked the dog early hoping it would distract me but all I could do was worry. I couldn't decide what to wear should I wear a coat or should I wear a jacket. I plumped for a coat and I'm glad I did because the day was bitter I wished I had worn my gloves too.

I couldn't eat breakfast, I was too nervous, I could feel the nerves through my body as I drove. My foot shook every time I pressed the brake pedal and keeping it still was impossible. I tried to distract myself with Radio 4 news but I couldn't concentrate on anything else, apart from who would turn up. I was dreading getting there and finding myself alone that was my biggest fear today. Oddly I didn't even think about what I would be saying to the MP. I knew over the last few months I had heard about so much harm it would be easy for me to talk about. I just wanted it to stop.

I needn't have worried though because as I turned the corner into the car park I could see a crowd of people but for one minute I didn't think they were there to meet me. I thought they must be waiting for something else as I didn't recognise any of them and they were in the wrong meeting place anyway. I had arranged to meet everyone at the entrance to the supermarket so I drove straight past that crowd. Just as I was thinking, 'if only they were here to meet me,' I saw another crowd at the entrance and that lifted my mood. Little did I know that the other group of people that I had spotted at the car park entrance was here to meet me, too. I was so relieved that was until the shop manager came out and asked us to move. "Move away immediately." He told us with as much force as he could muster. He was very unpleasant and one member of the group, Chris Dalziel, reproached him for it.

"Have some understanding. We're only meeting here, we're not causing any harm to anyone and we're going in a minute anyway."

Although there were a lot of introductions going on, as I hardly knew anyone, I remember thinking that she would be a useful member of the group and one to utilise. I was proved right as Chris Dalziel has proved to be a great campaigner and a dear friend.

Together there were around thirty people, all with banners. The surgery was being held across the road and we walked the short distance holding those banners high. Most of us had used the same slogan that we had discussed at the meeting, "Stop the neglect in our hospital," and it was meant for David Kidney. As we turned the corner I saw that the press were waiting for us. I had told them about the protest but didn't think they would attend, it was a real bonus to see them. The *Staffordshire Newsletter* was present but also the free local newspaper the *Staffordshire Post*. The *Staffordshire Newsletter* took pictures of us all and then went but the *Staffordshire Post* stayed with us throughout the meeting. Even their photographer told us that one of his relatives had been harmed at the hospital. People were coming from everywhere telling me of the harm the hospital had caused them.

I had never been inside the Chetwynd Centre before, it is a fantastic building and stands very imposing at the entrance to the town. In the past it had been the boys' grammar school and was now a 6th Form College. We all stood by the entrance while the photographer took the pictures, every now and again he asks us to move around. Moving around is keeping us warm and we are all hoping that we will soon be finished and allowed to go into the warmth of the building. The photos seem to take an age it is the first time that we have had photographs taken and we are inexperienced. Now it is different we are all experienced after nearly five years of being photographed as a group we all know what to do to get it over quicker for us all. But this was our first time and the photographer had to continually shout instructions, "Look this way," and, "Turn the placard to me."

Eventually, frozen, we were all shown into a small waiting area. We're obviously not expected as we are packed into a tiny room. You could clearly see the surprise on his assistant's face I don't think she knew what to do with us. I'm sure it was the first time she would have seen a bunch of protesters asking the MP for help to stop the deaths at our local hospital. Whilst we sit and wait for the MP, Dan, Laura's boyfriend, starts to interview those who had come along. Though I could hear them talking it wasn't until some months later when I saw it on You Tube that I realised what had been said. He continued to record our meeting with David Kidney. He did a fantastic job and it

can still be seen today

It was the first time I had met David Kidney and I was totally unimpressed with him. He shook hands with me and I felt myself trying to wipe my hand in my pocket afterwards. His hand shake was weak and clammy, I avoided it in any future meetings with him and there were several over the next few years.

It was one of the first times I had spoken at such a meeting but again I found that the words came easily, I felt I was speaking for the many that didn't now have a voice. The first thing he did was to deny that he had said he was happy with the standard of care at the hospital but that was exactly what his letter had said that he had written to me previously. I could

have kicked myself for not bringing it along but who would suspect that an MP would deny something he has written.

I didn't feel nervous at all, I was just so determined that something needed to be done urgently at the hospital to avoid anyone else suffering. Although I was reluctant about setting up a monitoring group at this point I couldn't see what else we could do. Getting someone to believe us that there was a problem was proving impossible. It was what the former PPIF members wanted and I was relying on them to advise me on the setting up of such a group. David Kidney seemed to jump onto this solution too quickly for my liking too. He said nothing about the poor care that we were telling him about instead giving us a lecture on the history of the PPIF. There we were standing in front of him with banners saying *stop the neglect of the vulnerable at our hospital* and there he was getting us to come up with the solution.

When I got home and reflected on the day I felt we had got no further in stopping the abuse at the hospital. The fight would need to continue as he seemed more concerned with getting me to meet Martin Yeates.

The following week both papers covered the protest on their front page but the main story on the inside cover was my criticism of the PPIF. During the meeting with Kidney I had said that the PPIF had proved ineffective and he had agreed. I had mentioned about the inspection report where they had mentioned a lid missing off a jam jar. My criticisms had inflamed the PPIF and the Chair, Ms Whysall, had listed their achievements at the hospital on the front page of the paper. 'Not much point if people keep dying,' I thought but at the same time I didn't want to fight with anyone. I was forced to apologise. I knew I shouldn't be apologising but the last thing I needed was to upset people I needed them to help. However nobody called for an apology from David Kidney, despite his agreeing with me.

Though I felt my apology exposed them for all they were worth and that was very little in my eyes. I said, "Of course we are impressed with the PPIF achievements and who wouldn't be but what concerns me is why no one is doing anything about the abuse of our most vulnerable." I added that I couldn't see the point of setting up a bus service to and from the hospital when patients were dying of neglect once they arrived.

'There's some odd folk about,' I thought, how strange to focus on peripheral concerns when there was so much suffering to address. Martin Yeates had added a comment praising the PPIF for all their hard work and all the improvements they had been involved in. He added "A number of improvements had been introduced at the hospital as a direct result of the forum's reports"

No mention of the abuse going on in the hospital or what action they were going to take to improve the care, nothing. I was shocked that they thought it was acceptable to write such an article.

A few days after the meeting David Kidney wrote to say that I needed to meet Martin Yeates to discuss the setting up of a monitoring group. He wrote to tell me that he had discussed it with Martin Yeates and he was in support of us monitoring the hospital. He wrote

"I have been on the telephone with Martin Yeates this morning and he would like to discuss this idea with you"

Again he urged me to arrange a meeting as soon as possible as it was important to start the dialogue between us. He even suggested he chaired a meeting between Martin Yeates and myself. I don't think he realised I doubted his integrity too. On reflection who would expect a member of the public to set up a monitoring group to monitor standards at an NHS hospital? I realised I needed to be very cautious here as this wasn't a normal response to allegations of abuse of our most vulnerable.

I was reluctant to start any dialogue with this sort of management either, the sort that was deeply in denial to the harm it was causing people. The reply I had received to my letter of complaint had confirmed this and reading an identical reply received by another member of the group a year earlier had made up my mind that this management could not be trusted but I was also realising that neither could I trust the MP David Kidney.

A few days later I was invited by one of the borough councillors, Ann Edgeller, to attend the OSC meeting where the hospital management would be present to answer questions raised by members of the borough council. We were greeted outside the chamber by councillor Edgeller. She was attempting to be polite but I could sense that she was looking down on me. She was done up to the nines with a beige satin suit that looked like she had squeezed herself into.

"When will I have an opportunity to speak?" I ask tentatively.

"The public aren't allowed to speak", she tells me.

"Oh, I didn't realise that," I add, surprised at her answer.

"No, as a member of the public you are not allowed to speak but your questions have been put to the hospital management"

"Whoopee,' I thought, am I not lucky and very honoured to even be invited? Laura came along with me and we sat in silence stunned throughout at what we were hearing.

The meeting was held in the Borough Council building in the council chamber. It was a grand, beautiful room with dark oak panelling, all very distinguished. Oddly this was the very room where the M.S.P.I. would be held three years later.

Some days I was finding it difficult to get up and get dressed. Some days everything was an effort. I made sure I did it every day, having the cafe to work on had helped. Today the tasks were easier, perhaps today someone would listen. Getting Laura to dress for the meeting was a real effort though I had dressed smartly and wanted her to do the same. But you know what teenagers are like, jeans and a t-shirt and she was comfy. She ended up wearing her work trousers and she looked a treat although we both looked out of place as we sat alone in the public area. Rows of chairs but just the two of us sat as if we were waiting for a performance to begin, neither of us spoke and no one spoke to us. Little did we know that it was to be a performance and it was solely for our benefit.

In the centre of the room sat the committee around a large wooden table and the management sat at the top of the table. Everyone wore suits and the women wore their finery, assorted perfume filled the air and every now and again tickled your nostrils.

The representatives who came along from the hospital were three heads of department, one being Helen Perrin, the head of communication. The three questions I had put forward were put to them and they managed with such skill to turn the concerns around and tell us about the fantastic job the hospital was doing and the wonderful care it was providing.

It was my first exposure to the hospital spin team and also the OSC, who were really impressed with the hospital management's performances. Not one of the councillors challenged them. They all seemed so old or uninterested in the proceedings, moribund and spent. Ann Edgeller, ally that I thought she was, ended the meeting by thanking them profusely for coming along to address the committee.

She was the Chair of the committee and I won't bother to describe her just think of Marina from "Last of the Summer Wine". Anyway she proved to be of little use.

As the meeting progressed I could tell the way it was going to end and I just wanted the ground to swallow us up. There we were telling them that the hospital was so bad it was abusing patients and they were completely ignoring us and believing the management, they seemed to be hanging on their every word. The three questions I had asked were completely dismissed by them and they managed instead to give a presentation on the high standards of care they provided, the low infection rates and on and on went the spin.

They even mentioned a Red Tray system to help to identify the vulnerable who needed feeding, they implied that they had this system in place but I knew for definite they didn't. In fact it became a sore subject for me, the Red Tray system, and a source of great annoyance. Several managers since tried to imply that the red trays had been introduced onto the wards but in actual fact they weren't introduced to the hospital until 2011.

After the meeting I managed to speak to the three managers and although it was bitterly cold standing outside I spent a whole hour with the head of communication telling her that everything she had said to the councillors was untrue. I told her all about the eight weeks I had just endured on Ward 11, I told her about the other relatives I had met, I told her everything because of course she wanted to hear.

"My Mother suffered and so did the other patients on the ward," my teeth were chattering with the cold as the wind howled around us.

"I'm so sorry the hospital failed your Mother," she said with as much sincerity as she could muster.

"But what about those patients who are suffering now?" I ask as once again all of the failings are being spoken about as if they are in the past and I must tell her that.

"Everything you said in that meeting just isn't true." I'm trying to be firm with her but my teeth chattering doesn't help my argument.

We are stood under the Borough Council car park it is dark and spitting with rain. We couldn't have picked a worse place. We are exposed to the elements on a cold, wet February evening. Despite the cold every now and again the smell of urine fills my nostrils and then the wind picks up and moves it on.

"Come and meet Martin, come and discuss your concerns with him." Her teeth are chattering too but I get a sense of her determination when she pulls the collar of her coat up tighter around her neck. She's cold but she is going nowhere yet.

"Why what more can I tell him?"I had written everything in my letter of complaint, what more did they need from me before they started to improve the care.

"It's the only way forward." she tells me

"The only way forward is for the hospital to improve." I say it in a matter of fact way and I feel Laura at the side of me, her arm linked through mine. She squeezes it tighter, I sensed she was offering her support at my statement.

There was no challenge from her she accepted everything I was saying, her priority was to get me to meet Martin Yeates. Oh it was the best thing to do and the only way to move forward and get any improvements, although I had just sat through a meeting where they had been saying there was nothing wrong. In fact they were one of the top hospitals in the country or so they had just told us all. They were about to find out if they were to become a Foundation Trust hospital, at the time I had no idea what this meant but I would soon find out.

She was so convincing and I was probably worn down and at this point, I agreed to meet with the management team. At the time I thought, 'What have I got to lose? They can't eat me, can they'?

I was desperate, running out of options. But when I got home I worried that I had done the wrong thing by committing myself to a meeting, it just didn't feel right. That had been what had guided me all my life if something didn't feel right I didn't do it and tonight I felt that I had taken the wrong course. It just seemed that everybody wanted me to meet the management, the DoH, the MP, the councillors, the papers, they were all urging me to, particularly to meet with Martin Yeates.

The following morning I received an email from Helen Perrin with a few suggested dates for the meeting and an agenda. For the next few weeks I went back and forward challenging the agenda with her. The agenda she sent was very similar to the agenda that they had presented to the OSC. They would cover the complaints procedure, *Essence of Care*, infection rates, staffing issues and training. I told her I had heard all this before at the OSC meeting and that isn't what I wanted to hear about. It didn't matter what I said to her the same agenda kept coming back to me by email.

Sam had agreed to come with me to the meeting and on the agenda the hospital had put us down to discuss a monitoring group. Something that I wasn't happy with in the first place but those that had been involved in the PPIF had wanted this.

Alone I didn't think that this was something that we should be doing and I knew I certainly didn't have the skills or the time to monitor a hospital. It was with great reluctance that I had agreed to attend the meeting with the management. The following week it was reported in the papers and the date was given that we would meet with them. The hospital had given a statement to the press about the meeting as for the last couple of weeks they had criticised me openly in the press for not agreeing to meet with them.

Someone had even written a letter which was published criticising me for complaining but then not agreeing to meet with the management team. I suspected later that this was instigated by the hospital themselves to put pressure on me to meet with them. Throughout the campaign there have been several attempts to discredit me in the press but this was the first and the start of an orchestrated campaign against me. It was the first time I had ever been in a newspaper let alone my decisions and actions being condemned in one. All over the billboards one evening throughout the town was my decision to meet with the management "Hospital campaigner agrees to work with the management", they said and that felt really strange. It felt quite odd but at the same time I was starting to feel as if the group was worrying the hospital management.

It was just a pity that it wasn't worrying them enough to invest in improvements for patients at the hospital. By now a nurse had made contact with me anonymously and told me that nothing had changed and she was desperate to leave. Several more people came forward with complaints that their loved ones had been harmed. It was so difficult knowing about all

179

these cases of poor care and yet not being able to do anything about it. I decided to contact the HCC again and ask them what they were doing as the poor care continued.

I was told that an announcement was imminent, they couldn't tell me what it was but I would be pleased. Before there was a public announcement the HCC would contact me first to inform me. I could only think that this meant they would be investigating the hospital, my only thought was that the abuse would stop. At the same time I asked for some advice on a monitoring group and they advised that this wasn't a good idea, which was exactly what I wanted to hear. This was what I had felt all along and having it confirmed to me reassured me.

Also after spending more time with the former PPIF members I soon learnt that none of us had the skills or knowledge to monitor the hospital. The PPIF members that I thought could help didn't really have what it would take and they didn't appreciate the difficult task it would be. They had more of an idea than I had in specific areas but realistically we just didn't have the knowledge or skills that would be needed. We were amateurs and this hospital needed professionals.

I was also contacted by someone anonymously, it was the first time that someone had rung me and not wanted to tell me who they were, but as the campaign progressed it became common that I would be contacted with information and the caller wouldn't want to give their details. Once I was given information by a man who told me that if anyone found out it was him speaking to me he would seek me down and break every bone in my body. 'Delightful,' I thought. To make matters worse when I took the call I was sitting opposite the local BBC health correspondent, Michele Paduano, or Paddy as I would come to know him.

The caller told me that under no circumstances would the management allow us to set up a monitoring group and they were just stringing us along. Also that at the next Governors meeting the board would be voting on awarding the management a huge pay rise along with stopping unannounced inspections. I was so angry and felt so betrayed, whilst patients were dying of neglect the Governors were about to vote on awarding themselves pay rises! I was blinded with rage, the despair on Ward 11 kept returning in my head. The lack of pillows, blankets, mattresses, drip stands, hoists, commodes, the very basics were all in short supply. This failing management wanted to award themselves a pay rise whilst the wards were starved of equipment and staff. How dare they?

I called a meeting. I wasn't allowing this to happen, 'Over my dead body,' I thought. I rang around everyone who had attended the last meeting and arranged another for the next night. Although it was short notice most could make it, they were all very keen to meet again. I had also heard back from Baroness Masham and she had alerted Sir Ian Kennedy, the Chief Executive of the HCC. At this time his name meant nothing to me but that later changed as he gave evidence to the MSPI that the group later successfully campaigned for.

The rest of the group agreed that they shouldn't be getting a pay rise but it was at this meeting that I realised the division between some within the group. There were those that had lost and those that hadn't and the people that hadn't lost didn't seem to have the sensitivity to understand and want to listen to the bereaved. They didn't have the patience, they wanted action now. They wanted to put a sticking plaster on but we knew the cancer needed to be cut out, it went too deep. I knew this wasn't possible at this stage as we had no power but with numbers and more time we would.

It was at this meeting that I realised that within the group we had something special. We had a group of people who were prepared to give up their time to help others but at the same time there were others that were not group players and would prove to be a hindrance to getting anything done. They were unhappy with the amount of time that was being spent at the meetings listening to the bereaved talk about their loss but at the same time I knew before they were given the time and space they couldn't move forward. I had some counselling experience and it proved invaluable and I didn't realise how I had maintained those skills without knowing it.

Even more people turned up to this meeting than last time, all who had loved ones who had suffered at the hospital. New faces but people I had either communicated with online or had spoken to on the phone. For some I knew that they didn't want to sit and listen to people talking about the loss of their loved ones. I could tell by their body language and I could sense their impatience as I refused to intervene and move the meeting along. The information I gained proved to be invaluable throughout the campaign and now five years later the knowledge I have developed from listening to people helps me to guide families through the complaints procedure.

It was the first time I had met Deb, she was one of the first to write to me but she couldn't make our first meeting. She lost her dear Mother, Ellen Linstead, on 13th December 2006. She had gone into the hospital in remission for cancer but needing rehabilitation. They did that alright, she ended up with every HAI going and Deb telling us about her Mother's experience left many of us in tears. Her voice was quiet but clear as she told us about one day when she had been visiting her Mother. As she had opened the ward door she had heard her Mother screaming. She ran to her room and found Ellen hanging off the commode chair, she found out she had been left on it for hours, the nurse forgetting she had left her on it. Her Mother had suffered appalling care and even in death she had no dignity. She was told that because of the amount of HAI she had contracted in the hospital she would have to be buried in a body bag. Even after death her family were made to suffer as they were not allowed to say goodbye as they told the family she had to be sealed in a body bag to contain the infections.

Although Deb was devastated still at the loss and the nature of that loss of her Mother I could sense her strength and her skills that would be useful for the campaign group. Deb has been a tower of strength for me at times when I have needed it most. She has always been there when I have needed her and is now a dear and trusted friend. It's not that I am a needy person but there have been times when I have needed just her and no one else would do. You see like my Mum her Mum was her best friend and that created an unbreakable bond between us.

Deb was in her late 30s tall blonde and very thin but she had the most beautiful personality. The first thing that struck you about her was her eyes, talking to her it was difficult to focus on anything else. They were hypnotic. Like us all Deb was suffering and her grief was never far away. Deb was angry, angry that after searching for answers for two years she had been fobbed off. Deb and her family was one of the few at the meeting who had met Yeates. Although she was angry and that was never far away she could still support others and offer a shoulder to cry on for others.

I managed to lose those in the group who weren't team players by refusing to go along with the monitoring group plan. There was no big fall out, nothing as dramatic as that. We parted on amicable terms but I knew they didn't have the mindset that was needed and that was crucial for the campaign to work. It was those who I first thought had all the knowledge, far more than I, but they proved to be too isolated, lone wolves if you like, and for a group situation they were not suited.

Now in the Premier League

It was at this meeting that I also realised the cafe wasn't big enough to accommodate us all, the room was packed and we didn't have nearly enough seats for everybody. I went home thinking that we needed to branch out, we had outgrown our headquarters already.

The hospital's catchment area served several towns and Mid Staffs Hospital was made up of two hospitals, a small one in Cannock and the main, acute hospital in Stafford. People who used the hospital and were contacting me were mostly either from Cannock, Stafford or Rugeley. Our next meeting was arranged for Rugeley, the venue had been secured by a relative who had contacted me. She had lost her Mother at Stafford following her neglect. This had happened in 2005 and yet she was still no further in getting answers from the hospital. She had even involved the HCC but here she was all these years later still being tortured trying to find out why her Mother had died.

After our visit to David Kidney's surgery our story had been front page on both weekly newspapers, *The Staffordshire Newsletter* and *The Staffordshire Post*. I had contacted the *E&S*, our local daily newspaper, and they had barely covered the story. I wanted to know why when so many people were being harmed and I was left so shocked at their response. In fact it was another moment where I was left speechless and in tears. The reporter I spoke to said the *E&S* readers would not be interested in pictures and stories of older people dying in our local hospital and they certainly wouldn't be covering our campaign.

Peter Atkins was a local journalist who wrote a weekly column for *E&S*, he had once been editor of *The Newsletter*. I had recently been introduced to him by Jackie who had lost her young daughter. Peter had written a small piece criticising the trust board for wanting to award themselves pay rises once they had become a Foundation Trust. He had also mentioned our campaign, an indication he was supportive of us.

Now I just thought a hospital was a hospital and had never heard of a Foundation Trust (FT) or Monitor until early February 2008 when the hospital was awarded FT status.

A press release from the hospital on the 1st February told us that following a searching investigation the FT regulator Monitor had concluded that the hospital was well managed and financially strong.

Martin Yeates made a statement thanking the 3,000 staff for helping to take the hospital into the premier league of hospitals. He added,

"We have been on a remarkable journey as we aimed to achieve our aim of becoming a FT. After a rigorous process to check on our financial stability and our arrangements for ensuring the quality and safety of our healthcare, I am delighted to say *we did it*".

FTs are part of the NHS but have significant managerial and financial freedom. The aim is to develop services best suited to local needs, along with greater involvement from patients and the public in deciding what they want from their local hospitals.

As you can imagine I scratched my head when I read this. I was walking home from work and had nipped in to get the *E&S,* since the campaign had started I didn't miss an edition. "You need to sit down before you read it tonight," the newsagent told me. I smiled not really understanding or wanting to understand what he was saying, I'd had a hard day. "The premier league!" He said as he laughed. As soon as I saw the front page I realised what he meant. Both of us couldn't believe what we were reading, like me he had heard of many complaints about the hospital. Being a local newsagent he met with lots of people who had been harmed in one way or another by the hospital. Once you started asking it seemed everyone you spoke to had a story to tell and it wasn't a nice one either.

All the local press were now keeping a close eye on the hospital there was a story in one of the papers practically every day. There seemed to be either a press release from the hospital or some other story to be reported on.

On the day FT was awarded the patients were treated to a salmon dinner and the staff were each given a £25 M&S voucher as a gesture of appreciation from the management for all their hard work during the FT process. Ironically some of the staff were unhappy with the vouchers and sent them back to the hospital in disgust. We never found out why but I made a comment that the money would have been better spent on pillows and blankets for the patients. The vouchers had cost £70,000 and would have funded a couple of nursing posts.

The hospital being awarded foundation trust status was a huge shock and came completely out of the blue. Particularly when Martin Yeates's statement to the press had said the hospital was now in the *premier league*. The announcement had really rocked me and I had contacted the HCC once again telling them that more people had come forward with concerns and a flagship hospital Mid Staffs wasn't!

I was also contacted by the previous chair of the OSC who had now become a Governor of the hospital, Phillip Jones. Phillip was a lovely man very much a gentleman and very polite, perhaps too polite to be in a position where he should be challenging people. He made contact telling me that the Chair, Toni Brisby, was an authoritarian who ruled the hospital with an iron fist. He had several concerns about what was going on and had found out that now the hospital had been awarded FT status they were talking about closing their board meetings to the public. They were also considering awarding themselves pay increases that would see the Chair's salary rise from around £15,000 to £45,000 for a 15 hour week. He mentioned the next Governor's meeting and asked if we could attend.

I got in touch with everyone that had contacted me. At the group's second meeting we had tried to organise a round robin where we each contacted one person instead of me contacting everyone. This was proving helpful as it was saving me a lot of time.

I was starting to realise that getting press coverage was an important factor in any campaign and I needed their support. Every other local paper seemed to be behind us apart from the E&S and because it was a daily paper it was the most important. I had another run in with one of their reporters a few days later when we protested at the first Governor's meeting we attended.

It was bitterly cold as were most of our protests in those early days. The attendance was even better than to the MP's surgery protest and I was totally overwhelmed at the amount of people that turned up, and in such terrible weather. *The Staffordshire Post* reporter was there and *The Staffordshire Newsletter* reporter along with *The Cannock Mercury*, a weekly paper that served the Cannock area. The reporter Jane Hartwell had printed a letter I had written the previous week and had been out and interviewed me. She had told me that the editor of the Mercury, Lindy Young, was very supportive of our campaign and would cover our stories when she could, I was overjoyed. I felt it was a breakthrough as we were now reaching the people of Cannock.

Taking the pictures seemed to take an age though as the wind was hampering everything. It was freezing and the wind was howling around the Postgraduate Centre which was situated at the back of the hospital. Most of those that turned up were older people and I was concerned that they were getting so cold.

As soon as the pictures were finished Helen Perrin, the communication manager, seized her opportunity and invited us in for a warm drink. I didn't hesitate when she offered, I knew some of the group were shivering. Whilst she served us all hot drinks she also told us that the Chair, Toni Brisby, would allow us to address the board of Governors for fifteen minutes. Whilst she was telling me this Toni Brisby, who I had never met before, walked over and introduced herself. With her white hair and ghostly face she instantly struck me as cold and alien.

"I'd like to take this opportunity to tell you that I will no longer be accepting a pay rise." She's trying to win me over but I know she wouldn't have hesitated to put her snout in the trough if we hadn't created a stink. The bitterness in her voice reinforces this.

I didn't get chance to reply as we were immediately shown into a room and around a large table sat fifteen governors.

187

Squeezed at the edge of the room were ourselves, who stood, and also the management team who were seated around the edges. Little did I know but right next to me sat the one and only Martin Yeates. Never again would I get so close to him.

Now this Chair did look a formidable character and my observations proved to be right. I am pleased to say that I have very few regrets about the way I have handled this campaign. But I do have one regret that still today, nearly five years later, manages to eat away at me when I allow it.

"This is an unprecedented occasion." She began, "Never before has the public been allowed to address the Council of Governors. You shall each be allowed two minutes to tell your story. Please, raise your hands if you want to speak." She reminded me of a sadistic schoolmistress.

Those brave enough do raise their hands, I think there were four of us. She instructs me to begin. I start with

"My Mother entered Stafford Hospital a strong, wonderful woman and she lost her life through a combination of neglect, abuse and indifference." I'm terrified but I have no reason to be because as soon as I open my mouth the words are there and before I know it my two minutes are up and I have told them some of what I have seen people suffering on Ward 11. What surprises me is that each time I speak about the horror during those eight weeks, unconsciously something else comes out of my mouth. I feel as if I have buried so much and each time I speak it gets easier but today it doesn't, I find myself in tears. I try and choke them back, I want to concentrate on what the other patients suffered. Again I must let Mum take a back seat and accept I have lost her, it's about stopping it happening to others.

When I have finished Rebecca Davis speaks and I fight to hold back the tears as she tells us about her proud Grandmother who the hospital destroyed. You can hear the pain in her voice but I can also sense the bravery. Her Mother stands at the side of her holding onto her arm too raw to speak herself. As she starts her voice echoes within the room she tries to control herself but every now and again the pain within her breaks through. She tells us that her Grandmother only went in with a broken arm and ended up a shadow of her former self.

I later learn that this woman gave her life to the sick, a nurse all her life, caring for the vulnerable. Even after retirement she continued to care as she was a volunteer for St John's Ambulance. Rebecca has bought along pictures of her Grandmother there is one of her as a nurse and others taken during her stay in the hospital. In front of us sits a small petite woman, beautiful with eyes that would melt the heart. She looks so proud in her nurse uniform she looks immaculate as she sits in her starched outfit. The picture shows a wise but kind woman. Her smile is radiant and displays a warmth to her that the picture is able to capture.

In contrast the ones taken in the hospital are no different from pictures you see of a woman returning from the concentration camps. She is covered in bruises, unkempt and broken. In one she sits slumped in a chair, she has given up, it looks as if she has already died or wants to. Her matted hair covers her face and her eyes look dead, dead like my Mum's did.

"Look. Look what they did to her."

I struggle to fight back the tears, the air in the room is stifling, everyone is in silence apart from the Chair herself, who stops her in mid flow and tells her, "The two minutes are up". Rebecca is so close to me as we are squashed into the door way. I can feel Rebecca's breath on my shoulder and if I listen even her heartbeat. She wants to say more, her body rocks side to side as she ponders what she hasn't been able to tell them, has she missed anything important?

She then points to the next person who has raised their hand. Although I have heard what these families' loved ones have suffered hearing it again is no easier a second time and in the room you could hear a pin drop.

Jackie is next, Jackie has come along with her husband and they have attended our two meetings. Their daughter, a young woman, had her life ended at Mid Staffs. The hospital had given her chemotherapy when she hadn't needed it. She had acquired C. Difficile and other HAI during her admission and the family watched over a period of weeks as the hospital destroyed her.

"She was only twenty six."

The hospital had even messed up her death certificate putting the wrong date of birth and not recording she had a HAI. Jackie spoke so bravely, I just couldn't imagine what it would feel like to lose a child. I hugged Laura close to me, at least I had only lost my elderly Mother and I was finding that hard enough to live with.

"That's two minutes." Brisby sensed the mood well and realising how unreasonable she was sounding, she added, "We have a very busy schedule today and we don't want to be here all day do we? It is important we stick to time."

Nobody says a word there is silence apart from the sound of a few people crying from those that have spoken. I can see Jackie's face, the pain of her loss shows clearly and I want to reach out and comfort her.

Chris Dalziel spoke next she had lost George, her dear husband of 42 years, at the hospital. George had walked in a proud man and had been reduced to half the size he was, they had practically starved him to death. He gave up destroyed by the uncaring environment, begging for pain relief.

Following his death and the reading of his case notes, they found George was never given any pain relief, even the morphine that he had been prescribed. Even his death surrounded in mystery and very soon I was to hear of many similar deaths with the hospital using the same scenario on other families.

"He died in agony. Screaming in pain."

"That is enough we now need to move on" The Chair rudely stopped Chris talking. At that moment a relative who I had only met last week put his hand up, wanting to speak. Hearing us speaking had given him the courage and he now wanted to tell the others about his poor wife's death.

The man had rung me the previous week and I had gone out to his house to meet him the day after he had buried his wife of sixty years. It was a dreadful evening, pitch black and the rain was coming down in buckets. I was frozen but the first thing that struck me was the warmth, not only from his home but from Jeff himself. It felt like I was meeting a friend who I had known for some time. I felt so at ease sitting with him and as I sipped tea he poured out his heart and talked about the suffering of his dear wife, Irene. He showed me pictures of Irene when she was young, pictures taken on their wedding day and pictures taken more recently. Her smile was enigmatic and she was a very attractive woman. Little did I know at this stage but her smile would help to light up my room when I would hang her picture proudly in my cafe when I created the *Wall of Shame* the morning the Health Care Commission Report was

190

announced on March 18th 2009, a year after I first met him.

He was heartbroken following her death, the guilt had got to him and at times it was hard to sit and listen to. Irene suffered with dementia and although elderly himself he had been her full time carer. Jeff was seventy nine, himself and although small in stature he was a strong man still.

Irene had gone into hospital with a urine infection and over four weeks he had watched her waste away through neglect. It must have been dreadful for him to see her so uncared for after he had cared for her so well, it was heartbreaking. He told me through tears that his wife had been a proud woman and they hadn't even put a comb through her hair in all the time she was in the hospital. She hadn't been bathed, left so unkempt and yet there wasn't a damn thing he could do about it. Another proud woman they had destroyed and one that he had loved and cared for himself so well.

She hadn't died in the hospital, they had sent her home in the middle of the night, a bitterly cold winter's night, in her nightdress. Later I learn that she is one of many that I hear from that have been sent home with cannulas still in their arms. Some either returned to their GPs or to the hospital where one elderly Mother I met with was made to wait five hours in the A & E department to get one removed after being discharged sick the previous day.

Luckily for Irene her son was an ambulance driver and was there in the early hours to meet the ambulance, getting her into the house he realised she still had the cannula fitted in her arm. It was bad enough that the hospital had discharged a sick elderly woman during the middle of a winter's night without leaving that in her arm.

Jeff had worked all his life, once working down the pit and eventually retiring from his own business making stone fireplaces. They had both had a wonderful life and a very close marriage until Irene developed dementia. The wonderful retirement that they had planned was cruelly spoilt by her illness and instead Jeff spent his retirement caring for his dear wife. He tries to fight back tears as he tells me of the struggle to get anyone to help at the hospital. Sadly it's beginning to sound all too familiar, the struggle that families are having to face when they have tried to raise concerns at Mid Staffs.

"I'm afraid you had your chance. You should have put your

hand up at the beginning."

Why didn't I speak up for him? Why didn't I tell her that he had just buried his wife? The wife that her hospital had destroyed. But I didn't and the moment moved on. In fact I hadn't noticed but a couple of the Governors were in tears.

"We need a break after what we have just heard," Councillor Phillip Jones meekly raises his hand.

"We have a very busy schedule to get through". The chair bites back.

Another brave soul asks for a break. She wipes her eyes as she looks at the Chair, hoping her tears will convince her. She's a small woman with grey hair. Her face is kind, and although it's too soft to stand up to this one she continues as the Chair shakes her head.

"I'm too distressed to continue," she pleads looking at the others for support.

"Yes. We need a break," another adds her support. The Chair's anger is evident as she slams down her pen, the irritation evident in her voice she asks for hands to be put up to vote for an adjournment. Those wanting the adjournment won by one vote and we all begin to file out the room. As I turn and before I have reached the door Martin Yeates pushes past me and tries to race out of the door. It's the first time I have seen him in the flesh and the description I have heard from relatives comes to mind. I have only seen him in pictures and he is much smaller than I thought but he does remind me of a used car salesman or an insurance broker, just as I'd been told. Without thinking I chase after him and Chris is by my side, she calls out to him.

"What are you running away for, Mr Yeates?"

I stand at the top of the stairs whilst he runs down them and I call out, "I thought you wanted to talk to me." Alongside him I see he is with the E&S reporter, they both look up but say nothing. They both continue to run down the stairs together and Chris and I return to the others who have now congregated outside the meeting room. Seeing the reporter with Yeates later plays on my mind and I'm confused as to why the reporter would be with Yeates and not us, particularly after what they have just heard. Was that why the E&S didn't want to cover our campaign? Were they too close to Martin Yeates?

As soon as I return to the others I am surrounded by a group of Governors, these particular Governors I later learn are very supportive of the Chair and the current management team. One person who came and spoke to me and who stuck in my mind was a staff Governor, Sandra Barrington. Being a nurse herself she was horrified at what she had just heard, or that's what she said. I thought she was saying all the right things until she went on to tell us that now things had improved at the hospital. Her advice was to meet with Martin Yeates and the other Governors who were with her said the same thing.

I couldn't help myself because as soon as anyone said that I needed to meet with Yeates it set off warning signals inside me and I could feel my anger rising.

"But he has just run off," I remind them. "He's a coward! Only a coward would run away. That hospital hasn't improved. Nothing's changed. Jeff lost his wife last week. In fact three other families have contacted me this last week."

"We have been tirelessly following the Essence of Care and implementing the correct care pathways to ensure that the hospital provides a much improved service in the future." This Sandra Barrington could twitter on about the Essence of Care and the care pathways but recent cases were evidence the hospital was neglecting patients and the wards were still starved of staff.

"Eight weeks ago Helen Moss announced more nurses as a result of the staffing review. Where are they? 'Cos the families ringing me haven't seen them." I reply.

Their faces tell me everything, they are worried that they haven't been able to pacify me. At the same time though I realise that it doesn't matter what we have told them, they are convinced that the hospital is doing well. That really is a worry, they are like robots.

As I pushed my way out the door I noticed how many police had been present. I hadn't noticed them on the way in but outside stood four policemen. All male, all in uniform and all different sizes. I always think how intimidating their uniforms look and today my impression is no different. 'Now come on!' I thought, 'We are hardly dangerous.' The average age of the group is around sixty and the majority use walking sticks. May Day anarchists we weren't.

Following our first protest at the MP's surgery I had been visited by the police. It was the following day to be exact and they put the fear of god into me at first. After I went home and thought about it I realised that that is exactly what they wanted me to feel. I suspect they wanted to frighten me so that I wouldn't protest again. Of course it was all very pleasant and he had called in to see me for my own good. And of course the best advice he could give me was to meet with Martin Yeates.

That put me on alert straight away and then he told me that I had actually broken the law by organising a protest and walking across the road with the group. When I questioned him on this he had said I was allowed to protest but I had to give three weeks notice of my intent. And as for a walking protest that was a different matter. If one of the protesters had been harmed walking the 50 yards across the road to the Chetwynd Centre I would have been liable, it was Health and Safety law. I shook my head as he spoke as there he was quoting health and safety law to me and there was a hospital up the road that was allowing people to die in dreadful circumstances. I said nothing but I think he realised that if he had intended to put the frighteners on me it hadn't worked.

Four years later I had the privilege of speaking at a conference in relation to the law and the NHS. I spoke about the lack of support vulnerable patients have had from the police involved with MSFT hospital but also throughout the NHS. One grieving woman came to see me following the death of her husband at the hospital. He had tried to escape from the hospital as his care was so poor and he was being left without pain relief. The police had found him on his way home and physically dragged him back to the ward fighting and screaming about his poor care. I also spoke about other poor care I had heard about and yet no action has been taken against any of the staff despite clear cases of abuse.

Over the next year at every protest we organised the police would be present despite us always protesting in silence and the group being mostly elderly. Some even turned up in wheelchairs others on mobility scooters but they still turned up to watch over us.

Even the police wanted me to meet with the management and I just couldn't understand why. Someone had once said to me if you report a hole in the road to the council would they be asking you how to fix it? But that is exactly what the hospital were expecting.

Why would I want to speak with the management? Hadn't they shown to me that they were not interested in my Mum's care? The DoN completely dismissed what I was telling her. The least she could have said was that she would check. She could have looked any Saturday night and found what I was describing but she hadn't. Even if she'd paid lip service to me, told me she'd look into it, that would have at least pacified me for a bit, at least I'd have felt something was being done. The reply I received from my letter of complaint confirmed they weren't interested in learning from complaints. They hadn't even mentioned the medication error that the nurse had made and nothing about her attitude. This error led to my Mum's death a few hours later and not even a mention of it.

The headline following the Governors meeting we attended wasn't as you would expect to be about the poor care and the suffering of our loved ones. No the headline was, "Pay rises put on ice". I suspected they wanted to take the focus off the poor patients and paint a positive picture of the Governors. The management were still insisting that the high death rates were down to problems in the way they had been recorded. "It was the coding," they continued to tell us.

Incidentally they got their pay rises before the HCC concluded their investigation. In August the remuneration committee approved the rise which saw the Chairs salary increase from £18,000 to £40,000 for three and a half days work a week. This was around the time that I was appealing to the hospital for basic equipment for vulnerable patients.

Is Anyone Independent in the NHS?

The morning arrived when I was due to meet with the management team. Just the thought brought me out in a sweat. Reluctantly Sam and I had spent the weekend working on our presentation. I planned to work the morning and meet Sam on the way. I'd spent another night tossing and turning. I was getting to the point where I was thinking of approaching my doctor for something to help me to sleep.

I had taken out a five year lease on the dog grooming salon and was still responsible for paying the rent. To cover this I would normally groom a dog a day either early in the morning before the cafe opened or late afternoon when I shut the cafe. At the time of the call I was trying to groom a dog when the telephone rang. It was Helen Perrin, herself.

"Hello, Julie. Just calling to say how much I'm looking forward to meeting you today, and I know Martin Yeates is too. Also we received a call today from the HCC. They said that following an unannounced inspection they will be launching a full investigation into poor care and high death rates at Mid Staffs. Had you heard?" She says it so matter-of-factly, so flippantly.

Once again I found myself on the floor in floods of tears but this time it's tears of joy. At last something will be done about the abuse.

"I'm afraid in that case I shan't be able to make the meeting today, Helen. I think it is best to postpone until the HCC investigation is over." She wasn't very pleased

"Over? But that could take a while." She pleaded with me to keep the meeting.

I was going nowhere near the lion's den and I told her so. No, until the HCC had concluded their investigation I wouldn't be meeting with them. After I put down the phone I stood in shock, the relief, I could actually feel my body relax and I closed my eyes for a minute. They soon opened though when I realised the dog I was grooming had taken a shine to my ear and was licking it like it was covered in chocolate

Later that day I was contacted by the HCC and told the investigation had been launched and next week they would be opening up a phone line for people to get in touch with their concerns. People would be invited to ring in and book an appointment to be interviewed by the investigating team. These interviews would form part of the investigation. Even whilst I am talking to them I am thinking of getting in touch with everyone who has contacted me.

That night the local papers covered the story that the investigation had been launched due to high mortality as the average expected death rate should have been 100 and Mid Staffs mortality was 127 for the previous year. The headline said, "Probe into hospital trust's death rate." The HCC said the investigation would be focusing on admissions to the hospital as emergencies and also the quality of care for older people". Nigel Ellis the HCC head of investigations said, "An apparently high rate of mortality does not necessarily mean there are problems with safety." If he had looked at the hospitals complaints he may have thought differently.

Martin Yeates made a statement saying that the mortality figures were normal for a hospital the size of Mid Staffs and he stressed that services were completely safe at the hospital. His statement said,

"We have worked with the Strategic Health Authority and investigated this apparently high mortality rate and concluded that it was due to problems in the way we were recording and coding information about patients".

More denial, I thought and that denial continued for the next year and long after. Today, even after three inquiries into the hospital, people are still in denial as to the extent of the problems that our loved ones had to suffer.

That evening I had met with a young woman who had been taken to the hospital following a road traffic accident, she was in her twenties. She told me if it wasn't for her friend coming in to feed her and to give her the correct medication she would be dead. She had broken both arms and was totally dependent on the staff. She told me that she was still tortured by the suffering she saw on the ward and this was Ward 8. She had never been dependent like this before and so vulnerable. She dreaded her friend going home as she had to fend for herself. She cried whilst she told me that she had been made to wet the bed as she had waited so long for help. Then she had to lie in wet sheets, covered in her own urine, until a member of staff would change the bed. She sobbed as she told me about the rude staff and the looks they gave her when they found she had wet her bed. Whilst she was talking something struck me that this case is different because this is a young woman and even the young aren't safe in that hospital. It's not just the elderly it's anyone who is vulnerable and dependent on the staff. She tells me as she wipes her eyes, "If I had been old I would have died." Her tears continue to flow and I can sense how frightened she had felt, powerless.

She makes me another drink but I'm anxious to leave as I have so much to do but I can see this woman needs to talk. I think it's becoming so vulnerable so quickly and then finding out that those that should be there to care for you aren't. You just don't expect to be in your twenties then made to use your bed as a toilet and then have to lie in it for hours. I leave encouraging her to make contact with the HCC once the number is published. At this point I still wasn't familiar myself with the NHS complaints procedure, not like I am today but I encouraged her to write a letter of complaint to the hospital immediately.

Today I would advise anyone to first get a copy of all of your case notes. Write your letter of complaint and send copies to the GP, Clinical Commissioning Group (CCG) the group that will shortly replace the PCT. Send a copy to your MP, the Care Quality Commission (CQC), the Chair and the CE of the hospital. Tell as many people as you can and your local press are always worth informing.

I thought at the time that it was a bit odd that the HCC had told me that they would be printing a special number for complainants to ring and it would be printed in the local newspaper. During the next week I made contact with everyone who had contacted me with concerns and told them about the need to call the HCC once the number had been published. I couldn't be more specific as I didn't know which newspapers it would be in. I was shocked though when the number was only printed in the Stafford weekly paper, *The Staffordshire Newsletter*, which I knew would only reach the people of

Stafford. The majority of the people who had contacted me were mostly from the Cannock and Rugeley area. To make matters worse the advert had said that people only had until the following day at 4pm to book an appointment.

That evening I once again rang around people now giving them the number to ring. At this point I didn't know until the following day that the number that the HCC had actually given was the hospital PALS number. The PALS office was part of the hospital, part of the problem not the solution. Mid Staffs PALS was staffed with former nurses, it wasn't impartial and certainly didn't feel as if it was there to offer the patients advice.

I suspected they would try and bat off people as that is what they tried to do when people tried to make a complaint. A common theme that I found from people that I had spoken to was that the first thing PALS staff would say is, "You are concerned about your loved one's care". Only being concerned avoids an official complaint being made, this helps to keep the number of complaints down and they can hit their target. This usually means that nothing is recorded and no lessons are learnt.

I was beginning to worry about the impartiality of the HCC and their plea for people to come forward. I didn't know myself when I rang to book an interview that I was ringing the hospital and they certainly didn't pass my information on to the HCC.

When I did ring the HCC to ask them about the number they had given, I was told there had been a mistake and the hospital had given the wrong number. "The wrong number?" I asked her.

I wasn't convinced that this is what had happened and I suspected the HCC had allowed the hospital to print their number and manage the calls. I was so damn angry I thought that is all we need and I am not putting up with it. After so much hope that the HCC would now help me I wasn't going to allow this to happen.

I hadn't yet contacted the Labour MP for Cannock and Rugeley, Dr Tony Wright. His constituency, a former coalfield with a rich mining heritage, had always been a Labour seat unlike Stafford which was more of a marginal seat, swinging between the two main parties. A few people who had attended our meetings had mentioned that they had already contacted him over their complaint about the hospital but he hadn't helped them much. I believed this Dr Tony Wright had been elected to represent the people and he should be representing them. I wrote and told him that the HCC investigation into the hospital would be flawed already if it didn't hear from everyone who had concerns. What was he going to do about his constituents who had been unable to get in touch with the HCC investigating team. Many of his constituents had been harmed by the hospital and they now wanted an opportunity to give evidence about their experiences. I wrote and reminded him of his responsibilities as an MP, that he should be representing his constituents.

I also contacted all of the press and informed them of what had happened with several of the papers running a story on my concerns. It was around this time that I was first introduced to Shaun Lintern, the E&S journalist. After our first protest at the MP's surgery and at the Governors meeting I had contacted E&S editor complaining about the lack of coverage from them. In December 2007 when I launched the campaign they had printed a very small piece about me but that had been about it. I was angry that other papers were covering our activities, even the *Staffordshire Sentinel* which mainly covered the Stoke area and not Stafford, while the E&S ignored us. Spotting one of their journalists with Martin Yeates had been nagging away at me too.

The day after the protest at the MP's surgery I received a call from a journalist from the Stafford office. This was another occasion when I was left shocked and in tears wondering who cared. I had no idea who I was speaking to as I didn't know any of the reporters at this time.

It was early one Saturday morning and I was just about to start bathing a lively Labrador. Whenever the phone went when I was grooming a dog it was a real inconvenience and I would normally turn off the phone but I had forgotten today. Dogs are often like naughty children and when they are being groomed any distraction of your attention and they will take advantage. He did. As I was on the phone getting shouted at by this journalist he jumps out of the bath and starts shaking water all over me. I try and dodge it but really I don't care as I'm too interested in what is being said to me.

"Our readers don't want to hear about old people being

200

harmed," he tells me in the most aggressive voice I have heard in a long while. I have nothing to say to him I have no challenge at all. I feel as if a weakness has overcome me, I feel defeated and hurt.

The onslaught continued, "Why do you think our readers would be interested in old people?" I must have answered him but I have no idea what I said to him and no idea what I would say to him next. I just wanted the call to end and with as much effort and courage as I could muster I tell him, "You really are an incredibly rude man. Goodbye".

On and off I cry for the rest of the morning. I try and get the dog groomed but every now and again I find his big tongue licking my face whenever he senses my tears. Dogs are very sensitive to moods and this one tries everything to distract me but it feels like a cloud has descended upon me and today I just cannot shake it off.

I suspect he is right, that is the problem and from my experience so far everyone I have asked for help just doesn't seem to be interested in older people. I knew getting publicity was crucial for the campaign it was the only thing that was getting a reaction from the hospital. As yet it hadn't resulted in improvements but the positive thing was they were talking about them.

As a result of this I was introduced to Shaun Lintern. He rang me one morning and apologised for the way I had been treated by one of his colleagues. "Let's start again," he said, ever the optimist, and he introduced me to a keen journalist, Chris Gorman, from the Stafford office as Shaun was based in their Cannock office at this time.

Many people are critical of journalists, and they have every reason to be in some instances, but I can honestly say that in nearly five years of campaigning I have met some of the most professional of them. Some have been a real credit to the profession, treating us with the upmost of respect and they have helped us to expose many of the failings within the NHS.

Shaun has stood out though, a jewel, a real credit to his profession and I know he will be very embarrassed when he reads this. He is the type of lad you would be very proud to have as your son. From the very first time we spoke I knew he cared, he cared about people and that if there was a story it was told and he made sure our story was told. It's not just people he cares about it's the ethics of journalism, he is a true professional and his integrity shines through.

I received a letter back from Tony Wright immediately and also a call from the investigating team telling me that the date to book an interview had been extended. The following week all of the local papers carried an advert from the HCC investigating team asking for anyone with concerns to contact them and this time the correct number was printed. The deadline was still very tight but there was little more I could do. I felt my efforts trying to contact everyone who had contacted me had paid off and most people would be heard.

For the next week I was inundated with calls from people who had been trying to get an appointment with the HCC to be interviewed. Laura had tried for two days practically constantly to get a response from them but the number was constantly engaged. In the end she managed to leave a message on their answer phone and they did eventually ring back with an appointment but Sam wasn't so lucky. Laura and I now had an appointment arranged but Sam could only get a telephone interview.

Shaun Lintern picked up the story and I gave a comment urging, "It is important that people don't give up and that they keep ringing the number until they get through". The HCC commented that, "The helpline had been overwhelmed with calls over the last week but it is settling down now". They assured us that everyone who wanted to speak would be contacted back.

At the same time as this was happening in Stafford something very different was happening in the corridors of Whitehall and within the NHS. This is a piece of evidence that was uncovered during the MSPI. It refers to a conversation David Nicholson the Chief Executive of the NHS had, had with Anna Walker the Chair of the HCC about our group. Bearing in mind that I had started the campaign in December 2007 and he was implying the campaign had been in existence for "some time".

Mid Staffs Public Inquiry — *Extract from Exhibit NE40 — an email dated 19 May 2008 from Anna Walker to 'CHAI Executive Team', copied to Nigel Ellis, Richard Hamblin and other HCC staff, regarding a meeting that she and Ian Kennedy had had on*

14 May 2008 with David Nicholson: David Flory and Mary Newman were also present.

***

"Investigations into Mid Staffordshire

David was clearly concerned about the investigation into Mid Staffordshire. I explained that the current position was from the brief that I had been provided with (thank you very much for that Jenny). I explained that we had an overwhelming response from local people on the questions of quality of care. Our first formal visit to the trust by the investigation team was this week. David said that there had been a local campaign group in existence against Mid Staffordshire for some time. Clearly patients needed to express their views but he hoped the Healthcare Commission would remain alive to something which was simply lobbying or a campaign as opposed to widespread concern."

In the meantime people continued to contact me with their concerns and one caller told me about an advert they had seen in the local paper advertising that the Chief Executive of the Primary Care Trust (PCT) would be holding a surgery that night. I phoned around a few people and around ten of us turned up and met Stuart Poyner for the first time. At this point you see, I just thought that the more people that were told what was going on at the hospital, the better. Stuart Poyner was the Chief Executive of the PCT but I had no idea who the PCT were and what they did. They are about to be erased with the recent health reforms but at the time they were responsible for managing the contracts between the patient and the hospital.

The meeting was held at the Rugeley Health Centre and there was only one other person who turned up apart from us. We all piled into this small room that had been reserved and then he told us that no one usually turned up for his meetings, it was obvious really as I don't think he knew what to do. Although I had never met him before he didn't need any introduction. He was quite small, chubby with dark features and a receding hairline. As most male NHS managers I had met he was an oily type, full of his own importance. He just seemed to stand there umming and ahhing and shuffling papers with a grin on his face. He spent twenty minutes telling us all about himself and I sat there thinking, 'He thinks he's in a job interview, not here to listen to us.'

As his CV had taken up so much of the time we barely had time to tell him our concerns. At home later as I thought about the evening and what had happened I wondered if that had been intentional. Why spend so much time talking about yourself when all of these people are here for your help. What he did find time for though was to advise me to meet Martin Yeates and he insisted that the HCC was independent as I had mentioned my reservations about them. In hindsight it should have been his independence that I questioned and not the investigating team's.

Because of his time limitations he asked if he could attend our next meeting to hear more from us. He would bring along doctors and nurses to listen to our concerns. I was over the moon and gave him all the details of our meeting at a local pub. I felt a little bit embarrassed that here we were meeting at a pub in Rugeley, it didn't look very professional did it? But the room was the best we could do without any resources and it would hold sixty people. I knew there was going to be at least fifty coming and I was very grateful for the offer.

The following week the meeting took place and Stuart Poyner and a couple of his female colleagues arrived with him to the meeting. I could see they were shocked at the amount of people who had attended, it was packed. Some I had never met before and that made the meeting difficult and Stuart Poyner being there added to those difficulties. To make matters worse it wasn't just one big room, there were different areas. I tried to encourage everyone to move to the middle of the room to make it easier to talk to them but then that made it awkward for seating I battled on but having a quiet voice didn't help either. I suggested to Poyner that he should speak first and then leave us to hold our meeting. I was relieved when he did go.

He stood up to talk and half of the room continued to talk over him which was a little embarrassing. In desperation I tried to intervene in the hope that he wouldn't give us his personal details presentation again. That would not have gone down well at all and looking at their faces he wasn't exactly getting their attention. As he stood in front of me and listening to the grumblings in the crowd I could sense that they saw him as no different from Martin Yeates.

Poyner was very similar to Yeates not really in appearance but mannerisms and of course full of spin. Perhaps the NHS breeds them, I thought. He struggled to get his words out and didn't exactly fill any of us with confidence that he was going to champion our cause. I stood there regretting that I had invited him along but I thought, 'It's too late now'.

Basically he told us that his team (I think there were two others) would take contact details and make contact with people over the next week. They could then listen to their concerns and help them with their complaint. There were so many people that turned up for the meeting and half of the faces I didn't know, I agreed it was the only way forward as it was all very chaotic. At times I struggled to hold everything together and to keep the ground rules upheld.

It was at this meeting that I realised the lengths the management team at the hospital would go to. Jackie, who had lost her young daughter, stood up to speak.

"Well I have to tell you all that the other day I met with Martin Yeates," those not speechless gasp at this. "And I must say what a thoroughly nice fellow he is and I am sure…I am sure that he can help us."

The room is like a bear pit, shouts from all corners. Though, Jackie, is oblivious to the bad feeling.

"He's like a used car salesman! He lied to me. Telling me the hospital was improving!" Deb can't contain herself, her anger boiling over. There are shouts and insults thrown. Jackie has stirred things up but she goes on.

"He's a nice man." She points at me, "And by refusing to meet him you're hindering any improvement to the hospital."

The room was in uproar everyone was shouting out, "Rubbish," and, "he's nothing but a liar." Though I felt wounded by the attack on me I had to move the meeting along.

It wasn't easy but I managed to draw them together by getting them to talk about the meetings that they had attended at the hospital. I wanted to highlight that many of them had met with the management and what had they achieved? Jackie at this point sat there in silence and in her defence it sounded like Yeates had used his charm on her, promising her things. I was exhausted, the tension in the air was draining but then I sat back and listened and I didn't like what I was hearing.

Something dawned on me that night that destroyed any hope I had that the management could provide a safe hospital. What I heard from the complainants was that this management had heard all of our complaints before and yet they were making out when they spoke to families that they were shocked at what they had heard. At meetings they were telling relatives that they had never heard about such appalling care before and then a few weeks later they were telling other relatives the same. The same names and the same faces would sit in meetings and pretend to relatives that they were so concerned. The DoN had heard many times the failings and abuse that I had told her about when she had told me that she walks the wards night and day and had never seen or heard the poor care I had.

I went home sickened, how could they do this to people, families that they have failed, harming their loved ones. I despaired but what could I do about it? Who could I tell? Who would listen? Once again I felt isolated, nobody wanted to listen and they were only old people anyway. Fortunately whenever I felt low and in despair like this I would get strength from somewhere and tomorrow would be another day filled with opportunities. Mum always taught me that there is always something good in everyone and out of something bad comes something good. That thought alone would help to keep me sane over the next five years.

The following day I received a call from one of Poyner's assistants who reiterated what we had discussed the previous evening. The PCT were very grateful for allowing them to attend one of our meetings, she told me. But they were shocked at the amount of concerns and the severity of them. What they would do now is make contact with those who were at the meeting and help them through their complaint and whether I would like help.

"What is the point?" I ask. I had had a response to my complaint, months ago now. I told her "I have lost my Mum there is nothing you can do to change that but could you please help me to stop the suffering at the hospital".

She asked, "How can the PCT do that?"

I couldn't believe it. I was in the middle of Cannock Chase at the time walking the dog. I struggled to hear her as the wind whistled around me and every now and again the phone crackled because of a poor connection. She was pleasant enough and I suspected genuinely didn't know what she could do. I was annoyed with them anyway as they just seemed to be part of the hospital's PR team and why they thought I should meet with Martin Yeates I just didn't know.

"But that isn't our role," she pleads but I wasn't quite clear what their role was.

"You want to help? Easy. Just make sure the hospital gets more mattresses, chairs, cups, footstools, pillows, blankets, hoists, drip stands." Basic equipment but all were in short supply at the hospital. Because of the poor line I asked her to confirm what we had discussed in writing.

She did and she probably lived to regret it as 3 years later in the MSPI, I submitted it as part of my evidence. You see the PCT denied that they had agreed to help me with ensuring that basic equipment was increased on the wards.

This coincided with Martin Yeates making another statement to the press saying that they treated 30,000 people a year and only had 160 complaints. That was the figure that Moss had quoted in January. Now I had met with at least 20 people who had made a complaint since and yet the number of complaints hadn't gone up. At the time that struck me as odd but it wouldn't now, not after the evidence we heard during the MSPI. The NHS and all who work in it, call it *gaming*. CTNHS call it *lying*, fraud in some cases.

Giving evidence to the HCC is one of the most difficult things I have ever had to do. I was still finding it difficult to cope with Mum's death or even to think about her and I knew it would be a tough day. Once again it was at the Borough Council offices and into the Councillor's Suite. I had attended another OSC meeting in the same room the week before and heard the same denials as at the last meeting from the hospital management.

My involvement with Ann Edgeller had been brief and she had barely spoken to me but she was Mayor now or about to be. Following the first OSC meeting I attended I rang Edgeller and told her that the management were not being honest with the committee. I had written to all of the OSC telling them all the same but I followed up my letter to Edgeller with a call. Unfortunately she could help me no more as she was about to be made Mayor of Stafford. "But surely as Mayor you would have more power to help us", I argued. She didn't quite under-

207

stand that and thought her new role was to kiss babies and put her feet up in the Mayor's Parlour.

At the next OSC meeting I thought I would update her on the recent cases that families had contacted me about but I didn't, I didn't get chance. At one point I thought she was coming to talk to me. Of course it was the least she could do but no, instead of wanting to speak to me she practically pushed past me to get to the hospital management. As soon as the meeting is over she makes a beeline for them in her sycophantic way. I leave her laughing and giggling with the managers from the hospital with not a care about the disaster that is happening on her patch.

I had spoken to Dr Heather Wood on the telephone but it was the first time I had met her. Alongside her in the room was a note taker who wrote everything down as I spoke. I found the experience so very painful but I was determined that my story was going to be told I had fought for this investigation. I had now spoken on several occasions about what I had seen on the wards. What I hadn't done was talk about the way my Mum had been treated and what had happened to her. Heather was kind and made you feel at ease she just sat and listened to me for a long time. She was probably late fifties with short grey straight hair a round face with glasses. She looked a typical university lecturer, confident and astute.

When I got out of the meeting I had been in there all day and yet I felt I had left so much unsaid. She gave me no lead, she just let me talk. Every now and again she would ask a question and I would become aware of the note taker writing but most of the time I was oblivious to them both.

The intelligence I had gathered from relatives about the hospital frightened me and I needed to share it with someone. Over the last few months I had found it hard to know what I now knew and not having anyone to share it with. I had to expose the hospital and this charade of wanting to learn from complainants. I had to expose how cruel they were being to families and how they were adding to their suffering.

The first stage of this game is that the families are invited to a meeting at the hospital. Usually it is the ward staff but the persistence of the complainants determined who the meeting was with. Some got as far as meeting with Yeates himself and they were the very persistent complainants, those that the hospital realised they couldn't just bat off, they needed more work.

Sometimes the Medical Director would be present, other times the DoN and that was what had occurred to me at our Rugeley meeting. When I had rung Helen Moss a few days after I had lost my Mum the day she had told me that she had never heard complaints like I was telling her. Well she had, over and over again and I had seen it for myself in the letters that had been sent to me.

Another scam was the format of the meetings they usually opened by the families being asked what they knew or thought had happened. The staff would usually apologise profusely, very often usually the Matron or the Sister of the ward would shed a few tears telling the complainant she had never heard about such appalling care before. I had heard this same scenario described by over fifty relatives each one oblivious to the extent to which the hospital had gone to convince them that they would change. Lessons had been learnt and of course it would never happen again. Each family left thinking that it was an isolated case and that nobody else would suffer like their loved one had.

The charade continued as the hospital tried several tactics to ensure the families felt the complaints had been taken seriously. Some would be asked to help to train the staff to work with the hospital as part of the training team. Their relatives experience could be used as a training tool for the staff or they could even come in and talk to the staff. They would tell them anything to pacify them. Many of the families I had met with had gone and spoken to the staff thinking they could help change the poor care. Sitting and watching their faces when they found out that nothing had changed and they had only wasted their time was heartbreaking as they thought they had helped others. From all the people I have spoken to I believe that is what drives people, it's not wanting others to suffer like your loved one has, it's the main reason people complain.

One family I heard from was sent a cheque for £400 out of the blue following a meeting with Yeates. They had told him that all they wanted was to ensure others didn't suffer like their Mother had. In the post a few days later was the cheque with a letter from Yeates himself saying, "the money is for out of pocket expenses." The family sent the money back to him saying they hadn't suffered any out of pocket expenses.

Although my interview with Dr Heather Wood lasted for the

whole day I tried to tell her everything but I still got home and thought I had missed so much. Tissues were offered and I cried my way through the afternoon and way into the evening after I had returned home. I had found it so difficult talking about the lack of Mum's care and all she had suffered. Blocking it out of my mind had been much easier than having to recall it all. Sleep will be impossible tonight despite me being exhausted.

***

So far we had had plenty of coverage from the local press and media but nothing from the national press. It was early one Sunday morning in April when I was contacted by the reporter from the Mercury she told me to take a look at the *News of the World*. I was on my way to the cash and carry in Wolverhampton and although I was late already I couldn't wait to find the next newsagents. The cafe had been doing well and despite the campaign I was managing to earn a living through my cooking.

I found the story on page seven. It was a full page coverage with a picture of the undercover reporter, Dan Sanderson. He had been in the hospital undercover as a cleaner during and following a deep clean. He had swabbed parts of the hospital after the deep clean and still found areas contaminated with HAI. The article even had a picture of a smiling Martin Yeates. A year later I looked at the PCT's board minutes and found that the story had been discussed and our group had been blamed for being involved with the reporter. I never found out why the *News of the World* had chosen Mid Staffs but we had nothing to do with it, despite the PCT thinking we had.

The following day I received a call from a cleaner from Cannock hospital who told me about the conditions at Cannock. To cut costs the cleaners were being made to cut corners and to water down cleaning solutions to unsafe quantities. This cleaner was frightened that the expose in the *NotW* would result in them getting blamed when it was what they were being forced to do.

I contacted Dan Sanderson after I had spoken to her but he was concerned as Martin Yeates was threatening all sorts of action against him. Instead of being concerned that someone had managed to get into the hospital without any reference checks or police checks he was criticising the reporter for going in undercover. If he had found nothing I could have understood it but the infections were widespread within the hospital. The amount of people that were contacting me and telling me that their loved ones had died with their bodies riddled with HAI was staggering but there was nothing I could do. The spin coming out the hospital was still that they had low infection rates for all HAI and were meeting government targets. Three years later at the MSPI we found out that the hospital stopped putting HAI onto death certificates for a period.

Just before my interview with the HCC I had been contacted by the local BBC health correspondent, Michele Paduano. He was interested in coming along to the cafe and meeting the group. I had also contacted and spoken with Adam Brimelow from the BBC national health team. I had told him what was happening at Mid Staffs, about all the complaints I was receiving and he said he would be keeping touch. I wasn't sure what this meant at the time and was just so relieved that he had made contact.

It was really strange speaking to someone I listened to each morning on the radio. Knowing that they were now interested in us and the situation at our hospital was really encouraging and I always mentioned it at our meetings. He had told me that once the HCC had concluded their investigation the BBC Radio 4 team would be more interested. I was really proud that a BBC health correspondent would eventually be interested in our campaign. Little did I know that in a few months time I would be inundated with requests from journalists not only from the radio but from every TV channel and newspaper following the HCC report. After the report was published the global media were interested in our campaign and we spent days filming with television companies from all over the world.

Because of the number of complaints I was receiving and the amount of people that were contacting me with current complaints happening right now on the ward I contacted the HCC once again. I asked what they were doing? I was becoming increasingly frustrated it seemed no one was protecting the patients. I was told that this was a HCC investigation and they were unable to give me specifics about what that involved. They would pass my message to Dr Heather Wood. I waited but I heard nothing back from her. It was sometime before she did make contact with me but when she did I sensed immediately her concern for patients.

Our numbers continued to increase and I was over the moon when I was contacted by a fellow campaigner in Cannock, Ethel Powell. She had raised over a million pounds for the hospital and although her interest was Cannock hospital she was a real source of information despite her age. She was very unhappy with the management team and gave me lots of contacts who may be able to help. I went to her home and met with her and we hit it off immediately. Though elderly, I think she was eighty six at the time, she still had a fight in her and she had recently stayed in Mid Staffs where she had to beg for a blanket.

They still had none available and this was now June 2008, seven months since my Mother had been refused one. This is despite me asking the PCT to ensure that basic equipment was being provided on the ward. What was happening? Why was this being allowed to continue? Did no one care?

Well that was what it felt like, it just seemed the more cases that came to my attention the more I believed that there had been little improvement. Mortality statistics for this period along with other performance indicators, are evidence that little had changed.

Ethel kindly hired her local church in Bideford Way, Cannock for our next meeting. The first time I saw it was the night of the meeting and my first thought was it was enormous and far too big. I never thought for one minute that we would fill the room but we did. It was packed with around eighty people all either grieving relatives or those who had been harmed by the hospital in some way.

If we'd been there for his sermon the vicar would have been overjoyed, I bet he rarely saw his church so full. It was sad to see so many people but at the same time I thought my efforts are paying off. I was still out most evenings delivering leaflets that now had advertised our current meeting. I would pin them to bus shelters in the hope that people would see them and keep my fingers crossed that I wouldn't get into trouble for fly posting. Each evening after meeting with relatives on my way home I would stop to post leaflets, nothing would stop me.

It was at the first Cannock meeting on Ethel's suggestion that we formalised the group and voted in a committee. I was voted Chair and a Deputy was elected, along with representatives for Cannock and one for Rugeley. We voted for a Treasurer, Event Organiser and a Press Officer, Secretary, Complaints Manager. Sam got landed with publishing a monthly newsletter and a survival guide for patients.

At this point we now had a core group of people who I considered to underpin the campaign, an inner circle. Though lots of people were coming to our meetings it was mostly to get advice on their own case. That was fine but I needed people who wanted to help others or who were at a point where they felt they could help others. I felt guilty about this because it seemed almost as soon as I had lost Mum, I had focused on trying to help others. Logically I knew it was the right thing as people were still suffering but in the early hours of the morning or when I was alone the guilt weighed heavy on my mind.

Getting the committee together made it all very official but at the same time a relief to me that I would now have some help.

I opened each meeting by setting ground rules and tonight was even more important after the hostility from our last meeting but tonight Jackie hadn't turned up. I always relayed anonymously the complaints I had received since we last met and any communication I had had with anyone. We then focused on moving forward and what our next move was.

I had been contacted by Peter Atkins, the esteemed local journalist who I had spoken with now on a number of occasions to get advice. He had rung to ask if we had made contact with the MP for Stone, Bill Cash. Bill was Deb's MP and at the meeting she had agreed to contact him to get him involved. Although he was in opposition Bill Cash had a reputation as being a good constituency MP coupled with quite a high profile for a backbencher.

I came away from the meeting full of positive thoughts because although care hadn't improved our numbers were climbing and soon someone would have to listen. Like Ethel had said having a committee would help share the load.

I had been trying for weeks to speak with Steve Powell, the head of the consortium group of local GPs. One of the group thought that he may be able to help us. I wasn't sure how but I thought it was worth a meeting and I had nothing to lose. We knew that some of the GPs in the area had concerns about the hospital. At one of the meetings a few people had mentioned that their GP had referred them to other hospitals instead of Mid Staffs saying it was safer. Eventually I had managed to get an appointment with him for a few days later and I asked the newly elected Deputy to come along with me. It had been the first time I had included anybody. I had done everything myself and it felt odd not being alone.

Although Powell sat and listened to me for over an hour I could sense his lack of concern for the vulnerable. It could have been the lack of eye contact between us or how every now and again he would check his email as I spoke and at times cried. Once more and like so many his priority was getting me to meet with Yeates. I didn't like him and I certainly didn't trust him and my intuition was right. As soon as I had left his office he wrote an email to Yeates, laughing at me, mocking me. He emailed Yeates saying, "She doesn't know what she wants and I think she has started something she cannot control." Powell was very similar in appearance to Stuart Poyner possibly better dressed and slimmer but still that oily NHS manager look about him.

But he was right I couldn't stop people being harmed at the hospital, it was out of my control. The email was produced at the MSPI. It made me feel sick when I saw it, he was asked if he had got a reply from Yeates but he said he couldn't recall. I thought I bet you can't, that reply will now be destroyed as it would have indicated just how friendly he was with Yeates. Like Poyner, Powell had similar mannerisms reminding me of a used car salesman. Dodgy dealers, the lot of them.

I went home from the meeting suspicious. Why were all of these people, wanting me to meet with Yeates? They should have been on my side they should have been helping me and not trying to throw me to the wolves. What about all the patients that were being harmed that I had told him about? In Powell's email to Yeates he even mentioned one of his colleagues who had someone in the hospital at the time being neglected.

Complaints continued and any promised improvements never seemed to materialise for the patients. The hospital issued a press release telling us they had increased their staffing levels and had introduced a hand-held feedback device to monitor standards. On closer inspection the hospital had increased the number of Matrons from three to twelve. I wasn't impressed it was nurses, that were needed. The Matrons were normally office based and from the relatives feedback they were having no impact on the wards. I had also found out that this was a national decision to increase the numbers of Matrons within the NHS and not Mid Staffs taking that decision. But it was more spin for them to fill our newspapers with a positive story.

Everybody who had contacted me with their experiences was at a different stage. Some were strong and wanted press coverage for their story to be told. Others wouldn't and were not strong enough to share their experience. It was disappointing for me because I saw my priority to expose all that I was hearing but I had to be astute enough, to sense, who would benefit. We were lucky because all of the local journalists were very sensitive to people's needs and I was able to provide a steady stream through to the press.

The hospital hit back by telling us through a press release that they had now introduced a high tech device to measure patient feedback. The Patient Tracker (PET) was basically a hand held computer. Helen Moss told us through a press release it would provide invaluable information from patients. "The annual NHS Patient Survey provides us with valuable feedback but by the time we get a response it is 10 months out of date". This statement also helped with damage limitation as a vital question in the 2006 staff survey was, "Would you want one of your relatives to use the hospital?" Only 27% of the staff had said yes but to soften the blow it was 10 months out of date remember! The survey had also said that the staff at the hospital, were the most disgruntled in the country.

Yeates commenting on the PET told us, "This new technology will help us to keep our finger on the pulse of opinion about our services and step in to take swift action to put right any aspect of patient care that is not up to the high standards we aim to provide".

Feedback that I received from relatives and patients was that the hand held devices were handed over to patients by the nursing staff. The nurses stood over patients while they responded to the questions such as, "Are you happy with the care you are receiving?" I had a vision of some poor old dear lying in a bed with Nurse Ratchet standing over her.

Under no circumstances would I have criticised my care if I

had been an inpatient, not when you are at the mercy of the staff. I had memories of the night my chair was removed by the staff and I had made sure that I hadn't criticised the staff during my complaint. The spin continued. The PET had been telling the hospital how pleased the patients were with their care or that is what they were saying in statements to the press. Sadly relatives were telling us something very different, they couldn't control the feedback we were getting and it seemed they couldn't stop harming patients. It was a pity that they didn't use their complaints as feedback on their performance.

The Chair of the Local Medical Committee, Ian Wilson, also made a statement to *The Staffordshire Newsletter* along with Liz Longstaff, the regional representative for the Royal College of Nursing (RCN). Both said in their statement that the hospital was a good hospital. Longstaff went as far as saying that the trust bosses were, "Committed to patient care and safety." It didn't end there as she added, "As a champion of the nursing profession, the RCN works with Mid Staffordshire and many other trusts in order to ensure they have the right numbers of nursing staff in the right places with the right mix of skills to provide high standards of patient care."

After the next statement from Moss telling us, "We are investing over £1.1 million in new nursing staff and already job offers have been made to some 50 trained and skilled nurses," I called for Yeates resignation and the rest of his management team. I told the press his time was up and he had had long enough to improve care at the hospital. They had now been telling the public since January that they had identified a shortage of staff and only now were they recruiting.

I was livid. I had also been contacted by a niece whose Aunt was on Ward 10 suffering, an indication that little had changed. There was little I could do apart from pointing her towards the press who featured her case. She described the hospital as, "Like being in a third world country." Sadly her dear Aunt died suffering in the hospital despite her raising her concerns to the ward and then to the press whilst she was alive.

It was laughable really as at the same time as the RCN was telling us the staffing was adequate the hospital management was telling us something different. I commented in the E&S that this was a, "Knee jerk reaction," to increase the staff but they had no idea what to do with them. I said that "We have had enough of this management and it is time to bring a new management team in". They seemed to have no idea as to what was needed or that some of the established nurses on the wards needed investment in their training, many lacking the skills that were required and the RCN seemed to have absolutely no idea what it was talking about.

It wasn't the only blunder that the RCN made during this disaster which exposed the fact that they were far too close to the management, especially for a union. I knew little about the RCN at the time but at the time when I got the paper and read their comments it was like being hit with a hammer. There was I trying to expose the poor care and here was a local doctor and a nursing representative telling us something very different. I think in the same edition were letters allegedly from families thanking the hospital for the wonderful care their loved ones had received.

As for the other blunder, while Sammy and the group were working on our Survival Guide the Chief Executive of the RCN, Peter Carter, visited the hospital in May 2008. We were hoping the Survival Guide would help families to look after their loved ones whilst they were in the hospital. It seemed the hospital was doing little to improve the care or whatever they were doing it wasn't improving the care on the wards. Complaints were continuing to come to our attention as people were contacting me in a constant stream but more importantly those complaints were nearly always after someone had died.

I was also conscious now that those who could help us hadn't, therefore we would have to do something ourselves. I just couldn't bear to allow people to continue to suffer in this way. I was hoping that having the protests and getting the media coverage would shame them into doing something but it hadn't. It seemed they were just getting better at putting out well timed spin.

Over that spring and summer of 2008, we stood out in the wind and rain trying to raise awareness of the suffering that was happening at our local hospital. What we needed to do was to offer advice to those who could still be saved or to their families. It was up to us to do something if we couldn't stop people going into the hospital to be harmed then we should offer them some advice for what to do to help themselves.

While we were advising the community, "Stay with your vulnerable relative as much as possible to avoid them being harmed". Peter Carter the Chief Executive of the RCN was saying something very different, endorsing the hospital in our local newspapers as a safe place.

After his visit to the hospital he wrote to our local papers telling the community that he was impressed with what he saw and his impression of the staff was, "a highly motivated team, very much in touch with the contemporary issues in nursing".

To say it was a blunder was putting it kindly and his evidence to the MSPI a few years later was toe curling. Despite our campaign and the HCC in the hospital investigating high mortality and poor care he made a public declaration that he thought differently. He wrote to all our local newspapers and told the community:

On May 23 2008 I had the opportunity to visit the Mid Staffordshire NHS Foundation Trust and spent a morning at Stafford Hospital. In my job as CE of the Royal College of Nursing I travel extensively throughout the UK and visit a wide range of hospital and associated healthcare provision. I am therefore in a very good position to be able to judge and comment on standards of care.

I thought your readers might find it of interest to hear my views on my visit to your local hospital.

I found the hospital to be well managed it was clearly a very clean and efficient hospital and the quality of nursing and other health-related care was of an exceptionally high standard.

I had the opportunity to talk in private with patients and their relatives all of whom expressed a high degree of satisfaction with the standard of care.

I feel it is important that I write to share these observations as we all know from time to time in the NHS things are not as we would all wish and there are occasions when the RCN has to be highly critical of the standards of care we observe.

Clearly this was not the case at Stafford Hospital and I believe that all of those involved particularly the chairman CE and the Director of Nursing and staff, have every right to feel proud.

Proud! Who could be proud of some of these staff? They have harmed so many people and tried to cover it up at the same time.

Our meetings continued and our numbers expanded, at some meetings we had around 80 people and I estimated over 120 people were now in regular contact with me. My phone bills were costing me a fortune and the time I was spending on the campaign was phenomenal but I had to. Little did I know that our very next meeting all that could have changed and I could have been forced to walk away from it all.

We hadn't heard from Jackie since her outburst at the meeting in Rugeley and seeing her at the entrance unsettled me straight away. I knew this meeting wasn't going to be an easy one. It was the one and only time that I came close to walking away from the group. Jeff had arranged the meeting hall and was there early to put out the chairs. He had arranged the seats, it was unusual but the Committee was sat at the front with the rest of the chairs in front of us. Sammy couldn't come to this meeting and I had travelled alone, although Chris was now out of hospital herself after missing the last meeting.

Seeing her calmed my nerves she had become a great friend and a confidante when I needed one. Although I had now organised several of these meetings I could still feel myself shaking inside I was nervous. Strangely, as soon as I opened my mouth something took over and I felt calm again. Whenever I was talking at a meeting I felt that Mum was looking down on me, even standing beside me and encouraging me to continue with the campaign. It was strange but that was when I felt her close to me as if she was trying to give me the strength to continue.

I opened the meeting as I usually did by feeding back anonymised complaints since our last meeting. I had now heard from over 120 people and there were some awful cases that I had to feedback. I was just telling the audience about a family that had contacted me from Cannock. They had lost their Father on Ward 8, another one robbed of his dignity. I really don't think people realise the impact on a person when they first have to use their bed as a toilet. It really must be dreadful, a total loss of one's dignity and then to have to lie in your own waste must be unbearable.

"According to the recent Picker survey and the results from PETs care from the hospital is now rated at a high standard and the services and care at the hospital have improved immensely." Jackie stood up and interrupted me, mid-flow.

I hadn't spotted the survey in the press and I was now

making sure that I read everything. Every piece of spin that came out of the hospital I either read or someone told me about it. How could I have missed this?

"I've met again with Martin Yeates and he again assured me that things are improving. He asked me to give you this Picker survey as evidence." I had evidence to the contrary, the complaints were still coming in thick and fast.

It was also hurtful for those in the audience who had been brave and attended the meeting. Some I knew attended our meetings despite not being ready to attend such an event. Grieving is different for everyone and many attended still so raw in grief. Given the choice they would never have come along and spoken out but some saw it as an opportunity to get advice. Everyone I met thought they were alone, just as I did when I lost my Mum. It was usual for me to receive many calls the following day telling me that people who had attended felt so much better being able to share their experience. To know they were no longer alone gave them great comfort and helped to empower them.

Getting that balance was sometimes difficult when someone would want to open up and share their bad experience. I had to be skilled enough to draw a balance between what others were ready to listen to too. It would have been easy to spend the evening as a counselling session but it was important for those who attended that each person got something from the meeting. I was beginning to develop those skills and I was finding it easier to control the flow of the meeting.

I was also gaining so much knowledge but what frightened me was I was hearing the same things over and over again. I was also starting to hear the same names of doctors, nurses and managers. I would shudder when I heard certain names it was becoming all too familiar.

I knew tonight in the audience were some who had suffered very recently and June Chell was one of them. June was in her 80's and although physically frail she was mentally very strong and astute. She was a tall woman and very much a lady, her accent and her dress sense told me so. I warmed to her straight away and as she had sat telling me what her husband, Ron, had suffered I had wanted to hold her close. I felt as if I had known her for years, parts of her reminded me of Mum. It was her strength and her courage even at her ripe old age.

June had lost Ron, who was eighty years old, on Ward 10 and she was still in shock although it had been the previous year. She was still distraught at the lack of care he had received and how he had been treated. Ron had suffered a severe stroke and was immobile and so very vulnerable when he had been admitted to the ward. While in bed one night he was attacked by another male patient. The man jumped on his bed and tried to strangle him, because Ron had no speech he was unable to call out for help. He died a few days later but the hospital hadn't even told June he had been attacked, it was another patient who had witnessed the assault.

Ron died in pain and torment, covered in bruises. Thinking of Ron and all that he must have suffered has kept me awake on many a night I cannot imagine how difficult it must be for his family to have to live with. Can you imagine how it must have felt to be unable to do anything at all whilst you are being attacked? Lying there so vulnerable but only yesterday being strong and able. I still wince at the thought.

Jackie continued to challenge me. "Martin Yeates promised me that my daughter's death certificate will be changed and the doctor involved in her complaint would be disciplined."

I just wanted her to be quiet I wanted her to go away but she wouldn't, I felt she was a thorn in my side during the meeting and just wouldn't be quiet. She kept on about the Picker survey and how I should read it. I had turned off to be honest and thought her motives were for her own reasons and not the groups. Jackie was someone who was unable yet to move forward to look at the bigger picture, she was stuck and she had every right to be. I could sense that Yeates was taking advantage of that.

"He wants to help us."

Unexpectedly the organiser for Cannock spoke. He wasn't agreeing with Jackie but saying that whether or not I met with Yeates should go to a vote. I sat there devastated and it is the closest I have ever come to walking away from CTNHS. 'A vote! A vote!' I thought, 'but *I'm* CTNHS, am I not?' However if they had voted to meet with Yeates I would have walked away and the campaign would have been over for me.

"I have met him and look where it got me." Deb called out.

"I met him too and he gave me no answers," a woman called out from the audience.

Helping Each Other?

We needed to step up our campaign as nobody was listening and people were still being harmed. We decided to take the fight to the hospital and one of the group had the great idea to hold a candlelit vigil there. It would be a lovely tribute to those we had lost but it would also be an opportunity to attract the media. I had realised by now that the hospital hated the bad publicity and they always tried to counteract our press coverage with their spin. We needed to intensify the campaign and get out into the community more. It was after this meeting that I sat at home and filled in the calendar for the rest of the year with events for the group, events that would attract the press and also inform the public that despite the spin the hospital was harming patients. At each protest I would bring people up to date with the recent complaints I had heard about and the harm it had caused people.

I would make a press statement declaring our intentions and inform the press of our dates for the future. I made a plea to people to stay with their relatives to help to ensure their safety. Better still if they have an option stay away until after the HCC have concluded their investigation.

It was now June 2008 and once again I contact the HCC to ask what they are doing to protect the people of Staffordshire. Our survival guide is published in the hope it will protect the vulnerable and give the family some advice.

Survival Guide

We have put together the following points to help to ensure everyone receives the treatment and care they should expect regardless of age or vulnerability as a patient.

1. **Everyone has a right to be tested for MRSA and C-diff on admission to the hospital.** Ask to be tested on admission to ensure you are not taking the infection into the hospital– some hospitals will offer the tests as they do not want someone bringing infections into the hospital.

2. **Everyone should have a care plan.** This sets out the plan for you or your relatives care. Ask to see it, inform staff you want to be involved with your relatives care provide as much information as you can. Ensure you have regular communication with the doctors and nurses. Ask when the ward round takes place. Inform staff you want to be present. Ask questions, you have a right to be kept informed of test results and any changes to the plan of care i.e. medication. Ensure you know who your relatives 'named nurse' is and that they know who you are.

3. **Try to spend as much time with your relative as possible.** Try to get there other than at visiting times, especially meal times. You have a right to stay, ask to be shown the relatives facilities i.e. bathroom.

4. **Ensure your relative is receiving the right nutrition and fluids.** Ensure you have access the nutrition and fluid charts. If you have concerns and one is not in place ask for one. If they are not being filled in by the staff, ask why. You may find 'refused' has been put on the chart. If so question it. If your relative is unable to feed themselves ask what system is in place to ensure your relative is given food and fluids.

5. **You have a right to an assessment from social services.** This is for anyone who is classed as a vulnerable adult. Ask for one.

6. **If you are not happy with any treatment or service you or your relative is receiving, ask to see the ward manager.** You have a right to ask question and make a complaint. This should be done in writing and addressed to the Chief Executive Martin Yeates. Send copies to your MP and Cure the NHS. Get and include any evidence – times, dates, witness contact details.

    Cure the NHS members hope this guide will help you or your relatives during their hospital stay. If you have any other advice that we could add please let us know and we can include them.

Before the candlelight vigil takes place, out of the blue, I am contacted by the police and invited to a meeting the following afternoon. I'm frying eggs at the cafe and I explain that I cannot make it. I ring around the group and a couple from Rugeley who were voted the group's event organisers at our meeting in Cannock will attend instead.

Bob and Joy had been involved with the group from the beginning following the death of Joy's Mother. She suffered appalling care at Mid Staffs and died at University Hospital North Staffordshire (UHNS) who tried to save her life after Mid Staffs had destroyed her. She was too far gone for UHNS to repair her and she died a miserable death which was totally avoidable. Reading Bob's letter which he wrote to me describing his Mother-in-law's death was heartbreaking and stayed in my thoughts long after.

Bob and Joy attended the meeting but never attended another it was to be the last time we saw them. Bob's health deteriorated shortly after the meeting and I never saw either of them again but I would have understood if they'd been frightened off by the police.

The police were there in force, and so was the management. The outcome was if we protested at the hospital we would be arrested. No "ifs" no "buts", that is what would happen if we tried to protest at the hospital. You see the Governors' meeting that we protested at was away from the hospital and really only the management saw us. This was different as we would be in view of everybody and their dirty laundry was about to be aired in public.

Bob told me that several of the management had been present along with several police officers, telling him that under no circumstances were they allowing us to go anywhere near the hospital. If we insisted we would be arrested immediately. I could sense Bob's reluctance to proceed with the protest as we would all have to spend at least a night in a cell.

The hospital immediately made a statement to the press that said we would be arrested if we proceeded with the planned protest. The papers all carried the story the following day it made the front pages. Not only that it, was all over the billboards in Cannock, Stafford and Rugeley.

But the police didn't frighten me and they didn't frighten the rest of the group we met and it was agreed that the protest would go ahead. I contacted the press, I thought that would be the last thing the police would want on camera. Staffordshire Police had commented that they would ask us to leave because the rally was "unlawful". I couldn't think what they could arrest us for if we didn't stand on the hospital grounds but at the entrance just outside the hospital.

I tried to get the BBC regional news team along to the vigil or at least to be aware of the threat by the police. I emailed Michele Paduano and told him about our intention to continue with the vigil. My email tells him that, "I have now been contacted by over 120 people and heard about some dreadful care".

Unfortunately the BBC couldn't come along and I'm really disappointed as I wanted them there as I thought the police would be unlikely to arrest a group of grieving relatives if they were being filmed.

I was determined that the protest would go ahead and I wrote an open letter to Yeates that was published telling him, "You have pushed our loved ones around but you are not going to do the same to us." I was determined that the protest would go ahead and I reiterated, "It will be a peaceful protest. All we want to do is to raise our profile and let people know they are not safe in the hospital". We had every right to stand in silence in respect of our loved ones and that was what we did.

Peter Atkins wrote his column that week supporting our protest and encouraging others to come along to support us, they did. There were so many people the entrance to the hospital wasn't big enough so we decided to stand at the bottom of the hospital field instead and light our candles. It was a very emotional time but there were so many people and as the morning passed more and more people joined us. People were getting off the buses to join us and as cars passed they pipped their horns in support along with the buses and the ambulances visiting the hospital.

Despite the BBC not being able to cover us the press seemed to be out in force all taking pictures and negotiating between themselves who would take the next. Even *The Sentinel* was there, it was the first time that they had covered our campaign. I had contacted them originally but their health correspondent had told me he was far too busy with his own hospital, UHNS. I was so pleased at the amount of coverage and the attendance at the vigil confirmed our support.

I had been disappointed when I contacted the *Cannock Mercury* to tell them about the vigil. It was a new reporter who I hadn't spoken to before, it seemed Melanie had left. It was a Sam Schofield who wrote an email back telling me that the hospital was out of their catchment area as it was based in Cannock. I thought this was odd as a few weeks ago Melanie had written telling me that the editor was keen to support us.

I was so busy at the time but a thought did cross my mind, had the hospital increased its advertising with the newspaper? Would spending more money with them influence what stories they covered, it just seemed too suspicious for me. I should have done a Freedom of Information request but I had no idea at the time I could get such information. And as we have found out from the Leveson inquiry some editors have few morals. I later found out that this particular journalist later moved to the hospital as part of their press team. That could have been a coincidence but everything now caused me to be suspicious.

On the day of the first vigil the police stood by looking silly, silly because there we were doing nothing wrong but lighting a candle for each loved one we had lost. We were a group of relatives, mostly elderly, who wanted to stop the poor care within the hospital. We stood there in silence with all of the photographers taking pictures. It was a really miserable day and hard for us all to stand there remembering our loved ones for long as the rain soaked us through. I had brought a bunch of irises,

Mum's favourite flowers, though she loved any flowers and had been a keen gardener. That's when she had had a garden, her life had been very hard and most of it was spent working instead of enjoying herself.

We had been at the vigil all morning and I was desperate to use the toilet, I kept putting it off and putting it off. Reluctantly I would have to use the hospital toilets, I had no option. I didn't give it another thought, apart from deciding which chocolate bar I would buy from the hospital shop. Entering the hospital didn't come into my head until I started to get closer. I could feel a knot in my stomach getting tighter but I tried to force myself not to think about it. "Which chocolate bar would I have?" I tried focussing on that instead and I tried to hold a vision of a Turkish Delight in my mind. It wasn't until I entered the toilet when it hit me like a sledgehammer my legs buckled underneath me I felt strange, my heart was racing.

I found myself holding onto the sink with my legs feeling like they belonged to somebody else. I hold onto the sink I feel it is the only thing that is holding me up, I hold on tighter, tighter. The room begins to spin and my head feels as if it is moving alone, a strange sound fills my ears. What's happening to me? I begin to wonder if I am here, is it me? What is wrong? I've got to get out of here quick. My heart is racing, something has happened to me. I must get out the door and out of here.

But I can do nothing I find myself frozen at the sink holding on scared that if I let go I will fall. I can feel my nails grasping at the sink, frightened that I will lose my grip as my hands are shaking so much. I can't breathe, my heart is racing I can feel it banging against my chest. "Let me out, let me out," I can hear my voice as an echo, I'm not sure that it is me saying it. I'm scraping back the toilet lock and the first thing that hits me is the smell, my mouth goes dry, I'm going to be sick. I can't stop I just keep running I push past people and before I know it I'm out of the hospital. I'm running, "faster faster" I tell myself, I just focus on getting away. Sweat pours from me I'm drenched and as I sit down on the grass I find I have wet myself. I'm terrified of that place.

Over the next week the papers are full of pictures and details of the deaths of our loved ones. They have all covered the vigil and the response has been overwhelming. People continue to make contact telling me of the poor care their loved ones suffered. The hospital tried to imply that we were intimidating visitors and the staff. We never did any such thing, we kept ourselves at the very bottom of the hospital. The only people that saw us were people in cars or on the bus and as I said people were getting off the bus and joining us. Again they tried to paint a picture of us that just wasn't true.

Yeates made a comment to the press, "Our staff are very hard working and should be allowed to arrive and leave work without feeling threatened or demoralised." When I read that I just thought, 'What is he talking about?' But then I realised what he was trying to do. People are reluctant to criticise anyone in the NHS, it is seen as sacred and he was hoping to pitch the staff against us. Sadly he achieved what he had set out to do and the staff played out their support for him, live on TV for all to see the following year.

It wasn't at all like that. We were really proud of the caring staff and I often shed a tear at how they had struggled to help Mum on the ward. No, it was the uncaring staff that we were against. But under no circumstances would we have even approached them, let alone 'threatened' them. We were there to protest, to grieve, not to intimidate.

Nobody was there to help us. All the people I had contacted and were aware of what was going on had done nothing. The group continued to attend the OSC to try to tell them of our concerns but they barely spoke to us. I felt they had not been elected to represent the people, they were there to cosy up to the management of the hospital. I had had no further contact with the MP David Kidney, I hadn't seen or heard from him. He wrote me a few further letters implying the only thing to do was to, "Meet with Martin Yeates". It started to feel like a mantra, a well rehearsed line they all took. I didn't reply to his last letter and he went quiet.

That is until we find out that during the summer he carried out a PR stunt for the hospital again telling us, "Everything is fine at the hospital". Unbelievable I know but in the summer of 2008 as we stand out on the streets of Stafford calling for the abuse to stop, our MP is inside the hospital on a two week work experience working alongside cooks and cleaners. Now it would have been a different matter if he had gone onto the wards and checked on the vulnerable patients but he didn't even do that. The press release when he had finished the placement said the priority for the hospital needed to be better recycling of their waste, he had seen nothing similar to what I had seen. I was shocked when I had opened that week's paper and a picture of him in a chef's outfit staring back at me.

At first I felt sick and then I thought "How dare he"? The man has been elected to represent the community and instead he is doing this. You see by this time I had heard from several more people who had asked for his help over poor care at the hospital. Every person I listened to with their concerns I would help them with their letter of complaint but I would also pass their details onto the press with their agreement. This combined with cases coming out of the coroners court ensured that throughout that year there was a constant flow of awful cases being featured in our local papers.

Hate Campaign

During the summer of 2008 I started to receive a lot of hate mail and menacing calls. Some sounded as if they were coming from the hospital as I was very familiar with the sound of the ward at night. At first I would race to the phone thinking it was Laura but I soon realised that this wasn't going to stop.

When it first started I would stand there in the dark terrified. Most of the calls were just silent apart from the sound of footsteps along a corridor. Others there would be a male voice warning me to, "Shut your mouth," or swearing at me. One night I stood in the living room holding my phone while a man with a Scouse accent told me he was watching me. I was frightened I spun around looking in the dark room daftly thinking that someone was in there with me, terrified I dropped my phone and ran up the stairs. That call was the final straw and from that night for a long time after my phone was turned off as soon as I went to bed.

After each protest or meeting I would normally receive an anonymous call from a man with what would seem to be a fake accent. Sometimes it was a Geordie, Scouse or Scottish accent but always a northern accent. He would always ring after one of our meetings he must have been in the audience as he always mentioned something that we had discussed. It gave me the creeps and I became conscious of who was walking behind me on the street, even whilst I was out shopping.

I became paranoid and so did the rest of the group. We started to be suspicious of anyone new. The first time I met our current MP I thought he was a spy and possibly the man who was ringing me. I've never told him this and it seems daft now but at the time I was really frightened by it all.

We were holding the meeting in the Trinity Church in Stafford. I was standing talking about the recent cases when Deb hands me a piece of paper and written on it is 'I think we have a spy in the room'. Well to cut a long story short he wasn't a spy, he was the town's Prospective Parliamentary Candidate for the Conservative party and he had recently experienced care he was concerned about but from another hospital. It's not until we are nearly at the end of the meeting that he introduces himself and it is such a relief to hear he is not a spy. He raises his hand to speak and I'm dreading what he is going to say. I glance over at the others who have sat at my right hand side. We are all nervous and expecting him to disrupt the meeting and it's a huge relief when we find out he isn't a spy but Jeremy Lefroy, now the MP for Stafford.

The threats continued throughout the year but alongside the calls were the abusive emails. I received dozens of letters many I suspected were from staff members or their families. Some threatening, others bitter, nasty, telling me to leave the poor staff alone and to stop causing trouble. Others were from members of the community telling me to stop lying and shut up or I would get the hospital closed. The most threatening were anonymous obviously from the most cowardly within the community.

I still have some of them saved on my email, a record of all the denial of the harm the hospital was heaping on patients. Some were arrogant enough to include their identities, they just didn't care. One was even from a doctor. The first one was in December 2007 about a month after I had lost my Mum and they haven't stopped. I still receive offensive letters, the denial continues and that is despite three major investigations into the hospital, all saying the same thing.

They had no idea of the impact they would have on me but overall they only made me stronger, more determined. Some hurt more than others and it also depended on how I was feeling that day. One, and it was one of the first I received, told me that I was probably feeling guilty about my relationship with Mum and the campaign had nothing to do with exposing poor care. That hurt more than anyone can imagine as yes, I was feeling guilty. Some days I would call out, "Mum, Mum," and think I had gone mad.

Guilt consumed me, some days I felt so guilty for allowing Mum to die that I would find myself pacing up and down the room racked with feelings of guilt. Realistically what more could I have done but at that time I felt I could have done a lot more, I wasn't being rational. I was also feeling guilty as I couldn't bear to think about my Mum, that was still too difficult. Meeting others though had made it a little easier as I knew I wasn't alone, others who had lost felt like me. I was beginning to realise that there were a lot of people out there who didn't want the poor care exposed.

The weekly newspapers who I sometimes felt were part of the hospitals PR team printed critical letters that named me. Over time we could detect a pattern to some of them as they would use a similar format. The letter started by telling us that they had been well cared for at the hospital. They would tell us about the fantastic staff from the domestics through to the Consultants, how kind they were and how hard working. They would tell us that they had used the hospital for years and never had a problem. They would finish the letter by criticising those who were complaining about the hospital care. They all seemed to follow a similar pattern as if they were using a set template. There also seemed to be an active campaign to discredit me by some within the community and an active campaign to intimidate me.

A man phoned me one morning while I was at work cooking a bacon sandwich.

"If you don't shut up I'm gonna fucking kill you." At first I had trouble understanding what he was saying as the extractor fan was on full blast and he had a strong Asian accent.

"I'm sorry, I can't understand you. Can you say it again?" I turned off the extractor fan and then I realised that it was a threatening call. It was the middle of the day yet I was left terrified I stood and shook I wanted to close the cafe there and then. His voice was chilling and I certainly didn't want to walk home alone. I got over it but for a long time I was really careful where I went.

It was the knowledge that someone felt so strongly against me, those negative feelings frightened me. Who would help? I didn't feel the police would be there to help me. I suspected they would say, "Told you so".

I didn't even say anything when I arrived at work and all over the cafe windows somebody had daubed bitch on both windows. It took me hours to clean off. To make matters worse the cafe is situated on a busy main road going in and out of Stafford and the cafe is right in front of a set of traffic lights. That morning I dreaded the lights turning red. As the cars queued I cringed and the tears flowed as I scrubbed as fast as I could. I wanted to give up and go home, to return when it was dark but I braved it out, wiped my eyes and got stuck in. It was all I could do. It would have been easy to give into them and at times I wanted to but then I would recover and strength would surge through my body. Mum would feel close by and I could feel her telling me it was time to move on, get over it and begin the fight again.

Little did I know that this was nothing, the following year after the HCC report things got a lot worse for me. The denial from the hospital was unprecedented. The staff, management and members of the community would begin to criticise me publicly. And it would end in violent threats against me which were posted all over the internet. It would also cause me to become practically bankrupt and forced to rely on handouts to survive.

All through that summer not a weekend went by where we didn't either protest or hold a road show to raise awareness that something was terribly wrong at the hospital. We stood in the middle of Cannock, Rugeley, Penkridge, Stone and Stafford, all our local towns. We took it in turns to visit each town once a month and we also held a monthly meeting in each town. Most days I would be out after work until the late evening either meeting a family or delivering leaflets. I couldn't stop because whenever I stopped thoughts of Mum and the suffering that was continuing filled my mind.

Following the Cannock meeting Deb had made an appointment to see Bill Cash her MP and I joined her at his surgery. Mine had been hopeless and going to the meeting we were full of hope that Bill could do something. His advice was to now wait for the HCC findings and I suppose that is all that he could say but I still wasn't sure about the HCC's impartiality. Both Deb and I left frustrated, thinking that was a waste of a day. He suggested that we get a Committee together to formalise our group. Both Deb and I didn't have the heart to tell him we had done that, months ago. It wasn't until we had left that we realised how pointless the meeting had been and Deb wrote and told him so.

Although the Committee has been formed I found that it is mostly easier to do things for myself. I understood it was difficult for the others in the group as they are either working full time or elderly. Pete as secretary does all that he can along with working full time. He far exceeds his role of secretary he takes the minutes, helps me with letters and keeps us online with the website and our email.

Chris, Pete's Mother-in-Law, as we sadly found out was far too raw to act as our Rugeley representative. The idea was that the Cannock and Rugeley representatives would take over the cases for those areas. The plan was that whenever anyone contacted me from these patches I would forward them to the representatives.

The first time that Chris had met with a grieving relative she had ended up distraught herself. I would like to have said she just wasn't ready but I realised she would never be ready. The death of George had destroyed her and listening to others who have lost only brought back her loss. Not for one minute was the loss of George far from her mind on any day.

The same with Jeff who had been elected as our Cannock representative, he just wasn't ready or strong enough emotionally himself to listen and empathise with someone grieving after losing someone they had loved so much. The training I had had in counselling, be it very brief, helped me enormously.

It was difficult for me trying to take on so many roles but I think this was why the group has been so successful. Nobody challenged me or disagreed with me there has never been any infighting. They all knew that whatever I did it was to try and help the vulnerable that was all that was driving me. They also knew that whatever I did it was to make sure that others didn't suffer like our loved ones had. They all trusted me and believed that whatever I did I would be speaking for them too.

The first time we stood in the centre of Stafford it was another bitter day with the rain every now and again coming down in sheets. We all had our raincoats on and it was hard to stay positive at times. We were handing out application forms to join the trust and if we didn't have our banners we could be mistaken for part of the hospitals PR team. We had received some really positive feedback from the survival guides and we were handing those out too.

I'm standing alone as the others have split up and gone into the crowd and a woman on a mobility scooter drives towards me. She's a large woman with short jet black hair that is secured at the sides with clips and a rose. She's wearing a large smock dress and no coat which is odd on a day like today. For a minute I think that she is going to steer straight at me and I am about to be a victim of a hit and run. I try to dodge her but all she does is place something into my hand and drive off into the distance after telling me to, "Keep up the hard work you are our only hope," In my hand I have a letter she has written telling me all about the harm she has suffered. It leaves me in tears standing there in the middle of the town, I know that the hospital has caused so many people so much harm. I must now do everything I can to expose it, we have suffered enough. It feels a monumental moment to me and I vow there and then that I will expose all that hospital's failings.

Standing out in the wind, snow, and rain isn't easy and some days I just want to go home. It's not everybody that would either and if we weren't desperate for the suffering to stop it's not something we would have chosen to do on our Saturday's. Whenever anybody new contacted me I would encourage them to join us at our next protest or meeting but for some they just wouldn't entertain it. We felt we had no choice because people just continued to be harmed at the hospital and I felt that if it wasn't for us raising awareness even more would be harmed.

We would normally stand in the town centres of the towns that the hospital served. That would either be Cannock, Rugeley, Penkridge, Stone or Stafford. We alternated between them and in between we would try to attend the board meeting although as soon as they had been awarded Foundation Trust status they made their board meetings private. Once a Foundation Trust they say that they now have commercial interests unsuitable for the public's ears. Despite this we just stood outside in silence and only spoke when we were approached. It was usually the communications manager who as time went on I came to realise was only interested in positive communication. She always made out she was listening and for a long time she had me fooled.

We always stood in silence with our banners waiting for people to approach us and they normally did. At Cannock and Rugeley people were pleasant to us and many people approached us who had suffered too. It just seemed everyone you spoke to had been or knew someone who had been harmed at the hospital.

Stafford and Stone were different and unlike Cannock and Rugeley we usually faced hostility from someone during the day. Both Cannock and Rugeley were former mining towns and the people seemed different, kinder, much more down to earth with a healthy community spirit. Cannock had its own hospital which was part of MSFT. It was a small one but the community had raised thousands of pounds towards its upkeep. They were proud of the hospital even though they accepted it was failing the vulnerable.

In Cannock and Rugeley we felt that the community was behind us and whenever we were in town we were always joined by strangers who would stand alongside us in support, they cared.

Each time we protested in Stafford we always faced abuse from someone within the crowd. It usually felt as if it was a planned attack as they were always well rehearsed and normally related to someone working at the hospital. Now having the press coverage all of our protests and meetings were being advertised widely and people knew where we would be each week. This made us a target and they usually picked on the older members of the group, just like on the wards.

What some people in Stafford failed to understand was that we supported the caring members of the staff, it was the ones that were harming patients that we were against but I don't think they wanted to listen to our reasoning. The priority was to either, get us to meet with the management, be silenced or discredited.

Stone was another town where we faced hostility and challenge from members of the community. It was normal for me to be challenged and targeted by someone in the crowd they seemed to seek me out. After the first few occasions I became familiar with their tactics and was able to handle their criticisms but the attack on Chris was deliberate and by a grown man too. He was such a bully to challenge a grieving widow in this way.

I suspected that Chris was still in shock that first year and her tears were never far away. It all happened so quickly and was totally unexpected. We had all gathered in the Market Square there was around twenty of us, all in silence with our banners. As usual the rain was never far away and no sooner as we took our hoods off the rain would once again appear. I was stood away from the group as I had been talking to Brenda.

Brenda was another Brummie like Chris and she had a

similar personality. Once strong and determined but the loss of her husband had rocked her very foundations. Brenda walked with a stick as she had recently hurt her hip and every now and again she would wander off and rest her legs on a bench. She had just gone to sit down and I was making my way towards Chris and June who were standing across the square handing out the hospital membership forms.

I didn't have my glasses on but I could just see them talking to a middle aged man. He was tall and imposing and looked late fifties. I thought that was just what was happening until I saw him spit at Chris just missing her coat with his saliva. I could see Chris looking down and checking her clothes as the man walked in the opposite direction. Although Chris wouldn't admit it afterwards I could see she was physically shaken when she reached me. Before he had spat at her he had been verbally abusive telling her she was disgusting for criticising the hospital.

"The hospital had saved my life on several occasions," he snapped at her. I suppose it is natural to want to defend something that has helped save your life or that of someone you know, but at the same time they shouldn't just dismiss that your experience is different to theirs. And what about all the cases of poor care that were being highlighted in the press?

But we never seemed to get this response from anyone in Cannock or Rugeley just the opposite in fact. That community seemed to accept that others experiences could be different and they seemed more willing to consider the vulnerable members of their community. Far more people from Cannock and Rugeley attended our protests and our meetings.

Sonia is another member of the group who was left shaken following a protest in the middle of Stafford town. It was a Saturday afternoon protest and we were all scattered away from each other when it happened. We usually tried to stand together thinking we were safer in a group. But as the afternoon wore on we had become separated it happened easily if you were talking to someone alone. Sonia had found herself alone on the other side of the Market Square when it had happened. Again a well-built, middle-aged man began shouting at her for criticising the nurses. I think at the time Sonia was holding a banner saying, "infection control is out of control," and it was but this grown man thought differently. Sonia was shaken when she returned to the group and to think a grown man had tried to bully her and Sonia wouldn't hurt a fly.

Sonia was a strong woman she had practically brought up her three children single-handedly after losing her first husband to cancer. Peter was her second husband but you could tell she adored him and had hung on his every word.

She attended our first meeting but I had first met her a little while before the campaign started. She lived opposite the grooming salon and had come in one day all guns blazing. A petite woman in her early sixties with thick silvery grey bobbed hair. The first thing that struck you about her was her round rosy cheeks and her eyes expose her kindness. She reminds me a little of a school teacher or even a farmer's wife. She's a devout Christian and I'm certain her faith has helped her through the heartache that the hospital caused her. She has been a great support and a dear friend to me.

She had seen a dog foul the pavement and the owner hadn't cleaned it up. Sonia thought I may know the owner. I didn't but her spirit struck me straight away. Originally from Cambridge she hadn't lost her accent and her first words to me were, "A dog has just fouled the pavement opposite my house." My first thought was, "Well what is she telling me for?"

Sonia is now a valued member of the group and a real campaigner. Last year alone on Remembrance Sunday she stood at the cenotaph at Alrewas in protest at the war and the loss of our soldiers. Sonia is the definition of *Strong and steady wins the race*. She is very methodical and likes to think about every angle. In fact I would say that that is one of her problems, she thinks too much, but we all do.

At that moment I wasn't really living, it wasn't a life, I was just surviving I didn't feel able to enjoy anything. I hadn't spoken to friends for a long time I just didn't have the time and what would I have said to them? I feared if I did speak with them they would think that it was time that I started to move on. 'What does that mean? What does moving on mean?' I ask myself. Does moving on mean that I will not wake during the night and find myself back on the ward? Or does moving on mean that when I wake the first thing that goes over and over in my mind isn't why I lost my Mum? Or is moving on when I am able to even think about Mum and smile as I remember those happier times that we shared together? Is moving on when I can think about her suffering on the ward and not wince, physically, feeling the pain myself? All of these questions go through my mind and the sad thing is I know I am not alone, the others in the group face the same questions and Sonia is one of them.

Sonia was Peter's main carer as he had dementia and the guilt she feels is evident in her face when she talks. Her eyes say it all and her pain is written all over her face you can tell she is hurting. Whenever I speak to her it's very often the same conversation, "Why didn't I spend more time with him on the ward?" But guilt consumes us all as I tell the group I couldn't have spent more time on the ward and yet I lost Mum and some days the guilt can take over my day leaving me wounded. It wouldn't have mattered if Sonia had spent more time on the ward it's likely the neglect would have continued. You see Sonia wouldn't have been able to not say anything to the staff, it would be her nature. She would say something thinking she was helping them and I suspect they would have asked her to leave.

Peter, her husband, had gone into Mid Staffs with breathing difficulties, although he hadn't died in the hospital he had been robbed of his dignity and was sent home a weak imitation of the man Sonia knew and loved. Peter was a world renowned typographer and was an active peace campaigner known throughout the country for his views. They destroyed him, reducing him to begging for the toilet, medication and food. It's a real tragedy that Sonia still carries the guilt around with her, although she could do nothing, none of us could.

In October the HCC had issued a press release about the conditions they had found when they had inspected A&E in May. I had received lots of complaints about A&E but I wasn't expecting the failings to be as bad as the HCC had found. Throughout this period the hospital team had constantly been telling us that the hospital was safe. Now we were being told something very different and it was worrying that instead of the HCC telling us this in May when they had found it they had waited until October four months later.

The press release said how shocked they had been at what they had found in the department. There was a lack of staff generally but instead of four senior doctors they had found one and no leadership in the department. When the final report came out in March we heard things had been far worse than they had reported. They had found vital equipment turned off as staff didn't know how to use it. Patients were being put at risk from the moment they entered the building.

Yeates made a statement telling us, "Patient safety is our highest priority and we are committed to driving up standards throughout our hospitals. We welcome the involvement of the HCC and their acknowledgement that we are taking rapid action in resolving the issues they raised".

I thought *"Rapid action"*? The amount of people that were contacting me isn't an indication of a *rapid reaction* and to be honest I was struggling to see *any* action they were taking. I had heard from so many people who had been harmed in the hospital. I just couldn't understand why the HCC were saying things were improving.

At the time I wondered why they allowed it to stay open as they were telling us it was so unsafe. I had heard from several relatives who had lost loved ones in A&E, several people had even died on the grounds of the hospital. One woman had been discharged from A&E, told she was fine, only to die outside waiting for her son to take her home. I heard from many other complainants all telling me about the failings within the department. The day after the HCC Report was announced the floodgates opened and the cafe was inundated with people who had been harmed at the hospital. I then heard from many who suffered within the A&E and John Moore Robinson was one of them. John was only 20 when he died after being discharged from A&E with an undiagnosed ruptured spleen. His parents Frank and Janet have become friends and their struggle for justice for John continues to this day. They are now part of the group but because they live in Leicester they can't join us as often as they would like.

The first thing I thought when I read the press release was how the hell, could it have been left open. From what I knew and from what I was reading it was a dangerous place. We now know from the HCC Report 2009 that it was a very dangerous place.

After a series of complaints I once again contacted Dr Heather Wood, I felt it was important to keep someone informed of the complaints that were coming to me.

241

Heather, who had interviewed me for the HCC, has a soft Irish accent and a no nonsense attitude and she was the only person I could tell about the suffering. At the time I felt she was the only person who could help me as it was obvious that the hospital management were doing very little. I felt I could stand it no longer. Why were so many people still being harmed despite the HCC involvement? Heather took all of the details from me and said that she would let the DoN know. I told her that I had little faith in the DoN.

I had absolutely no faith in Yeates and after his frank interview with Shaun I had even less. He told Shaun that he had suffered, "18 months of hell," but accepted that patients had not received adequate care. But then he gave us his excuses, "When I arrived in 2005 we found a number of issues within the trust and a serious financial situation. We had to save £10 million in that first year, staffing levels got worse because of that deficit." Optimistically he told us that, "The hospital was at the point of turning the corner. The HCC would find evidence of poor care but it was not the reality now."

"Spin, spin and more spin." I thought.

The AGM

When I saw that the hospital's AGM was advertised in late September, I thought it would be an ideal opportunity for the group to go along. Yeates and the others needed to know that the hospital was turning no corner, it was still harming a lot of patients. And as for reality, why didn't he know what was really happening inside his hospital?

It was awkward for me as it was an afternoon meeting so I had to shut the cafe but I thought, 'Enough is enough." The hospital and the public needed to know that care wasn't improving and neither were conditions for the staff. I was hoping I would get an opportunity to ask the hospital management team, "Why are people still suffering and dying?" I was also hoping to speak to the DoN Helen Moss asking her why she told me that she had never heard about the poor care I was describing when we had spoken in November 2007.

It was September and there was the threat of rain again, I had checked the weather forecast. We were getting used to the rain and our banners were covered in plastic to protect them. It just seemed every time the group protested the weather was awful and the AGM for the hospital was no different. It was held at the Civic Centre in Cannock I had never been there before and when I arrived I was really pleased at the turnout.

Each time we protested more people had attended and it was the same with our meetings. More and more people were coming forward and telling me that conditions were still the same, the vulnerable continued to suffer. There were always new faces at each event sometimes I never saw them again, they would come and just get whatever advice they needed. I kept a list of everyone who did attend and as we would arrange an event I would ring everyone on the list. As you can imagine this took up a considerable amount of time, effort and money.

Today there were a couple of new faces and I found out later that one lady had lost her husband in 2004 and was still seeking answers over his death. Over the last year I had met with lots of families who had lost loved ones years ago and were still trying to get answers as to why they died and even to what happened to them in their final hours. I had now met with several families who had been given conflicting information surrounding the death of their loved ones. Each time I listened I could see the torture in their face as they tried to piece together the circumstances.

I was beginning to see a pattern myself, particularly around the time of death and at one meeting it was all exposed in public. One woman who I hadn't met or seen before attended one of our Cannock meetings. She had similar features to me, petite with mousy hair but hers was long and she had it held in a ponytail. She raised her hand to speak and when it was her turn she told us her Father had died recently in Stafford. He had been in the hospital a couple of weeks with a chest complaint which had improved. Like us all she had had to battle with the staff just to get basic care for him. One afternoon she had gone in at visiting time and found him dead, lying in his bed with his buzzer sounding out.

She told us she had just screamed out for the staff but they didn't even respond to her calls. She had approached the nurses station crying for one of them to go to her Father but all they did was raise their eyes to her and tell her they were about to ring her with the news. She knew immediately there was something suspicious, she said their faces gave them away.

The Matron had arrived and told her that her Father hadn't died alone, a nurse had been with him when he had died, "It had only just happened". Furthermore they had, "Worked on him," she went on to tell her. The daughter knew this was rubbish as her Father's eyes were wide open and his face was contorted as if in great pain and he was cold. She was inconsolable, he was lying half in the bed and half out and there was no way anybody had been to him. As for a nurse holding his hand - one had been stuck down the side of the bed and the other was next to his head. He hadn't been old either and had only recently retired He had caught C.Difficile in the hospital and had been placed in a single room because of his infection and away from anyone. The family were convinced he died alone and in misery they felt guilty that they had allowed this to happen.

But if that wasn't bad enough an older woman spoke out loudly above everyone else. Even standing up you could tell by her face she was angry and you could sense the anger in her words. "Its rubbish," she called out "they said exactly the same to me, and they told my neighbour the very same thing." The room went silent for what seemed a long time but could have been just seconds. I was conscious that there were others in the room who had told me the same thing had happened to them and Chris Dalziel, was one of them. I scanned the room and my eyes met Chris's and the others who had told me about a similar experience that they had. I wanted to reach out to them but all I could do was to close my eyes and shake my head. I was choked. I suggested an adjournment but all I wanted to do was to be home so I could cry alone. That's what I did do when I got home and I suspect so did others it was one of the hardest meetings for me as it had all been exposed, the hospitals dirty laundry had been washed in public.

It wasn't the first time this had happened either, I think it was at one of our Rugeley meetings when something similar happened over incident forms being completed. When I thought about it many of the people who had contacted me told me their relatives had suffered harm in the hospital usually from a fall or a drug error but no incident form had been completed to help them to learn from the error. I found out much later that the reason for this is that once it is recorded as an incident it is logged and added to their statistics. Not recording incidents allows things to stay hidden and it sure helps them hit their targets and raises no suspicions.

We had arrived at the Civic Centre in plenty of time it was the hospital's Annual General Meeting. I wanted to be waiting when the members went into the venue I wanted an opportunity to tell them about the recent complaints. They all needed to know what was happening at that hospital and today I was prepared to tell them everything. But as we stood I lost track of time as I was trying to welcome the new faces that had come along. It was the first time I had met Mary who had come along with her daughter. She had lost her husband, Ron, in 2004, another case of dreadful care and another unnecessary death. Mary was in her early sixties but didn't look her age at all. She was tall perhaps 5 foot 6 inches with dark wavy hair and she was smartly dressed. Her daughter had very similar features to her Mother, dark and attractive. As we stood talking about her husband's neglect I forgot the time.

Suddenly I realised that the meeting was expecting to start shortly and yet no one had walked past us to get to the entrance.

We had been tricked! Everyone had been contacted by Brisby and told to come in earlier to avoid us, they were told we were unpredictable. They were all shown through a side door at the side of the building to avoid seeing us. This I found out a few years later after reading one of the Governors evidence to the MSPI.

The police were out in force too and there was also what looked like security guards at the entrance we were standing at. We had no intention of going in although we were now members.

I found out that those that we thought were security staff were actually part of the management team from the Heart of England NHS Trust. I had no idea what they were doing at the AGM for MSFT. They came over to the group and introduced themselves, asking if they could talk with us. I could then see they were not security guards, their suits were too expensive.

We positioned ourselves at the side of the main entrance I always made sure that we created no obstruction or bother. At each meeting when I am trying to arrange a demonstration I remind everyone that it is important that we are seen to do nothing wrong. We must remain courteous at all times and never cause anything for them to challenge us about. I can sense that they are just waiting for us to do something wrong and even when we have done nothing wrong we have been accused of it, such as at the candlelit vigil.

We were standing at the edge of the car park in silence, we always stand in silence. We stand and we hold our banners high, most have made a new one for today. The printers next door to the cafe has been really kind and helped us keep what we have written on the banners fresh. Today I have a banner that reads, "Infection control is still out of control," although the hospital is telling the public their infection rate is low I don't believe a word they say now. I have had families coming to me where no infection has been recorded despite their loved ones being infected. I have also had others telling me that they had caught the infection in the hospital but on the case notes they have seen, "Contracted in the community," recorded. Others have been discharged with an infection only to be read-mitted the following day with the infection recorded as, "Contracted in the community."

It's usually at the last minute that I try to think of the right slogan to put on the banners. During the day I have to run the cafe, take complaints and at the same time think of something that is relevant but with just enough words to put on a banner. Until the campaign began I never gave it a thought when I saw banners with slogans on. Don't underestimate the work that goes in to this and I do mean those that are made by grass roots protesters, the home made sort. Often I will ring the others in the group and ask them for suggestions. Very often the glue is still wet and we hope that they'll hold together as we stand protesting for the deaths to stop. That day was no different and although I had made my banner waterproof I feared the rain would still seep in.

Some of the group were willing to share their experiences with the managers from the Heart of England FT, I can almost see them wincing at what they are hearing or am I imagining it. I'm pleasant with them but to be honest I'm more experi-enced now and I have been down this road time and time again, over the last year.

It's the usual patter, they tell us they're there to listen, that they want to help. Chris has bitten and so has Jeff, they are both talking at the same time to different people. It never fails to affect me and I have heard about Irene and George's deaths a number of times but there is always something each time I hear them talk that hurts me. Something different is remem-bered each time that I hear one of the group talk about their loved ones death.

Both George and Irene had been Jeff and Chris's first and only loves and they had met when young. As I sit here today I feel I know them as over the last five years I have heard so much about them. Now the memories of Irene and George are part of me too I have a clear vision of them in my head. George would be the life and soul of the party and a wonderful family man. George was hardworking, a provider, and Chris adored him. He was a charmer and a real showman. Still today she places a red rose next to his picture and each day she talks to him as if he was home with her. Irene is the opposite of George,

247

Irene would have been shy and reserved and very much a lady. She too was a hard worker and a valued member of the community that she lived in. Irene was a giver, she was always helping someone. Irene and Jeff only had one son, although I can imagine them with a house full of children running around. They had both spent a lot of their lives caring for the older family members. After she retired she spent her retirement doing voluntary work for the benefit of the community. She had worked at the local primary school and kids loved her. Huntingdon where they lived is a very small community and the children she knew have now grown up but still remember her fondly. One child who Irene had watched over in the playground is now closer than a daughter to Jeff. She has become his main carer and perhaps even closer than his own son.

It's a thoroughly miserable day but I find myself lost in thoughts of George singing along on the karaoke, some Frank Sinatra number, singing away and enjoying, himself. Alison his daughter absolutely thought the world of him and he had been a wonderful Father. Alison had followed in her Father's footsteps and had been a singer herself but his death had had a profound effect on her confidence and she was now a shell of her former self, along with her Mother. The day before George had gone into hospital he had been dancing and singing at the Birmingham Jazz Festival, another fine man destroyed by those that should have been caring for him.

I'm soon back and I can hear Chris telling them about George being offered a banana sandwich as that was all that was on the ward for him to eat. He had just had major bowel surgery and had had nothing to eat since the surgery a few days before. I feel myself shaking my head at the thought of poor George and I'm back listening again

The Heart of England team, just as I expect, tell us that our experiences can help the hospital improve and the best thing is for us to talk to the management. "Martin Yeates?" I can't help but interject in a sarcastic tone. I avoid telling them but if I had earned a tenner for every time I had heard that I would be a millionaire by now.

I feel all eyes on me and I try to think on my feet and realise everyone is looking at me waiting for an answer, "Why don't you come on inside and talk to the Governors, they can spare you ten minutes." he repeats. I think 'Why don't I? What have

I got to lose?' All of a sudden I feel I have nothing to lose and everything to gain. I can tell them about the recent cases and the absence of alleged improvements on the wards.

I can see the relief on the group's faces particularly the older ones, the chance of a seat and perhaps even a hot drink is enough to seduce them. We are escorted inside and I know before I have even sat down that we have been set up. Alone I am escorted to a particular table behind which sit four Governors. The rest of the group are escorted to other tables where other Governors sit.

I'm shown to four particular Governors who I consider are closest to the management the Governors who were part of the Foundation Trust assessment and the annual self assessment. The most trusted Governors, those who would toe the line and could spin the party line, the inner circle. As soon as I saw them I knew it wouldn't matter what I said, there was no point but I said it all the same.

I had already decided as I was being shown in that I would talk about the two worst cases I had advised. That was all I would have time for as I am thinking this I am scanning the room for Helen Moss, I need to see her but she is missing. I catch sight of the communications manager and my hair stands on end. That woman has heard my concerns a dozen times and yet poor care continues, why?

As soon as I sit down I know they are not listening, their eyes give it away and the way they look at me says it all. I sit facing them as they sit behind a wooden table, despite the table I can still sense the hostility towards me. It doesn't matter that they are not listening as I tell them about the recent cases that have contacted me. I tell them about the man in so much pain he had tried for two weeks to get them to give him pain relief but nobody believed he was in that much pain.

"He was in so much pain he tried to jump out the window in the hospital, Ward 11 where my Mum had died nearly a year ago". I draw breath and check if I have eye contact. I do, at least one of them is listening. "Instead of believing him and giving him medication the hospital sent him for a psychiatric assessment. After he had passed with flying colours they began to investigate further and they found he had terminal cancer". I feel myself wanting to shake them as I want them to listen. But the younger, of the four has maintained eye contact so I con-

249

tinue "He died in agony a few days later and he never received any pain relief".

They say nothing just blankness, no emotion at all but I continue, this is an opportunity too good to waste. You see at this stage I have no idea what the powers of a Council of Governors are. I have no idea that they are usually carefully selected to protect the hospital. I have no idea that three of the four sitting opposite me had all been nurses themselves and knew the staff at the hospital well.

I continue and repeat my case, "Why, if there are improvements, are people still dying? Why are people still contacting me?" Nothing is going to stop me, I'm conscious I only have ten minutes.

I tell them about the man who was left overnight on the toilet. The family were promised that the nurse who had left him there would never work on the ward again. They had promised that she would never work as a nurse again. They had believed them, trusting what they were being told. But that's the problem you do trust them and they know it and that's why they can tell you anything and you believe it.

Six months later their Father was readmitted with another complaint but went on to the same ward. In the middle of the night he rang his daughter to collect him after waking and finding the same nurse standing in front of him. Despite the hospital telling the family she would be dismissed, six months later she was still on the same ward.

He was terrified of her and without a thought he discharged himself and went home with his daughter in the middle of the night. Instead of the hospital doing something with the nurse she had been allowed to remain even staying in charge of the same ward.

Six months earlier she had taken him to the toilet around 11pm and left him sitting there until 5am in the morning. He had called out screaming and shouting for all those hours, he must have been in agony. Once she had found him instead of apologising she tried to make out he was confused and had only been taken to the toilet a short time earlier. He was having none of it and persisted that she had left him the previous night. She then physically threatened him telling him that if he didn't shut up and forget about it she would make him.

Terrified he kept quiet until she had gone off duty. As soon as she had he alerted his family who immediately contacted the ward. An emergency meeting was held and that's when they were told she would never nurse again. No minutes were taken and the family had no evidence of the meeting taking place. I was beginning to discover that this was how they worked, everything I heard about was done unprofessionally in this hospital.

I look up at their faces. Blank. Nothing. Again I am in tears, "He died the following day at home". One of them opens his mouth to speak but I haven't been told I have used up my ten minutes so I try to continue. He interjects telling me I have spoken for long enough. I have, my mouth is dry and I need a drink but I need to tell them about the way they handle complaints and the pattern I have found.

No, my time is up as this guy begins to tell me about the improvements, there is MEWS, a new initiative that alerts the staff when a patient's condition is deteriorating. *The Essence of Care* has been implemented and care can be benchmarked against it. "Oh please," I think, "how many times have I heard that before?" But it doesn't end there he hits me with the final blow, "The hospital has just been awarded a good rating in the Annual Health Check by the HCC". I can see by his face he is, loving this and he can see by my face I am crushed, he has hit me with the killer blow.

I later find out he was once a nurse, this man had had a life-time of the NHS and was very much part of the family. He tells me he inspects the wards regularly and he has noticed that improvements are being implemented.

I get up from my chair, I am defeated I will leave before they advise me to meet with Martin Yeates I can feel that that's what is coming next. As I stand and begin to walk away all of the things I should have said fill my mind and distract me from his parting words. I stand at the side looking for the others at the same time feeling disappointed at what I have left unsaid and what I have just heard.

I stand watching the four I have just spoken to there is nothing on their faces that tells me that they have just heard about the most dreadful care possible. As they pass me they don't even look my way, I am nothing to them, nothing but an inconvenience. The doors shut and all you can hear is applause their meeting must be ready to begin. I feel so disappointed that I hadn't been more prepared. Each member of the group could have told them about a recent case that had come to our attention. Instead I suspect the older members of the group would have repeated their own loved one's experience. I look around for them as I know they will need comforting, repeating their loved one's sufferings hurts.

My eyes search the room and I feel like a hen looking for her brood as I try to gather the others close. Over the last year we have become very protective of each other and I know some of the Governors would have been unpleasant. I can see by their faces that their meetings didn't go well either. The rest of the group have found me and we stand together at the main entrance as Yeates begins his speech in the next room. Those that we had thought were security guards are showing us towards the door, it is time for us to leave but just as we do I hear Yeates telling his audience,

"2008 has been a fantastic year for Mid Staffs Hospital, what a fantastic year the trust has had, we are now in the premier league, we are a Foundation Trust", I shake my head and head out through the door. The man is deluded, he isn't listening to a word we have been saying.

"A fantastic year and the hospital is under investigation for high death rates and poor care?" I can't help but say out loud. The others nod and tut and agree with me and the general consensus from them was that the Governors believe the HCC will conclude that the trust has now improved.

With that one of the Heart of England managers who I had mistook for security overhears and tells me that that is what the HCC will say as the hospital has improved and they are already saying so. I shake my head in disbelief because I know differently by the amount and the nature of the complaints that I am hearing about and I tell him so. I'm not rude or anything like that, I never am and to be honest he's a pleasant fella despite his robotic persona.

He tells us he wants to engage with the group as he is independent and will work through our complaints. I smile to myself as he must think I am more naive than I look but I'm now prepared for him and what I should have told the Governors he will now hear.

"I lost my Mother nearly a year ago and my complaint has been dealt with. The only reason I am here is that I do not want

252

anyone else to suffer." I put my hood up as the rain had started again.

"How on earth can the HCC give a 'Good' rating when they are supposed to be in there investigating high death rates? What is going on? How can they rate the care as good?"

Of all of the complaints I heard that year there wasn't one that didn't expose dreadful care or extremely bad failings. In all of those years there has only been one case where I sat there and thought to myself, "I'm just too busy to sit here listening to such a trivial complaint". But it soon became clear, as the victim's daughter continued that more was to come and what I had thought was a trivial complaint was in fact very serious.

She had begun by telling me that the hospital had lost her elderly Mother's nightdresses. Looking back now I think she started with the nightdresses because that was all she thought she could complain about. She had lost her Mother in the end and she had suffered neglect on the ward but the staff had denied it all. She had not been given her medication and her daughter had begged the staff for pain relief. She had always found her Mother thirsty when she visited her and there was never a fluid chart completed in her file. The daughter had been anxious to get her Mother's nightdresses back as she felt that was all she had left of her.

I have put my hood up but the wind and the rain still hit my face and I can feel it dripping off my forehead as I continue with a now shaking voice.

"Helen Moss is a bare faced liar. She told me she had never heard accusations of neglect or abuse about the staff when I've met countless people who have told her just as I have. Sandra's Mum was on Ward 11 a year before my Mum, they did the same thing to her, robbed her of any dignity. Sandra had to pick faeces out of her hair in the morgue! Moss told her the same thing, the same line, the same spin, the same denial."

On and on I go but I can see his eyes have glazed over and I think he realises I need more than his help.

"If you want to help, look at the staffing levels. Patients are telling me that the wards are still starved of staff. However the RCN says staffing levels are fine. But if staffing levels are fine why is Helen Moss recruiting staff? It just doesn't add up. Someone's not telling it straight."

I tell him about all the recent complaints and I suspect he

has heard enough because he doesn't take the rest of the groups details as he said he would. After the sixth recent complaint which I tell him about, he makes his excuses and he is off inside the Centre. We are left outside with just the police for company as the rain beats down on us once again.

He Who Pays the Piper Calls the Tune

Out of the blue I was contacted by Robin who instead of working with us had been actively trying to make progress with the LINK, the patient group that has now replaced the PPIF. Robin had attended our first meeting and had visited the solicitor in the Potteries with me. Sadly nothing had changed with this new group, not even the faces, despite Robin's efforts to the contrary. I agree to attend the meeting to support him as he has been a lone voice and it was supposed to be a patient group.

They had already been given a huge amount of public money and as yet there was no evidence they had done anything. Poor care continued and CTNHS was doing far more for patients and their families. They were dogged with infighting and when we met them I could see why.

I rang around and a few of the others agreed to come along with me. It's the usual suspects Alison, Deb, Chris, June, Jeff, Sonia. It's being held at a church in the town, the Trinity Church where I had met the prospective parliamentary candidate Jeremy Lefroy in the summer.

It looks like the meeting has started when we arrive but we are at least twenty minutes early. As soon as they see us their faces say it all, we are not welcome. They are all seated in this small room and as we have walked in I can feel all these eyes staring at us. There are about fifteen people in the room and I can sense none of them want us there.

One man pipes up who looks like he is the leader of the group. He's a short fella resembles a studious librarian with tiny glasses perched off the edge of his nose. He's even wearing beige cord trousers and a checked shirt. He had an odd voice slightly squeaky, "I'm sorry," he tells us and he has got these eyes that seem to look through you. "This isn't a meeting for the public" he tells us.

Immediately Robin queries and I can sense that there is history between these two characters. "It is a public meeting for the public." Robin tries to clarify the situation and prove his point. Robin is sitting at the edge along with Ron who I suspect has come to give him moral support.

I'm not listening as they continue to wrangle over the specifics, all I'm thinking is where are we going to sit? This room is too small for us all but at the same time I'm determined we are coming in and June will need to sit down soon.

"No, no. This meeting is only open to members of LINK."

"We are all paid up members of the Trust and LINK" His face went bright red. He had no answer for it and just walked away. They had no grounds to exclude us, the only problem was the room was no longer big enough so we had to move down the corridor to one that we could all fit into.

That night exposed to me everything that is wrong with patient involvement groups within the NHS. These people had become defenders of the very body that they should have been scrutinising. The OSC was the same, made up of people who are on these committees to make themselves sound important. Most of them are retired and usually retired from positions of power and they find themselves at home with nothing to do. Others want power and join these committees to get the power they crave.

I know there are some people that join and they are productive but very often they are talking shops and achieve little. Very often that is what they are designed for, to achieve nothing other than ticking the box. Patient involvement? Check!

It's like a band wagon they get on and then they find themselves on other committees, eventually they have the all the local voluntary groups in their hands. I know there is the argument that nobody else would do it but nobody stood a chance in Stafford, it was all sewn up.

The first thing this group should have been was democratic but it wasn't, they had elected a committee when only a handful of people had been present, all of whom were voted onto it.

"I think it would make a lot of sense for us to elect a committee tonight as it will be much more representative." Robin's suggestion goes down like a lead balloon, their faces could have turned cream sour. The Chair continued to obstruct all night, like a Nazi border guard. There was also a woman in a wheelchair who said something cruel and hurtful every time she opened her mouth. She was much younger than she dressed and her miserable face was only broken by her poisonous tongue which she lashed out like a whip.

"You can't come here and just expect us to concentrate on the hospital we have other things to discuss" she snarled. She shuffled some papers in front of her and continued "We already have an agenda and the hospital isn't on it"

"But who has set the agenda?" Robin asked but nobody seemed to know, their faces were blank and nobody answered.

There were about ten of them and they took it in turns to introduce themselves. All of them were involved with other committees not just this one. In fact a few of them were on so many committees by the time they had read out the names of them all, we could have gone for a cup of tea and got back in time to hear them finishing. They all had their fingers in lots of pies and most involved the voluntary sector.

Then we had to introduce ourselves to what we could see was a very hostile crowd. They sat opposite like pack animals waiting for their prey and I sensed it was us but especially me.

"My name is Julie Bailey and I'm here tonight to ask for your help as I am horrified at what is going on at our local hospital. Around six people a week are contacting me with real concerns about their care or that of their loved ones. It's mainly the elderly that have suffered and continue to suffer, there is something terribly wrong in there. People are continuing to die despite the HCC being involved and all the publicity the hospital is getting. We all need to work together to stop it continuing as nobody seems to be doing anything. Please help. The people who have suffered are the most vulnerable in our community and they need our help."

I thought I would plead with them and offering them an olive branch might help them to work with us to stop the suffering. But instead they are on me just like I suspected, I am the prey and each stands and tries to tear me to pieces.

With that each stood and told us that either they or someone they knew had been in the hospital and had received wonderful care. One man had brought along all his family, four in total, all stood and told me that the hospital had saved their Father's life.

"If you want to help anybody you should shut up, think of the harm you're doing to the lovely, caring staff."

"What about staff morale, don't you care what this is doing to the staff?" one of the women snarled back at me.

The woman in the wheelchair said with almost a sneer, "LINKS isn't just about the hospital you know we have other priorities."

Deb had been quiet tonight, probably in shock at their behaviour towards us, but at this she lost her composure, they had pushed her too far, she's far too intelligent for them.

"What's more important?" she asks, they all look vacantly at her completely missing her point. So she makes it easier for them. "What could be more important than people dying through neglect?" she isn't expecting a reply but she gets one.

"Mental health is very important!" she's almost shouting, not just at Deb but at us all, at the same time she shuffles in her chair as if to show her anger.

"Oh for God's sake," snaps Deb, "Are you for real?"

"Julie we are better off without them" Chris has heard enough and she starts getting her things together to go. Alison is sitting next to her and is putting on her coat, "You should all be ashamed of yourselves." Alison, normally quiet, is unable to help herself, "We have achieved more with no one helping us than you are ever likely to."

"I can't believe what I am hearing," adds June whose face says it all, "We are wasting our time here". She too gets up and reaches for her coat. Jeff, the gentleman that he is, tries to hold it out for her to make it easier to put on. "I'm disgusted with the lot of you," he says as he turns and faces them.

I agree entirely with Jeff but I realise enough has been said, we will get no support from this bunch. I feel sorry that we are leaving Robin with these clowns but it is time for us to go.

But the Chair hasn't finished with us, it's his final show of power when he tells us "It's the private part of our meeting now and time for you to leave".

"Were off, We've heard enough" says Jeff.

When we are out of the door we breathe a sigh of relief that in our group there are no similarities of what we have just witnessed. It was galling though that they had so many resources available to them and we had nothing. We all moaned at the injustice but I reassured the group that they were too ignorant to achieve anything. And I was proved right, a year later the group is investigated and proved to be ineffective and a waste of public money. It's now about to be replaced with Healthwatch, the latest initiative for patient involvement.

I write to Stuart Poyner from the PCT again, those families that had recently come to see me had mentioned again a lack of basic equipment on the wards after all this time and after all the publicity. One family had again had to take in pillows and blankets to keep their loved ones warm. They had all mentioned the lack of staff and how uncaring they were towards them. I just could not believe that after all this time something as basic as pillows were still not on the wards.

I write and tell him I want evidence of his efforts, I ask him about the increase of staff we were promised, where they are and how the increase breaks down, ward by ward. I ask him how many hoists are now on the wards and what wards have they gone to. I ask him about the pillow situation and blankets. I practically fought to get patients pillows when Mum was on the ward, I ended up bringing them in from home. At home Mum used about six to help her sleep. On the ward I felt too guilty to ask for so many and they just didn't have them. But I knew how difficult it could be for people with respiratory problems to sleep not being propped up. I want him to confirm where they are on the wards but at the same time I am politely reminding him of his agreement to help.

A few days later I receive a reply from him telling me he knows nothing about my request for basic equipment on the wards. I'm so angry, I can barely speak without shouting. I pace, up and down wanting to scream. I make myself a cup of tea to try and calm myself down before I phone Dr Heather Wood. I have no one else now to tell just no one seems interested in what is still happening it just seems to continue. I tell her about Poyner and his denial, that he had agreed to ensure that basic equipment was increased on the wards. I photocopy all of my correspondence between myself and the PCT making sure I enclose the letter where he states he will help with getting basic equipment on the wards. I send everything to her in the hope that it will shame him into doing something to help the vulnerable.

I also send Poyner a copy of everything I send to Dr Heather Wood, I'm so angry with him as all along I was thinking that he was helping me and he did nothing. I have no further contact with him until he gives evidence to the MSPI in 2011. Despite his failings, and they were exposed further at the MSPI, he has now gone on to much better things, promoted through the ranks of the NHS despite his record of failure and incompetence.

A few days later I receive a letter from the hospital. Oddly it is another reply to my letter of complaint from ten months ago. It is not from Yeates but the deputy Chief Executive, the finance director, Mike Gill. I have to laugh to myself as inside the envelope is an action plan belonging to someone else. "They can't even get that right", I tell Deb and we are full of speculation as to why we suddenly have a deputy CE, we hadn't heard about him before. I telephone the others and speculate if Yeates has resigned or is about to resign.

Talk of Yeates resignation is discussed when we next meet Bill Cash a few weeks later, it seems my fears about the HCC have been unfounded and the talk is all about how bad the report is likely to be.

We meet him again in November just as the HCC were finishing their investigation and leaving the hospital. Peter Atkins, the local journalist, Phillip Jones, the Governor, along with Deb and I meet him in a pub in Eccleshall. It's a small village just outside Stafford and is part of Bill's constituency. It was a terrible night, snow filled the sky and the roads were treacherous. Peter had arranged to pick me up, I think I would have probably cancelled if I had to drive.

It felt so surreal when we did get there sitting in a pub with a roaring fire next to the MP while the snow fell outside, it was like something out of a Dickens novel. Both Deb and I looked at each other for reassurance as we pushed Bill Cash for information. We both knew that the time had passed to do anything about the hospital and the discussion tonight would be around the publication of the HCC final report. Had he heard anything? Did he know when the report would be published?

Deb took the lead tonight, as his constituent, and told Bill firmly, "We want accountability for the failings". Driving home with Peter I felt much more confident that something at last was starting to happen. I couldn't tell you what but I felt a strange mood was hanging over me. I felt that everything now was on hold, like we were waiting for something that was very close, and yet people were still suffering.

Doreen Duff was one of those suffering on Ward 11 around the same time. At the time I didn't know her but the following year I would be introduced to her memory as her husband, Jim, reminisces about her qualities. I will come to know her as I hear about her beauty and her laughter as her memory lives on, through him. Like Ron, June's husband, Doreen had had a stroke but she was much younger, sixty four. Jim admits that she wasn't a well woman but at the same time the hospital did everything wrong. Jim, like Jeff, had been Doreen's main carer and he had put her into hospital to be cared for. They hadn't. She suffered and Jim had felt guilty ever since for allowing it to happen. Like me and the others Jim was powerless to save his wife even though he could see the neglect but there wasn't a damn thing he could do about it. She was left without food, fluids and medication and eventually he lost her.

It's when Raymond Duke walks in to the cafe that I realise just how dangerous the hospital is. Since Paddy had featured the cafe on the regional news people had been calling in to see me with complaints about the hospital and Raymond was one of them. He appears at the kitchen door as if from nowhere and I barely have chance to take off my apron before he is in floods of tears. I struggle to console him as he tells me that his Mother had begged him to take her out of the hospital. He hadn't and he had felt he had left her there to die. Of course he hadn't, there wasn't a damn thing he could have done to help her but like us all the guilt has got to him.

Raymond is tall and stocky and towers over me. I can sense his kindness and his fondness for his Mother. The tears flow as he tells me of her suffering and lack of care on the ward saving the worse for last. It's never easy sitting listening to anyone in pain but this man is hurting and it is apparent.

He has finished telling me about the way his Mother had been treated and he looks down at his bag. I'm thinking he is ready to leave as whilst he has been talking the cafe has filled with late afternoon customers wanting a brew. I am conscious that they are looking over at me and yet there isn't a thing I can do about it.

Instead of reaching for his bag he undoes the zip and reaches inside for a blue folder. Before I have chance to interject and tell

261

him I am busy and could he come back when I am closed he opens up the folder and exposes the most awful sight I could ever wish to see.

There, staring back at me is his Mother. Pictures of her battered and bruised, from head to toe. She is undressed and black and purple bruising covers large parts of her breasts, legs and stomach. Another picture shows the back of her body and just below both of her shoulder blades is black bruising consistent with someone kneeling on her back. There is also one picture that shows a close up of her face and at both sides of her mouth there is black bruising.

I am suddenly oblivious to what he is saying and my thoughts now are racing back to the ward, Ward 11. I can see it clearly in my mind and at the time I never gave it a thought as most of the patients, elderly ones anyway had bruising but mostly on their arms and legs. But no I remember similar bruising on a few of the patients who roamed the ward. Particularly the patients who were confused the ones who wandered around with glazed eyes, particularly at night. They had bruising in the same place as his Mother, just around the corners of the mouth. The vision enters my head of the man they had pinned down, first on his back and then the porter had turned him over onto his stomach as he had knelt on his back. I had seen them trying to force something into his mouth before the doctor had arrived and given him an injection.

I feel sick because I suddenly realise what has happened to his Mother. Oh my god, oh my god! I feel physically shaken, 'Stay calm, stay calm,' I tell myself. I can sense that this man is not coping well at all and I am conscious that I have to be careful, I don't want to make it worse for him. This man is struggling to cope and far too needy for me to give him the help he needs. I try to probe about his support network and he tells me about his doctor and the support he is getting.

"I don't know what to say, Raymond. The only thing I can think of is to phone the police." I say to him.

"When she was a girl in Poland she was put into a concentration camp. On Ward 11 she told me, in Polish so the nurses wouldn't hear, "At least in Auschwitz I had friends. In here I have nobody."

The vision of his Mother stuck in my head for a long time and I tossed and turned it over in my mind. I just couldn't seem to get the pictures out of my mind as I suspected a similar fate others had suffered. It was the confused you see the staff just didn't have the skills to manage them. Everything would get blown up into a crisis situation and then they would be sedated, dragged into their beds. I expect some of the staff felt they had no option, they needed them in bed out of the way as they couldn't get on with their other tasks. You could see though that some of the staff relished the power they had over patients and I am afraid some of the porters were part of the bullying team.

Throughout that summer I made sure we attended each Governors and OSC meeting. They didn't want us there but I made sure we were. It was important that they knew we were still having complaints and little had changed. A couple of the Governors occasionally spoke to us, out of pity I suspect as it was always so wet or cold. Saying either "It is the system," "It's the coding," or "Mid Staffs is no different from any other hospital". Most didn't speak or look over, in fact most avoided even looking our way. Some managed a glance over at us, tutting as they did. We were an irritant that just wouldn't go away.

Stepping Up

It was in November that Ken Lownds introduced himself to the group, arriving just at the right moment as the campaign was about to step up a gear. I felt I was running out of steam and getting nowhere was taking its toll. He was full of ideas of where we needed to be concentrating our efforts. Suddenly my engine was stoked and I was ready for the final push. We all believed that it was the last stage of the fight for the failings to be exposed.

At this point you see, we all thought that once the HCC report came out the campaign would be over. The hospital would be forced to implement improvements and the suffering would be over, the care would improve once it had been exposed by an independent body. It isn't until much later that I realise the campaign is only just beginning, the failings have been exposed but nothing has been done to stop the poor care continuing.

Ken had been given my number by Paddy who had advised him to make contact with me. We speak for over an hour and I just feel so relieved that I have found someone who is listening to me. For the last year I haven't met one person who has said they are willing to help us.

Ken attends our next meeting and he is the first person who is independent to meet the group. He sits and listens to our experiences and he can hardly believe what he is hearing. I can tell by his face he is shocked and he pledges to help us in whatever way he can. Four years later he is still trying to help us Cure the NHS, but now he is very much part of the group. Ken is the only member of the group that hasn't lost a loved one at MSFT hospital but this doesn't alter his commitment to curing the NHS.

I feel as if for the last year we have been trying to run up a hill. Meeting Ken is like running up the hill but having someone to hold our hand, it is a huge relief. Ken is full of ideas to get the campaign moving and ready for the HCC concluding their investigation. We quickly find out that who Ken doesn't know isn't worth knowing anyway. Names drop off his tongue and there are occasions where he has lost the older members of the group as they have no idea who he is talking about. He seems to know everyone and has friends everywhere, a fantastic networker and just what we need to help cure the NHS.

The last year has been so difficult and all I have done is to react to the situation as it has happened. My priority was to inform as many people as possible locally, Ken helps us to inform as many people as possible nationally. His first task on our behalf is to get all of our press clippings of poor care together compiled into book form.

Seeing all of the cases of poor care together for the first time was devastating, I knew all the families and all of that harm could have been avoided. Most of them are taken from the front pages of our local papers and each case is so similar. It's either poor standards of basic care or a surgical error leading to death.

It was now the first anniversary of Mum's death and nothing has changed, the poor care continued and so did the spin coming out of the hospital. That first anniversary was so difficult but Ken arriving somehow made it easier, it gave me hope again that we could cure the NHS.

Together we drew up a long list of people who needed to be sent a pack and Monitor was one of them. I hadn't even thought about involving Monitor who had now taken on the responsibility of ensuring the hospital was safe and was financially strong. Once a hospital is awarded Foundation Trust status the hospital is answerable to Monitor and not the Department of Health. It felt as if the campaign had really stepped up a gear and we were breaking out from Stafford and into the wider arena.

I hadn't involved Monitor at all but Ken introduced us into the wider NHS. He wrote to its Chief Executive, Bill Moyes, and asked him what he was doing to protect patients and our community. Since the hospital had become an FT, Monitor had also been one of their regulators and as Ken pointed out should have been monitoring the poor care.

He also wrote to the Chief Executive of the NHS David Nicholson and sent him a copy of all the recent cases of poor care. *The book of shame* consisted of around 30 cases of poor care, some had gone to inquest others hadn't. I don't think we ever got a response back from Nicholson but then he had been involved in Mid Staffs in his previous role as Chief Executive of the West Midlands Strategic Health Authority. I won't dwell on this, I find it too difficult and it's really for another day. Suffice to say that despite his responsibility for the situation at Mid Staffs he went on to be promoted to the top job in the NHS and even received a knighthood.

Ken joining the group gave us an opportunity to have a strategic approach to ensure we were ready for the publication of the HCC Report. Ken is tall with an urbane air about him, always immaculately turned out and organised. His features are sharp but his manner is very gentle and he oozes confidence. His background is in the airline industry and his knowledge on quality and safety systems, both sadly lacking within the NHS but introduced years ago to other sectors like the construction and airline industry, is unrivalled within the group. It isn't until Ken comes along that we start to discuss the impact the report will have and the press interest it will bring. He even suggests that we need our own press officer, something we hadn't even considered.

I'm not convinced at first that the press will be that interested a year of trying to get people to help us has taken its toll. I listened to what he was saying but at the same time I could never have imagined the coverage we were about to be given. On the day one of the journalists told me, "If Jade Goody dies you'll be off the front page". That didn't happen and the press stayed with us for weeks.

Although we have no idea when the report will be out we start to plan our response and prepare ourselves for the day. The press make contact and some even do pre-filming ready for the day of its release. Sonia and I spend a whole day filming for a Dispatches programme that is due to be filmed alongside the publication of the HCC Report.

The BBC regional programme, Midlands Today, came and featured us on their programme. Paddy, the health correspondent, had come to the cafe during one of our meetings and filmed parts of it. It was really strange as everything was starting to take on a momentum of its own.

The complaints continued to come in thick and fast and it is hard to believe that Mum had been dead for over twelve months. It feels like yesterday to me. It's still painful every day but on her anniversary it was even more so. I wanted to think about her but I am still finding it too difficult to reminisce. I long to because I miss her so much but it's just too difficult and easier to try to dismiss her from my thoughts. Her grave brings me no comfort, it's just a reminder of the pain she suffered. I want to be normal again, to have my life back but it's now impossible. I realise I have started on this journey and I have to see it through to the end, I owe it to Mum.

We had taken on an air of confidence, we were now convinced that the HCC would be critical and their report would bring about changes at the hospital. With this confidence Pete writes on the group's behalf to the Governors and all the members of the board. He reminds them of their responsibilities and asks for their resignation as they have failed us and they have failed the community. He writes and tells them that the last three deaths that have been brought to my attention are evidence that little has changed at the hospital and they have failed to hold the managers to account. He tells them,

"As a board member you had a responsibility to ensure that patients were safe. You have failed in your responsibilities so do the honourable thing and resign".

These three patients had suffered only last week and all on different wards but with similar suffering and all dying in misery. They hadn't been old either, retired but not old. They were ill but certainly not ill enough to die. They all died in misery though and all after their families had pleaded with the staff to help them. One of them had been a Consultant at the hospital, for many years he had cared for the older members of our community as a geriatrician. It was his son, daughter-in-law and daughter who had come to see me at the cafe. It was a bitterly cold night and dark when they arrived and although I had the heater on it was still cold inside. I suspected they were a Malaysian or Filipino family but their English was perfect. The daughter lived in Australia and was in the UK until after her Father's funeral. By now I had heard from over one hundred and fifty people and not one had been connected to the hospital but here in front of me was someone who was one of their own. He too had been neglected and the family had begged them to help him. They told me that they had been ignored as if they were nothing and yet their Father had known some of the staff.

It was so sad listening to the poor care he had experienced as he had given his life to helping others. The doctor had been in his 70s, he should have been enjoying his retirement not fighting for his life amongst his own colleagues. I just thought if they can't help their own who could they help?

His family were shocked at the lack of care and the lack of treatment he received at one point they had even brought in a mattress as the ward had run out of them. They had also had to bring in pillows and blankets.

The family were so keen to join the group and wanted to do whatever they could to help. His daughter and daughter-in-law planned to come along to our next meeting and that happened to be a special Governors meeting.

It was a special meeting to get feedback from Price-waterhouseCoopers, who had been inside the hospital for the last six months. We had heard that they would be presenting their findings of an investigation they had been running alongside the HCC. I thought this was odd but it wasn't until the MSPI that we realised just how odd.

We didn't go to the meeting to gloat, no, I'm not a gloater we hadn't planned any further protests as we were now just waiting for the HCC report which we were expecting to be out shortly but the three families that contacted me indicated that people were still suffering We were out in force and it turned out to be our penultimate protest and one of the last Governors' meetings that we attend. It had been a long and difficult road and thinking we were nearing the end gave us all a confidence I hadn't seen from us before.

There were several new faces with us all relatives of loved ones recently harmed. The Consultant's daughter had come along with his daughter-in-law, they were standing alongside Chris who was talking to them. They were holding a banner that they had made themselves saying, "Start to care for your patients". They were both young, perhaps early thirties, and attractive. The daughter is the more vocal of the two and continues to talk to Chris as I pass them and smile.

John is also a new face and he has recently lost his Father after him being admitted for a chest infection. His loss has affected him badly and he vows to get answers from the hospital. I want to tell him that he doesn't stand a chance but I cannot do that, I know it's having that hope that keeps you going. After nearly a year now of talking to relatives who have wanted answers I haven't yet met one that has found them.

I have arranged to meet him at the hospital and straight away I sense something is wrong.

I can see him in the distance and I can tell straight away it is him, the man I have been talking to for long periods over the phone. It's a bitterly cold night and he has turned up in a short sleeve cotton shirt. John's a tall handsome man with a gentle nature. He is quietly spoken and he is standing alone away from the others. I greet the others but I first must speak to John I can sense he needs me. Within minutes he has broken down crying onto my shoulder like others I have spoken to. It's the guilt that has got to him. "Why didn't I help him?" He cries.

I know there is no point him being here it is too soon and I shouldn't have asked him along. In my defence it's so difficult to judge someone over the phone, I hadn't had chance to visit him at home. John had pleaded with the staff to help his Father, he hadn't been that unwell. He had walked into the hospital himself and before long had deteriorated rapidly. John suspected not being given his medication previously prescribed for his heart had played a big part but so had the neglect and the lack of fluids had finished him off.

I had read the letters that he had written to his Father's Consultant, pleading with him to help his Father. They were heartbreaking, a man pleading with a doctor to help his Father before he dies of neglect. But he did die and there was absolutely nothing more John could have done. Begging the staff from the nurse on the ward to the Consultant got him nowhere and his Father died a miserable death much too soon.

I can feel his wet tears on my neck. He needs to go home, he is far too raw but also I don't want to leave him alone, but I must today as I have a job to do.

I decided that I would walk with John back to his car that was until I spotted a familiar face. It was a face that very often entered my dreams and had the very night before when I had woken terrified. At first I froze when I saw him but then I thought, 'No, stay strong he cannot harm me and I won't allow him to intimidate me.'

My stomach felt as if it had turned upside down and for one minute I thought I may experience another panic attack. That was what must have happened to me when I had entered the hospital toilet some months before. I quickly pushed that thought away, it frightened me to have been so vulnerable but since that day I haven't entered the hospital, having that panic attack frightened me so much. I'd never had a panic attack before and I haven't had one since.

Having the others around me had always given me strength throughout this last year and today won't be any different, I thought. I leave John and join the rest of the group standing on our usual spot in a position that the Governors have to see us as they enter the building. There's no press with us tonight, it was all at short notice as this is an unexpected meeting for some reason. We have our suspicions that they have seen a draft copy of the report and Yeates has resigned. Our suspicions are heightened when Yeates doesn't turn up. We know something is going on, I can smell it in the air.

The porter is coming towards us but tonight as he is approaching us I can see he is wearing an overcoat and not his normal white shirt and trousers. On the ward he looked so much taller but tonight what strikes me is how small he is. His confidence has gone and he walks towards us cautiously. I suspect it's because he has no power over us unlike the vulnerable patients he bullies.

"You can't stand there," he tells us but without any assurance.

All eyes are on me as the rest of the group expect me to answer as their leader. They have no idea he is part of my past, no idea that this man terrorized the elderly on Ward 11 and they have no idea that this man often fills my dreams.

I snap back with as much force as I can, listening to John has left me tearful. "We always stand here." I retort.

"Well you can't today as there is a breast screening lorry about to park on this spot." He is now up close to me, far too close for comfort and I can feel the anger rising from deep inside me.

It takes a lot to make me angry and staying calm is one of my strengths but not today the man has pushed me too far in the past.

With my finger pointing towards him and my voice raised I tell him, "I spent eight weeks listening and watching you bully old people, don't think you can do it to us now."

The colour drains from his face and he is lost for words.

Whatever he is going to say next he doesn't, his eyes hit the floor and with his hands in his pockets he walks off.

It is our triumph and we remain in our position as usual with the rain beating down once again. Surprisingly tonight a couple of the Governors approach us walking across the path to speak, we feel highly honoured. But they haven't come to listen, instead they tell us that the meeting tonight is to receive feedback from the consultancy firm.

"It has been a difficult few years but now the hospital has turned a corner," they tell us full of enthusiasm.

"Corner!" my mood hasn't improved and I introduce them to the Consultant's daughter who has just lost her Father on one of the wards. It seems to go in one ear and out the other as they rush off telling us their meeting is about to start. But before they do they take the contact details of the family promising to be in touch. Within minutes the communications manager is out and inviting them into the building, into the lion's den. It's the last I ever see of them despite their enthusiasm to join the group. The following day the daughter rings telling me that she had decided to work with the hospital. The week after, she telephoned me out of the blue. She had gone home and was calling me from Australia.

"Australia?" I say. What on earth is so important she needs to call me from Australia? It's advice and I'm getting too long in the tooth for it to be honest as I have heard it too many times now. She had promised to speak to the press about her Father's suffering but I knew as soon as she went into the hospital we had lost her.

"The best thing you can do is to work with the management like we are," from her voice despite the distance of the call, I can sense her hope that she will get answers to why her Father died as he had.

I know straight away that she has been sucked in by the hospital team, "Come and work with us." I can hear them now, it's all too familiar I'm afraid as I have heard it so many times from other families. "We will make you think that we are listening to you. You are very important to us and we promise your loved one didn't die in vain as lessons have been learnt".

She has been sucked in hook, line and sinker but this is exactly what they do. She was an intelligent woman and so were the rest of the family but they cannot see that the hospi-

271

tal will do and say anything just to silence them. Also to make them think that they are improving things and of course it is one less family for our group but, more importantly, no bad publicity.

I suspect they are rubbing their hands thinking we will keep this one hidden it wouldn't have made a good story for them "Retired Consultant dies in misery in his own hospital during a HCC investigation".

I'm annoyed because having someone with medical knowledge would have been really useful. But they catch people when they are vulnerable through grief and that's what they did with this family. I'm disappointed and I tell her so but if she needs us in the future she knows where we are. The other thing to consider, and now experience tells me, is that the NHS is like one big family and they protect each other.

Ann on the other hand is a different kettle of fish. She is angry, angry that she has lost her Mother. I can tell straight away that this woman will not be sucked in, she is far too clever for that and so are her family despite them having no medical knowledge. They are astute enough to see through them.

I knew before I had even met Ann Giles that we would be good friends because her Mum had been her best friend like Deb's and Castell's Mum too. We all shared that bond that our Mothers had meant everything to us and when we had lost them we felt we had lost everything and we still do. Most Mums are irreplaceable but ours had been characters and perhaps if they had been alive together would have been great friends. We all believe that their deaths have to mean something. They didn't die for nothing, they have to stop others suffering in the same way, that is important to us all.

I had spoken to Ann on the phone, she couldn't make this Governors meeting but her husband and her brother had come along to support us. Roger, her husband, was now retired and had spent a lot of time with Ann at the hospital helping to care for his Mother in Law, Joan.

Roger introduced them both but it was hard to see their faces as they had both wrapped up warm for the evening wearing thick winter jackets, hats and a scarf. My first thought was, "They have done this before," I found out later that they both supported Stafford Rangers and regularly attended the soccer match on a Saturday. Roger is a handsome man with fair, greying hair. He is quietly spoken with what I detect is a slight Welsh accent. I find out he originates from Kidwelly in South Wales and that helps to break the ice. It's a part of the country that I am very familiar with as I worked as a social worker in that town for a while.

Wally is the taller of the two and strikes me as a confident man, he is tall and handsome with a lovely smile but with a sadness all the same. He too had spent a lot of time in the hospital with his Mother.

Wally is named after his Father, Walter, who died several years before his Mother. Both Wally and Roger have now both become members of the group and over the next few years we have become very close friends. Little did I know when meeting them for that first time that we would share so many experiences together throughout the campaign to cure the NHS.

Wally is the type of man who can put his hand to anything and is similar in personality to Ann. Both are strong, confident and perceptive. Just like when Ken joined us the family have added something special to the group they are all lovely people very kind natured.

We spend the evening there despite it being so cold, we want to be waiting outside for when the meeting ends. We always stand in silence and it's nothing new tonight although we are suspicious as to the whereabouts of Martin Yeates.

I just don't seem to have enough energy for anymore public meetings, we haven't held one since October. I have found that they drain me physically and emotionally and instead I see people individually now. After I have shut the cafe relatives will meet me there and ask for advice on what to do next. I have found standing in front of 70 odd people is hard work in itself but to listen to the way their loved ones have suffered is too emotionally draining for me. A room full of people all with despair to share with me is just impossible for me to listen to anymore.

Instead our efforts are concentrated on our group meetings and the protests. People are still making contact telling me of the awful care and they want advice on how to make a complaint. It seems little has changed at the hospital, the PALS is still functioning to protect the hospital.

Most people now visit me at the cafe, I take their details and try and advise them on how to make a complaint. Looking back now I probably knew a lot more than those who were coming for advice but today I would handle it very differently. Today I would advise anybody to get a copy of their case notes before they begin the letter of complaint but even that process isn't as easy as it sounds. The first shock is the cost, normally £50. What a cheek! They harm your loved one and then charge you for information on how they did it! But even then I was beginning to feel that the NHS complaints procedure is a process designed by the NHS to torture the complainant. It's hard to have to sit and listen to the same complaints but just from different faces. Each day it's the same failings, but with a different family sitting opposite me. It's horrible hearing the same doctors and nurses names crop up over and over again but they do regularly. It's more evidence that little is changing on the wards.

There were now around ten people who I considered to be the group, the ones who attended every meeting and who would stand in silence protesting. The inner circle, that I trust and rely on. To be honest though it just seemed to happen that way and I didn't do it consciously either. The cafe has twelve seats and it is easier to hold our meetings there. I was starting to find it difficult to hire somewhere as we had no funds available to pay for a venue. We had all chipped in together in the past and had tried to do a few car boot sales but there just seems so much to do and no money to do it with.

The core group just really evolved, looking back now I think we became attached to each other because of a similar experience. We had each lost somebody very special and we all shared the same aim, to stop it happening to others.

There were Chris, Alison, Pete, June, Deb, Castell, Rebecca, Ken, Sonia, Jeff in the group and Roger, Wally and Ann were about to join us.

When I first met Ann it was as if we had been friends for years. One of the first things that strikes me is she's as tactile as I am and we have a similar personality. We cuddle and it feels like we have done it many times before. The last year has been a difficult time and the group have become a family, we have all bonded. Ann, Roger, Wally and their brother Steve just seem to join the family as if we have been waiting for them. Having them around makes me feel far more secure than I have felt before. Also having younger men around when we protest has made us less vulnerable and today nobody approaches us.

We all stand proudly together in the centre of the town holding pictures of our loved ones. Most people don't approach us but they do look our way sympathetically, some smile out of pity for us. I suspect some people realise that it could be them standing here but others are oblivious to any failings within the NHS. Most people say, "The NHS is something to be proud of!" Just as I had twelve months ago. Some look at us with disgust some even tut as they are passing us, it hurts but we have just got to be strong standing together.

The Giles family are still in shock and today they are saying very little but I can sense they are just relieved they have found us. Ann is definitely still in shock she can barely talk about what has happened to her Mother.

Ann is similar to her Mother in features and I suspect personality. Joan had beautiful eyes and a beaming smile. The picture that Ann carries shows Joan with just that, a beaming smile and not a care in the world. The picture was taken a few months before her death and there isn't a trace of illness, she looks a picture of health but then many of our loved ones did until they entered the hospital.

Ann looks the opposite, her face is drawn and dark circles have formed under her eyes. She's a similar size to me in height but her personality can fill a room. She's always very smartly dressed she wears her blond hair short and is always well groomed. But today Ann has no smile and there are no laughs for her for a long time.

Ann had stayed with Joan on the ward, Ward 2. Coincidentally Joan had been in the same room as Deb's Mum, Ellen but three years later. There was three years between them being in the room but both complained about the temperature. It was freezing as it had no radiator working on either of their stays. Even, after complaining, it was never fixed but the families had to bring in extra blankets from home.

"I Was Duped"

I just couldn't understand that despite all of these failings the CE Martin Yeates was still in his post. I thought people resigned when they failed or when they couldn't do the job they were being paid to do. The evidence was overwhelming. However the monitoring of a hospital relies largely on self assessment, and self assessment relies on honesty, something the board simply did not possess. This team of managers were telling the HCC something very different to what was really happening and from the MSPI we know that Yeates had not been honest with the investigating team.

His resignation was a big shock to us all and an even bigger shock when we found out he hadn't resigned after all but *Stood down*. We were duped by him and that is just what David Kidney the MP said some months later. "I was duped," by Yeates he told the papers, but it proved too late for him

I only heard the announcement about Yeates by chance as the Governors meeting was in the middle of the day. Middle of the day meetings were really difficult for me as it meant I had to close the cafe to attend. Also unusually it was being held in a top hotel in Cannock which wasn't a regular venue either. We only found out through the press. The E&S were running a story about the choice of venue. I had added a comment criticising them for spending so much money when they had their own meeting room at the hospital. I should have realised that something was about to happen that we weren't expecting.

I had rung around for the others to join me but no one was available, I nearly had to go on my own but in the end I was in luck at such short notice. Jeff, Ann, Roger and I armed ourselves with a banner and off we went together in Roger's car. We had never been so few to attend a protest and on the way I had worried about it but I had come to the conclusion that it didn't matter how few in numbers we were. The fact was we were there and it would let them know that we weren't going away until the hospital had improved. I had given up thinking that the poor care I had heard about would have an impact on them. It just seemed that not one of them cared, apart from one of the Governors who would usually come over and speak to us. I realise now how brave she was but at the time I admired her that she spoke but she frustrated me that she was doing nothing.

We were just finding a spot to stand in the car park when I noticed a tall fella in a suit coming towards us. What struck me as soon as I got out of the car was that the police were missing but instead today there was a wall of bodyguards. Odd I know but they all looked as if they had spent their lives in the gym. And they were here because of us? A team of six stocky security guards to tackle, three pensioners and a 46 year old woman, who stands 5 feet 4 inches, in heels. I shook my head when I saw them in disgust, not only that the management thought they needed protecting against us, but the cost of hiring them.

They all stood in a line watching us, I could see the suspicion on their faces and the formal stance they had adopted, what did they think we were going to do? As we were talking I could see out of the corner of my eye one of them break free and start to come towards us. I felt my body freeze I didn't like conflict but I didn't like being pushed around either and wouldn't be now. I stopped talking to Jeff and instead watched the guard as he came towards us. As he came closer he seemed to relax and I sensed he wouldn't be a problem his stance was too sloppy for a clash.

"If you put your banners down and behave yourselves, you can go into the meeting," he told us with a slight Brummie accent.

Now I wanted to challenge him but at the same time I wanted to go into the meeting. I didn't want to waste this opportunity to meet with the management and the Governors. But he irritated me all the same, "Behave ourselves?" Who did he think he was and who does he think we are? But I said nothing, I bit my lip instead.

We were seated away from the Governors who were sitting in front of us at a large round wooden table. I don't really know any of them as since the hospital had become a FT we only got to see them when they attended a meeting and we were stood outside in the cold. We had written to them a few weeks ago asking for their resignation along with the board but, unsurprisingly, no one had written back or resigned.

We were waiting for the meeting to start and I was planning in my head, 'What is the best I can get out of this meeting?' I was toying with the idea of approaching the Chair and telling her of the recent complaints I had received. As I'm mulling it over Jeff is sitting next to me flicking through the board papers that are prepared ready for the meeting. Suddenly he nudges me with his arm and I'm surprised at the force he has used. He's pointing at text in the board papers and his face tells me something is wrong or, in this case right. His smile tells me everything, his face has lit up, he can hardly sit still. Although he's nearly eighty he's like a young boy waiting for the school bell to ring.

Just as I'm reading it and the four of us are considering what it is telling us the Deputy Chair opens the meeting. Before I have time to think where Brisby is we are all leaning over each others' shoulders reading the board papers that Jeff has showed us. "It is with great regret that Toni Brisby the chair has resigned and the CE Martin Yeates has stood down".

How the four of us stay on our seats and stay silent is beyond me but we do and it is a credit to us. To get to this point has taken a year but here we are in a room full of Governors, NHS managers and staff forced to be silent and still.

The Deputy Chair rushes through her opening and the announcement, "It is with deep regret that the Chair has resigned and the CE has stood down". At this all eyes turn to us, it feels like all twenty of their eyes boring through us. There is silence in the room. Each of us frozen in our chairs and the smile is wiped off our faces by the atmosphere in the room. As quick as a flash their eyes turn back to the Deputy Chair and she has moved the meeting on. She is introducing us to the Finance Manager who gives us the financial report.

It's surreal, you can sense that nobody is listening they are just going through the motions. She moves the meeting along as if we have misheard her saying that Yeates and Brisby have met their fate.

It's probably not good but nobody is listening to what the Finance Manager is saying, we want to get out and celebrate but the others feel differently. Throughout the meeting some glance over and stare at us but most are focused on their own thoughts. It's obvious they have had a pre-meeting and discussed all this earlier as I suspect this is all a charade for our benefit. They are too calm and controlled to have just heard this information like we have.

The Finance Manager has finished and next we have to sit through a presentation from the nurses on how care has improved. I sit and listen but all I want to do is to get out and inform the press. The nurses tell us all about the *Essence of Care* and I can't tell you how many times I have heard this presentation.

All eyes are on the three nurses who are waffling on about this pathway and that pathway but really not having a clue what they are talking about. The Governors are not really listening anyway and one even starts to clap before the presentation has finished. The nurse had only paused and carries on with her presentation but she's now embarrassed along with the Governor who clapped too soon. For further reassurance that there have been improvements on Ward 11 they end the presentation by telling us all how many thank you cards they have received from grateful relatives. All eyes revert back to us even the nurses giving the presentation look our way.

I'm used to it now, after the hostility we had experienced over the last year this is nothing I just wish one of the Governors had something about them and would ask, "In light of the improvements on Ward 11, have the level and nature of complaints reduced on the ward? Have the Serious Untoward Incidents been reduced?" I know they haven't but the Governors say nothing, that's not what Governors do, they are carefully selected to ensure they don't challenge or ask awkward questions.

It's over and we all start to file out but as we are leaving I overhear two of the Governors in conversation behind me. The one is a staff Governor, I have met her before, "I suppose they are happy now but it is the worst thing that could happen to this hospital."

I tense up but I avoid saying anything I just want to get out of here and contact everyone with the news. You see at this very moment I am on a high, all four of us were but really Yeates is planning to go nowhere.

The negative comments continue from a group now in front

of us, it's going in one ear and out the other. That is until one of them mentions the group and our intentions. I am forced to intervene and put the record straight.

"Our campaign wasn't a personal vendetta about anybody. Our campaign has been about trying to force you to improve care so others don't suffer like our loved ones did."

One of the Governors snaps back, "You've got what you wanted."

"Wanted?" I spit back at her. I'm conscious that the other Governors have started to gather round. The one I am focused on is no different to the others but she is in my firing range.

She's not unattractive but her face is unpleasant if you understand me, her eyes are searching and she has drool lines, the ones people get when they hardly smile. She's quite frumpy for her age which I suspect is late fifties, her dress has no panache or colour.

Roger, Jeff and Ann are still beside me but they are silent. I guess they are still in shock at what we have been told.

"All we want is for the suffering to stop," but she isn't listening. She raises her head as if she is tutting, dismissing me but without any sound coming out of her mouth. She slightly turns and starts to continue down the corridor with the others.

This just makes me angrier and I feel I cannot stop, "Do you know what it is like to live with the thought that the person you love has died in misery and you have let it happen? Do you? But people are still dying in misery and you are doing absolutely nothing about it." She has now stopped in her tracks and her face turns a whiter shade of pale.

"How dare you accuse me of allowing people to die!" Her face looks shocked and the tone of her voice has changed, she reminds me of an old school mistress now.

"But as a Governor you had a job to do and you have failed to do it." I suspect she has no idea that as a Governor she should have been holding the hospital board to account. I suspect she only wanted to be a Governor because it would give her a standing in the community, make her a VIP. She would be able to mix with people that she wouldn't normally mix with and think of the social occasions she would be invited to. I expect she had never been challenged before and she didn't like anyone doing that to her.

She was crying now and I had no sympathy with her, she was

a nasty piece of work. She was another one of the Governors who has passed us as we stood in silence, a group of grieving relatives, and not once has she spoken to us. To be honest she has avoided us at all costs, not even eye contact with me until now.

She reaches for a tissue out of her bag and tells me in a raised voice, "You have made me cry, look what you have done to me." Her eyes search the room to see who is listening to her and the others tut, tut at me.

I've heard enough and with the others we make our way to the door and we are gone. Within seconds our banners are back in the car and we are all on the phone to different people giving them the news. Our mood has definitely lifted and we can see a future for the hospital again.

The following day I receive a letter from one of the Governors, a Maureen Compton, who happens to be a County Councillor too. She hasn't spoken a word to me despite us standing outside their meetings for a year. Now all of a sudden she writes to congratulate us for sticking by the campaign to raise awareness of the harm inside the hospital. She tells me that, "The Governors were always asking questions as they wanted to get to the truth of the situation."

'The truth,' I think when I read her email, maddened. How dare she? All any of them had to do was to open one of the ward doors, they would have heard the truth, they could have smelt it.

I heard no further from her and I didn't want to but she was one of many that came to us as if they had not played a part in all of the denial. Ironically four years on and this very day I receive a leaflet through my letter box from the local Labour Party, she is the local Labour County Councillor there staring back at me is a picture of her. She is heading a campaign to save the A&E department from night time closure. I suspect she sees that more of a vote winner than helping the elderly in the community who continue to be harmed at the hospital.

Another strange thing happened following Yeates's and Brisby's decision which was a huge shock to me - the staff's response to their resignation. They were so upset at the news that they called a meeting at the hospital immediately and invited the press along. The meeting was packed and it was staff from all disciplines who attended. Many were in tears, they fully supported the Chair and CE, telling the press that both were "approachable" and "caring". They even went on national television saying so and blaming our group for forcing them out. Doctors and nurses wrote signed letters to the local newspaper in support of them both. All the staff blamed our group saying that the progress at the hospital had been down to their hard work and we had ruined it.

A Facebook page was set up by the staff at the hospital, allegedly to defend Yeates and Brisby but it seemed to be more a vehicle for people to launch personal attacks against us. I felt so hurt that they blamed us when all we wanted was a safer hospital and support for the caring doctors and nurses. We were forced into cancelling our latest protest that was due to take place in Stafford town centre a few days later. The staff had planned on the same day to march through the town and into my cafe. I was forced to make a statement to the press saying that, "We do not want to get into any confrontations with doctors or nurses and therefore the protest will not take place".

An interim CE was brought into the trust to take over the reins from Yeates but he was part time and had a background in accountancy. The opposite of what we needed but someone thought he was what the hospital needed for some strange reason. Eric Morton had come from a large hospital, The Chesterfield Royal in Derbyshire, but he failed in my eyes on his first day.

The first thing that Morton did was to stand in front of the TV cameras and say that everything now had changed at the hospital, things had improved. They hadn't. Mortality was higher than the previous year and so was the level of complaints. At the precise moment he was speaking to the cameras I was holding a woman's hand whose Mother had recently died in agony, covered in infected bed sores. Staff had tried to steer the family away from the press as they had been in the hospital at the same time. He seemed no different from Yeates. Once again spin, spin and more spin.

Involving the press was the only way I could get these cases exposed and I made sure that her Mother's experience was covered in the press and on the local news. I thought it was important that people could see that there had been few improvements, people were still dying unnecessarily.

Oddly my first contact from Morton was when he sent me a

letter telling me what the Red Tray System was and a description of it, as if I needed to know. When it dropped through the letter box I thought it was an invitation to meet with him. He had given a statement to the press saying he wanted to meet with the group so that was what I was expecting.

It was just like salt being rubbed into a wound as I had been trying to get the system implemented to ensure that the vulnerable were firstly identified and then helped with being fed for over a year now. Much later during the MSPI, I was to find out that Age UK had a scheme running at the hospital and they were being paid to provide assistance with meals and fluids to vulnerable patients. It wasn't just the statutory bodies that failed us at Mid Staffs it was the voluntary sector too.

It made me so mad when I had read Morton's letter and it gave no idea of when the Red Tray System would be implemented either. I met him a few weeks later at the first OSC meeting after the HCC report, he was no different to the other managers I had met before, no idea and no substance, oily.

In another one of his comments to the press speaking about the HCC report which was due the following week he said, "Next week will be a difficult week — you know that and I know that. But it's important we support the staff through it and allow them time for healing." In another statement he said, "I'm very impressed with the attitude of the staff. It's clearly been a very, very difficult time for them over the past twelve months but I think they want to move on and the new Chairman and I will be very keen to move things on over the next week or two."

'What about us?' I thought. 'Isn't it us and our loved ones who have been harmed by the very staff he is lauding? Move on? I bet they want to move on,' I thought. Does he realise that many of us will never be able to *move on,* we are damaged forever. It just seemed that the priority was all about the staff and how they felt but nobody was listening to us.

The MP David Kidney came out of his box too and dropped another clanger. We hadn't seen much of him since his work experience at the hospital but now he popped up to tell us, "Local residents should put their trust in Mr Morton along with David Stone who has been brought in as interim Chairman." The Chair had come from the large teaching hospital at Sheffield. Kidney's next clanger followed like clockwork, he told

283

Vindicated at Last

Now we knew that the HCC report was going to be bad because of what had happened to Yeates and Brisby. We began to prepare for the day of the report coming out and it was lucky we had because it was totally unexpected. I had been told by the HCC that we would get twenty four hours notice but instead we didn't get any, the report was leaked to the press and they were forced to release it a day earlier. I was also told that I would get a copy of the report before it had been released, I was probably the last to receive a copy as it happened. A courier arrived at the cafe at about 9pm, long after the release and long after I had to comment on it.

The first I heard of the release was around 11pm the night before. I was getting myself ready for bed when my phone rang. A call at that time was unusual but what I wasn't expecting was to hear it was from GMTV, the breakfast TV programme. They wanted to start filming at 5am at the cafe and I reluctantly agreed to 6am instead. It was a long, long night I tossed and turned not knowing what to expect in the morning.

I know before today begins that it is going to be a hard day but I have no idea just how hard it will turn out to be. I begin the day by telling myself I must be strong, the others are relying on me, it's more important today than any other day. I don't know if it's because I haven't slept but I'm crying already. I feel as if I have woken crying, which I often do now, but forgotten why I am crying. I go to sleep thinking about Mum and I wake thinking about her and all that she suffered.

It was the pictures that had started me crying. Last night having to look at pictures of Mum to hang on our *Wall of Remembrance* had been so painful. Seeing her face on a picture but not having her here with me was just too painful, still.

I get to the cafe early and the others have gathered too, Jeff has caught the early bus along with June and they arrive just after 6am. Both are looking tired already as if they too have had a difficult night.

Pete has brought Chris, Deb and her husband, Steve, and they help to prepare the room. There is a lot to do before the press arrive, the mood is sombre amongst us and we are all silent as we work. Roger and Ann have arrived and have started the task of hanging the photos. Seeing the photos of our loved ones hanging on the wall is hard for us as we stand watching the pictures mount the wall for the first time. At this stage we have no idea that in a few days there will be that many people that they will have to form a queue as they wait to hang a picture of their loved one who had suffered at the hospital.

People arrive from all over the country, people who have contacted me over the last year and have been waiting for today. The day when they will be vindicated after all this time, telling others about the poor treatment their loved one suffered at either Cannock or Stafford, yet not having the evidence to prove what they were saying. When I had looked at all of our replies to our complaints they were almost identical. Identical, in the fact that they just didn't care and they also didn't care if they were dishonest. We had all never encountered anything like this before as we were all of the opinion that doctors and nurses were honest people. This had exposed us to a side of the NHS that we just had no idea could happen and that was difficult to believe at first.

I often think about the first time that my Mum was trying to tell me about the nurse who had shut her door the second night she had been in the hospital. "I'm tellin' yer Jude," her voice stern with me, "She shut that door and I was calling for help". That still hurt that I hadn't believed my own Mother but now I know that that sort of behaviour is common on some wards. At the side of the *Wall of Remembrance* we have the *Wall of Shame*, it is the names of the people and organisations that should have helped us. We have been working on our Wall of Shame for some time and it sort of evolved. During our meetings we had decided between us who should be on it and who should be at the top of it. If you had asked me a year ago I would have had no idea who most of them were.

The press arrive and within what seems like minutes every TV station is in the room, BBC, SKY, ITV, Channel 4. I barely recognise the cafe, there isn't a spare inch in the place, it's packed. There are wires and camera's everywhere. Journalists are everywhere too, faces we recognise from the TV and faces we have never seen before.

The press are focusing on the *extra* 400-1200 deaths, that's the figure that had been leaked to the press we have been told by one of the reporters. They all begin their broadcast with, "A hospital where it is estimated that at least 400 people have lost their life unnecessarily".

To me it is meaningless. It's the suffering that I have heard about that hurts me more. All the people, all the families that have contacted me over the last year and it all could have been avoided. To the others in the group it is meaningless too and at this point we have no idea where the figure has come from anyway.

At one stage, just after a live interview with ITV at lunchtime, I take stock and glance around the room it is then that I realise that there isn't one unnecessary death in this room. All our loved ones would have gone into the hospital and been recorded as an expected death, their death would be recorded as natural.

'My God!' I shivered at the thought but there and then I realised there must have been thousands and thousands of the elderly who had died in that hospital, died without a trace, without anyone knowing. I had seen it myself day in and day out. One minute they were there and the next they were dead and being taken away.

Some days I don't feel like carrying on. I don't want to live knowing all about the suffering that I do. Some days I just find things just so unbearable when I am forced to think about my Mum and her death. There is nothing I can change about it none of us can, that awful experience we have to carry around with us forever. Mum would be cross if she knew I felt like this and that is what is driving me. I owe that to Mum and that's how the others feel. It is the least we can now do because we failed when our loved ones were alive and now we can make amends.

At the time I think that this will be our only opportunity to get our story told but it isn't. These people cannot believe what they are hearing. I can see by the journalists' faces when they are listening to us. It's like Ken's face the first time that he met the group. Over the next six weeks we have journalists from all over the world who arrive at the cafe to interview us. Little do I know but today is just the beginning of media interest that has continued until the present day.

Many are quoting Sir Ian Kennedy, the Chair of the HCC, who said today that, "this is the worst report in the history of the NHS," and yet there is no one here to support us, we have to support each other with the help of the press.

We are being shown live from the cafe for the afternoon and the evening news on all channels. Neither of us has any idea which channel we are talking to we just talk, we have to get our story across. We want everyone to know the struggle we have had to be heard and the harm that our loved ones suffered.

As well as live TV we also have to broadcast live to the radio stations, local and national, and every now and again I am taken to the Council Offices in the town to use their broadcasting equipment. I welcome the break, a chance for some air, but I run there and back and my feet ache and once I'm out I miss the support of the others.

Sammy had offered to handle the media for the day and at one point I glanced over at her, she had three phones on the go and was having three different conversations. Late afternoon I broke free and asked her,

"Are you ok Sam?" I could see the strain it was having on her emotionally too as she had lost a wonderful Nan. She was organising everything, arranging who would be interviewed and at what time and keeping us all updated when our time was due. As well as cameras pointing at us we also had the photographers to cope with. Sam was managing it all telling us who they wanted to take pictures of and in what setting. I could see she looked shattered and yet there was no one else who could help her out but I asked her all the same.

"I'm fine. Look you have Central next and straight onto Live at Five on this line," as she points to the cafe phone. Sam was Sam, if she had a job to do she would do it and do it well. I thought she may even get a job offer and we laughed about that the following day.

We try to speak but at times each and every one of us breaks down on camera. It's odd but I can usually detach myself, I've learnt to do it. It's a skill I've developed, a skill I didn't know I had. Today it's impossible. We stand and talk to the cameras but we really have no idea what we are saying, we just talk from the heart. It all comes from deep within us. It's mostly about what our own loved ones suffered, we focus on that as that is what the reporters want us to discuss. Every now and again someone hands me a message to say that the HCC have been in touch and my copy of the report is on its way. So far none of us have seen a copy of the report yet and we are relying on journalists to share extracts with us.

How we do it I just don't know but whenever anyone is being interviewed the others are silent. It's as if a hush comes over the cafe in waves and we respect what the other one is saying. We have heard about this suffering many times but today it feels different and I feel as if I haven't really heard it before. Sonia is talking about Pete, another strong proud man who went in to Stafford Hospital and lost whatever pride he had. Sonia has tried all day to be strong and to comfort others but now on camera her tears are hard to stop. She holds a hanky to her eyes as she tries to talk into the camera.

Ann and Roger sit together for most of the day. For Ann it has only been weeks since she lost her Mum and today she is in pain. The tears flow and yet she is so brave when the reporter points a camera towards her,

"My Mum should be with us today. She should never have died in that hospital, if that is what you can call it". You can sense the anger in her voice and as she is talking that anger is exposed. Roger stands next to her holding her hand, hoping he can give her the strength to continue. She does,

"The hospital was filthy, absolutely filthy".

Every now and again deep sobs echo in the small room and each and every one of us has to support each other. Whoever is sitting nearest when someone breaks down or whoever can get to them first offer themselves as support. We are all really, still in shock at what has happened to us, nobody could have prepared us for today.

June is being interviewed by a BBC reporter, he is holding a huge microphone to her mouth and I can sense how hard it is for her. She looks years older than she normally does, she looks weary but her words are clear,

"A dog would have been treated better." She continues "My husband was attacked and the police didn't want to know." She is angry and that is not like June. June has a lovely soft voice but today it echoes in the room, she is so clear and so determined to get her message across. Her eyes stay focused on the reporter as she tells him how her husband suffered. "Why?" she asks, "Why didn't anyone stop it?"

Although we are unable to see the interview one of the channels lets us hear what was being said in the London studio by Sir Ian Kennedy, the chairman of the HCC.

"This is a story of appalling standards of care and chaotic systems of looking after patients. There were inadequacies at almost every stage in the care of emergency patients. There is no doubt that patients will have suffered and some will have died as a result."

Jeff looked lost, he had all day. He was taking it badly. I could tell by his face it was difficult for him to even speak,

"Too right and our Irene wer' one er 'em". Deb comforted him putting her arms around him and holding him close to her. Jeff cried on her shoulder, you could hear the sobs coming from him. It was all too much, quietly he cried. Jeff wasn't the only one that Deb hugged, she hugged us all. We all needed her arms around us today.

The report concluded that patients were put at serious risk by, "Patients being left for hours in soiled or wet bedding, the wrong medication or none at all. The A&E department was understaffed and poorly equipped. A shortage of triage nurses led to receptionists assessing patients' injuries. Doctors were taken away from treating seriously ill patients to those with minor illnesses to avoid breaching the government's four hour

target for waiting times. Essential equipment such as defibrillators were missing or not working. Accepted standards in infection control were not maintained."

Most of the day when we are not giving interviews we find ourselves sitting in silence, numbed I expect at what today has brought. Although we are talking to the press each time we speak it becomes more natural that we do. Today for the first time we have confirmation that people believe what we are saying and that is empowering especially for me who has had so many knock backs.

But here it was in black and white everything we had been saying for the fifteen months and that was a huge relief. There were times throughout the last year that I thought today would never come and things would be brushed under the carpet, "There have been problems but now they are resolved," as Yeates had kept telling us and wanted us to believe.

I knew differently though because people were contacting me from the wards with up to date information and that had given me a clear picture of what was going on within the hospital. Yeates didn't really know what was going on in his hospital as there was no system of governance, no safety systems were in place.

The 66 points that I had sent to the HCC just over twelve months ago were all listed in the HCC report, everything I told them they would find they found and that was such a relief. The group had had their doubts all the way through the investigation about the independence of the HCC. I am now convinced that Dr Heather Wood the lead investigator was herself independent and we in this community who use the hospital owe her for her resilience.

The following day the Secretary of State for Health, Alan Johnson, stood in parliament and apologised to the families and offered each relative a case note review. Actually an *independent* case note review. Now after 5 years of looking closely at the NHS I would laugh at the suggestion that an *independent* case note review is possible within the NHS.

"We're Not Going Away"

The struggle for a safer NHS continued after the HCC Report and it still continues today. Has it become safer since we started the campaign? Evidence tells us not. With around 3,000 deaths a year that are avoidable. Today at 3pm as I was four years ago I sit here waiting for complainants to meet with me. Yet more harm and suffering at the hospital.

Nobody to date has been held to account for the failings and the unnecessary deaths that occurred at Mid Staffs. In fact many have been promoted and the CE of the NHS is still in post looking even more secure than ever. He has been exposed in the press for his extravagance with our money despite patients still being deprived of food and fluids. He doesn't care, he's stuck his fingers up to us just as he did during the HCC when he told the investigating team to be cautious with the group's evidence. In the end Yeates did resign and ended up with a huge pension pot for his failings. He didn't give evidence to the MSPI, he was suffering from some illness, I daren't say a mental illness because I feel that is an insult to all the people that do suffer but that is what he claimed to have.

We are now in a similar position to what we were the day the HCC report came out. We are now waiting for the publication of the MSPI, the inquiry that we campaigned hard for two years.

We have the same thing now as we did when the HCC report was due out. At a recent OSC meeting the current CE Lynne Hill Tout announced that the hospital will be putting systems in place to ensure that the staff who gave evidence to the MSPI will be supported. Further evidence that even now we are nothing to these people and our suffering isn't important.

It's now four years on and nearly five years since I lost my Mum. A lot has happened, far too much to tell you in this sitting. Just as we placed great hope in the HCC Report being released, we are once again in that position waiting for the

292

MSPI recommendations to herald in the changes that are needed to cure the NHS.

The very next day after the HCC report came out we started to campaign for the MSPI. We had no choice as the report left too many questions unanswered and the most important were why did we lose so many lives, why did so many have to suffer? What the report has told us is what has happened, we are evidence of that, but not why. It was a real shock to us all just how many organisations were involved in a monitoring role within the NHS, that had failed. This was all news to me, I had no idea what each organisation was responsible for. Although from the evidence we heard during the MSPI some of those that took the witness stand didn't know what their responsibilities were. What I did know was if it could happen at Mid Staffs it could happen anywhere.

Although the following day Alan Johnson stood up in Parliament and said that Mid Staffs was an isolated case, we knew differently. The evening after the HCC Report was announced I went home to over 700 emails. Most were telling me of similar experiences from all over the country, the only difference was these people were alone. They had no group like CTNHS they were isolated cases either being tortured by the NHS or their complaints procedure.

We had no idea the differences between different types of inquiries, it was the MP Bill Cash who put us straight on that and I think at one point he regretted it. Although we eventually got the MSPI it was a long difficult road that we had to travel for two years. We even tried a judicial review against the SoS for Health. Alan Johnson had moved to the justice department by this time and Andy Burnham was his successor, being only a Junior Minister at the time of the HCC investigation. But he played several roles in the disaster at Mid Staffs that he was challenged on at the MSPI during his testimony.

The Department of Health didn't play fair with us, a group of grieving relatives and they tried to scupper our chances of getting the MSPI. They thought they had succeeded when they came up with a series of investigations designed to get the least information and to damage our chances legally to get everything exposed.

The group was granted core participant status when we did get the MSPI and that was a real eye opener. It gave us access to all the evidence that was produced by all the core participants and it was often uncomfortable reading. Seeing how these huge organisations responded to a small group of victims like ourselves exposed clearly to us that the patient is meaningless within the NHS, we mean nothing to these huge organisations.

I know the NHS does some wonderful things, myself and my family can testify to that, but around sixty deaths a month is, I believe, hard to ignore. Like I said earlier that figure very often doesn't include the elderly who are hidden victims. Another thing to bear in mind is that today very often the elderly now live in fear of going into hospital. One thing I have found too is until it happens to you, just like I felt, it is hard to believe that the NHS can fail and harm you so badly.

In the summer of 2010 we organised a workshop and invited complainants from all over the UK. I was finding it too much of a strain trying to cope with all of these complainants but at the same time knowing they were alone, unlike us. As a group we decided that we didn't want one big organisation but instead smaller groups like ours, who try to hold their own hospital to account. On the day we provided them with a toolkit and advice for them to establish groups similar to ours in their own areas.

During the MSPI we saw that all the evidence was there that our hospital was failing and that is what we encourage groups to do. By looking at performance data that comes out of a hospital the public can see for themselves if their own hospital is failing.

Mortality statistics combined with Patient and Staff surveys are a good indication of a hospitals performance. Bring together this information with the hospitals complaints and serious untoward incidents and a picture starts to emerge. Another rich source of information about a hospital is gleamed from Peer Reviews which are done regularly on some NHS services. It's a time consuming process because the information is in so many places but this is what we have to do. We have lost trust in the NHS telling us the truth, about its own performance, sadly we have heard far too much, spin.

CTNHS is now made up of a unique set of people all different but all sharing similar experiences and aims. We gain strength through each other and over the first year we grew and developed together. Somehow sharing our individual grieving processes together has created an unusual bond. An attachment that will survive over a journey that at this stage we have no idea will need all of our tenacity.

We have all found each other, we have got the strength and we are determined to expose what needs to be done. As core participants during the MSPI we were able to submit recommendations and our blueprint for the NHS. If adopted it would ensure a safer NHS where the patient is a special person and a hospital is a safe, special place.

We still have our *Wall of Shame*. Many have been promoted, others have moved and are working for consultancy firms, some even knighted. Some would argue that this is our Society, the way we have become rewards failure. What I am about to find out is the NHS is full of the great and the good. Sirs and Dames litter the upper echelons of our health service but the letters and titles after their names do not excuse their absolute failure to protect the very people they were there to save.

Criticism of the NHS is difficult for many to take. The images of dancing nurses that were beamed all over the world during the London Olympics opening ceremony underline how deeply it is ingrained in the national consciousness. Although I feel it has become a dangerous *Sacred Cow*, above criticism for many despite its obvious failings. I have huge admiration for the thousands of hard-working doctors and nurses who give selflessly everyday. However unless we accept that not every doctor and nurse is a saint, until we accept the failures and shortcomings that are rife in the system we are in danger of losing one of our most cherished institutions.

Sir David Nicholson has presided over not only the failure at Mid Staffs but also the failure to rectify this and the attempted cover up that followed. He is at the centre of an institution that appears to be pathologically unable to improve. The resignation of Sir David Nicholson will not cure the NHS overnight but it would be a bloody good start.